P9-DUJ-999

HARLEM
to
HOLLYWOOD

HARLEM
to
HOLLYWOOD

Billy Vera

An Imprint of Hal Leonard LLC

Published in 2017 by Backbeat Books
An Imprint of Hal Leonard Corporation
7777 West Bluemound Road
Milwaukee, WI 53213

Trade Book Division Editorial Offices
33 Plymouth St., Montclair, NJ 07042

Printed in the United States of America

Book design by Kristina Rolander

Library of Congress Cataloging-in-Publication Data
Names: Vera, Billy.
Title: Harlem to Hollywood / Billy Vera.
Description: Montclair, NJ : Backbeat Books, 2017.
Identifiers: LCCN 2016046566 | ISBN 9781617136627
Subjects: LCSH: Vera, Billy. | Singers--United States--Biography.
Classification: LCC ML420.V338 A3 2017 | DDC 781.64092 [B] --dc23
LC record available at https://lccn.loc.gov/2016046566

www.backbeatbooks.com

"When I turned forty-five, I couldn't get arrested. Then I turned sixty-five, and I became a legend."

—BENNY GOLSON

CONTENTS

FOREWORD

June 21, 2014. Billy Vera takes the stage of the Cutting Room in midtown Manhattan, and he's not alone. I'm not talking about the swinging eighteen-piece band that exuberantly backs him on his loving tribute to the great black songwriters of America's last century. What I mean is he's brought something else up there with him. What he's carrying, tucked deep into his heart and soul, is a whole history of jazz, rhythm and blues, and rock 'n' roll.

On this night, in a set that pops with Billy's evident joy in the music, he grabs you with such moody and melancholic blues classics as Buddy Johnson's "Since I Fell for You," Count Basie's "Blue and Sentimental," and Billy Strayhorn's "My Little Brown Book," as well as his own "Room with a View," written with the great Lowell Fulson. True, this singer's not black of skin, but he sure ain't Pat Boone covering Little Richard. This is the cat whose soulful hit with former gospel singer Judy Clay preceded the duo's very first appearance at Harlem's Apollo Theater in the sixties, the one who shocks the pants off 'em when he walks out onstage for the first time and he's—white? B. V. knows of what he sings. He's walked the walk, witnessed the woes, and suffered the slings and arrows. And tonight at the Cutting Room he looks you in the eye and tells the truth—after all, Vera is the first half of "veracity," is it not?

So, wait, stop the music. Or at least hit "pause" for a moment. Because we are compelled to ask this former white kid from suburban White Plains, New York, a nagging but pertinent question: What did you do to be so black and blue?

Billy's answer to this and other musical questions is this book, and it's delivered in the cool, mellow tone of his distinctive voice. If you've ever had the pleasure of hearing Billy speak—on the phone, onstage, on TV in his many commercial voiceovers—that same hip, husky drawl is here on every page. It's after midnight, he's finished his last set, and the two of you are sitting in the back booth of some roadhouse over a couple of—well, in his case it's Pepsi—and he's laying it all out intimately, understatedly, again giving it to you straight, the whole fascinating, up-and-down trip that was and is his life. And he is that rare bird in music that's never dabbled in drugs or alcohol. The sixties? The seventies? He's not only been there, he remembers it.

Pick a musical period of the last fifty years and Billy Vera is there, almost Zelig-like, though hardly anonymous. As a composer, his songs have been recorded by Ricky Nelson (before he was Rick) and Michael Bublé. How's that for longevity? As a record producer and scholar of American music, his album notes won him a Grammy in 2013 for Ray Charles' *Singular Genius: The Complete ABC Singles*. And as a singer, my old boss Johnny Carson ranked him second only to the great Tony Bennett, booking him on the *Tonight Show* nearly as often. But don't let me tell you about Billy Vera. Let Billy tell you. Waiter, pour the man another cola.

MICHAEL BARRIE

Michael Barrie's work on *The Late Show with David Letterman* and *The Tonight Show Starring Johnny Carson* has earned him twenty Emmy nominations and absolutely no wins. Barrie lives in Los Angeles with his wife, the lovely Fredrica Duke.

ACKNOWLEDGMENTS

Unlike most books, where there's often dozens of people who helped out, this has been basically a two-person effort. After I wrote it from memory with an assist from my old date books to ensure accuracy, the task of finding someone to publish a memoir by a guy most publishers and agents deemed "not a big enough name" fell to my dear friend and fearless protector, Tamela D'Amico, who has had my back and encouraged me daily for the past six years.

As if that weren't enough, Tamela did the hours of tedious grunt work, editing and formatting all these pages into a proper manuscript submission. I thank you from the bottom of my little black heart. Also, many thanks to the Backbeat Books team, senior editor Bernadette Malavarca and publisher John Cerullo, who both believed my story deserved to be heard; marketing and publicity manager Wes Seeley for his enthusiasm and wonderful ideas for getting it out to the public; and to copyeditor Zahra Brown and designer Kristina Rolander, who made my words into a beautiful book. You are all professionals of the highest order.

I am also grateful to the generosity of the wonderful photographers who allowed us to use their work, adding the visual historical perspective that makes a book of this kind come alive: Vera Anderson, Barry Druxman, Carol Friedman, Mark Hanauer, Rob Lewine, and Stephen Paley. And for my author photo, my friend and homeboy, Richard Roundtree. Extra thanks to Dhana Taprogge for touching Richard's photo up to make my skin look as smooth as a baby's butt.

To the many talented musicians who have made my music come to life over the years: without you there would've been nothing to write about.

Finally, to my friends and family, both here and gone: thank you for your love, understanding, and acceptance.

INTRODUCTION

Tuesday, February 16, 1988.

It was a busy week, recording a duet of Percy Mayfield's "Please Send Me Someone to Love" with E. G. Daily for her album at A&M's studio. An early-morning radio interview with Rick Dees. An appearance on Will Shriner's TV talk show, goofing with Don Rickles. A screening of a movie I'd just worked on called *Baja Oklahoma*, where I got to sing a song with Willie Nelson and hang out all night with a beautiful young up-and-coming actress named Julia Roberts. I would close out with a pair of nightclub gigs with my band, the Beaters.

But the highlight of the week came on Tuesday at noon, when I was to receive a star on the Hollywood Walk of Fame, a long way from behind the counter at the Boss Record Shop in White Plains, New York.

Around 11:00 a.m., a crowd began to gather on Vine Street in front of the Capitol Records Tower, by the fenced-off section where the podium stood. I arrived in an old Rolls Royce driven by my friend Paul Gayten, the first rhythm-and-blues star from New Orleans to have a hit record back in 1947. Paul, who was exactly my mother's age, had adopted me when I first moved to Los Angeles in 1979 and had been my biggest supporter and cheerleader, through thick and thin.

A few days prior, I'd worried that some might criticize me, fearing I wasn't a big enough name to deserve this honor. But Angie Dickinson, who had nominated me, explained the process. After nomination, a committee from the Hollywood Chamber of Commerce decided, based on whether your fame had come as a result of your connection with that city. Having made a name for myself in local clubs, making records and doing movies, TV, and radio in Hollywood, I was deemed by the powers that be to be qualified.

I was wearing my nicest light-beige suit, a white shirt, a blue silk tie, and suede shoes. I was looking sharp when the honorary mayor of Hollywood, Johnny Grant, called Capitol Records' new president, Joe Smith, up to the microphone to introduce me. I'd asked Joe to do the honors because of my concerns about criticism. Joe was known as the great roaster, and I felt that his irreverent approach would set the right tone. From his opening line, he did not disappoint: "What do you say about Billy Vera? Billy Vera gets a hit record every ten years . . . whether he needs one or not." The resulting laughter put the crowd on my side, as I knew it would.

Joe then brought Angie up with her big surprise. She had flown my daughter, Maria, out from Stamford, Connecticut, to share in my big day. They both stood beside me as I accepted this honor and basked in the love of the crowd, surrounded by my friends and associates, including my agent, Danny Robinson; my attorney, Chuck Hurewitz; my manager, Jim Morey; and the guys in my band, who'd made this journey with me for the past nine years.

With a number one record, a movie, and a new album coming out, I was on the top of the world . . . or was I?

1
Roots

Long before that star ceremony, and way earlier than the Boss Record Shop, my father, William Jamieson McCord, was born on December 18, 1916, in Colville, a town of some fifteen hundred residents located in the northeastern part of the state of Washington. The local economy consisted of timber and mining. Twelve native tribes, collectively known as the Colville Indians, chiefly the Nez Perce, lived on a reservation nearby.

Quinn William McCord, my grandfather, was the local undertaker. He came from a Scots-Irish family of bridge builders who made their way north from the Cherokee Strip in Oklahoma, building structures in Colorado, Nevada, and Wyoming, eventually landing in Colville. Later, during the Great Depression, when there was little money for funerals, Quinn would prepare and bury the town's dead, often accepting payment in bushels of potatoes or other vegetables, even chickens. One day, a new, rival undertaker came to town and spread lies about Quinn, causing the family to move to San Diego, where they earned a modest living operating two small apartment buildings.

Dual tragedies struck during my dad's childhood. The family home burned to the ground and his mother died when he was ten, leaving his younger sister, Louise, and himself motherless until Quinn married a strict schoolteacher named Alva, who provided the family with a third sibling, also named Quinn.

Alva was a tough, controlling woman. Many years later, as a widow in her late seventies, she came home one evening from playing cards with the girls to find two men, escaped convicts, in her house. For the rest of the night she was brutally raped by these beasts. When I asked her about it a few years later, she said, "Well, it had been a long time since your grandfather died, but if memory serves, they weren't very good at it." If that's not a strong woman, I don't know what is.

Young William was dressed in the style of Little Lord Fauntleroy, the subject of a popular children's novel of the time, causing his classmates to cruelly call him a sissy. In high school, he learned to play the saxophone and performed for dances.

He spent two years at Purdue University in West Lafayette, Indiana, before striking out to find his lifelong occupation as a radio announcer, starting in Spokane, Washington. Jobs in Washington, DC, and Cincinnati followed before World War II broke out, when he enlisted in the Army Air Corps, rising to the rank of first lieutenant and becoming a bomber pilot.

Meanwhile, in the tiny unincorporated community of Bascom, in northern Ohio, Charles and Victoria Ridenour gave birth on January 24, 1920, to a daughter, Anna Rose, who would become the middle child of seven. She would also be the only one to graduate high school. The family was poor; their house stood a hundred feet from the Baltimore and Ohio Railroad tracks, where the long trains would cause it to shake to its foundation as they roared by. As late as 1960, there was no indoor plumbing, only an outhouse, where the chamber pots used during the night were emptied each morning—after the intrepid first visitor had taken a stick from the wall and stirred it around to get rid of the black widow spider webs. Baths were taken by heating water on the stove and pouring it into a zinc tub on the kitchen floor. The telephone on the wall was of the wind-up variety. An operator would answer and place any calls. Bascom was that kind of poor.

The family had its roots in the Netherlands and in Alsace-Lorraine, that often-disputed border between France and Germany. At the end of any given war, the inhabitants would be French or German, depending on which side had won the most recent conflict.

Bascom, which was halfway between the small cities of Fostoria and Tiffin, the home of Heidelberg University on the Sandusky River, has never had a population of more than five hundred residents. The town businesses consisted of a farm supplies store; Walt Kelbley's lunch shop, which also sold magazines; three churches; a "beer joint"; and Clouse's, a general store that had a bar in the back, where farm workers drank while their wives and kids sat waiting in the car or truck.

Unlike most similar hamlets, Bascom also had the Gem, a small factory that made wooden furniture. Charlie Ridenour worked there, losing one finger on his right hand. I remember staring at it as I held his hand when we walked to the post office to pick up mail, and then up the street to Clouse's, where he'd sit me on a barstool while he drank beer and I sipped a Coke.

The Gem's owner lived in the only nice house in town and, to give something back, built Meadowbrook Park, which contained an Olympic-size pool, an outdoor movie theater, picnic tables, the usual Ferris wheel and roller coaster, and a large ballroom where first- and second-tier traveling bands, including Glenn Miller, Benny Goodman, and Stan Kenton, would play for dancing. It was at the Meadowbrook that Anna Rose got her first experience singing.

Upon graduation at eighteen and armed with a new name, Patti Ryan, she went to Cleveland to make her way in show business, performing in nightclubs, where she met all kinds of celebrities and future stars, thanks to her good looks. In Chicago, the legendary theatrical portrait photographer Maurice Seymour took a famous picture of her in which she rivals the great movie beauty Veronica Lake.

She sang on bills with the likes of Danny Thomas and a pre-stardom Frankie Laine, who was her boyfriend for a while. Years later, she would tell her son, "He was a lot like you; he loved to hang out with the black musicians"—the guys who defined what it was to be hip, in Laine's generation as well as my own. One night, Frank Sinatra took her home ("He was a perfect gentleman; he didn't try any funny business"). Another night, Duke Ellington sat in with the band and played piano behind her.

In the fall of 1943, while working in Indianapolis with the quintet of jazz accordionist Art Van Damme, she met a handsome first lieutenant in a spiffy Army Air Corps uniform and fell head over heels. It was a typical wartime romance and marriage, and, nine months later, on May 28, 1944, while the serviceman was stationed at March Field in Riverside, California, teaching the boys how to fly B-24 bombers, the couple had a baby boy . . . me.

Some children are born of love. More are born of fleeting romance. I was one of these latter. I have never harbored any self-pity or resentment over this fact. It's simply the way things were. It didn't make for a pleasant childhood, what with the bickering my sister and I were subjected to as children of a loveless marriage. We often commented that we'd never seen our parents even hold hands.

With no close friends to confide in, my mother would later occasionally confess to her young son things no son should be privy to. Did I need to know that, two weeks after their marriage, she had come to the realization that she'd made a grave mistake? Was it necessary to my well-being to know that my parents had virtually no sex life and that my little sister was a result of a broken, seldom-used diaphragm during a rare coupling?

The strong find ways of coping, and my way was to avoid my family as much as possible, spending time with friends, observing that their families were not perfect, either. As I grew older, I gravitated toward families where I felt a certain warmth that I was looking for.

In 1944, Riverside had a population of some thirty-four thousand (it's ten times as many today). Wartime Southern California had a housing shortage, thanks to the influx of workers who came, hearing of openings in local factories. As an officer, my father was allowed to live off base. Our first home was a Quonset hut with no floor, just oilcloth over the earth. After a scorpion frightened my mother, we moved to a tiny house, a duplex shared with another officer's family.

I was slow learning to walk, but one afternoon, our neighbor, a pretty housewife, said, "Billy, if you walk I'll give you a big kiss" . . . so I stood up and walked around the house for the next half hour.

Daddy was soon set to be shipped out to the South Pacific. On the drive to the port of San Diego, while he was sitting in the passenger seat, a rock thrown by some dumb kid crashed through the windshield, blinding him in his right eye. He spent several months in an army hospital, enduring a number of operations to rebuild his brow with bone fragments taken from his hip.

During his recovery, my mom got a job singing on radio station KWTO in Springfield, Missouri, where her guitarist was a young Chet Atkins. When Daddy got better, he was offered his old job in

Cincinnati at WLW, a powerful clear-channel station that, during the early 1930s, could be heard in forty states and as far away as Toronto and South America, thanks to its five hundred thousand–watt signal. The government eventually forced WLW to reduce power to fifty thousand watts, which still covered a huge market, enabling local celebrities like Doris Day, Rosemary Clooney, the Mills Brothers, Fats Waller, Merle Travis, and Andy Williams to become national stars. Writer Rod Serling worked at the station at this time, before leaving to create *The Twilight Zone*.

WLW was owned by the Crosley Broadcasting Corporation, which made all kinds of appliances, radios, TVs, record players, and even a small automobile that was too far ahead of its time to catch on nationally.

My dad went back to work as an announcer, working on every type of show, from the after-midnight organ stylings of Gladys "Hap" Lee on *Moon River* to live big-band remotes across the Ohio River in the Covington, Kentucky, nightclubs operated by Cleveland mob boss Moe Dalitz. In later years I asked him what it had been like, working around Dalitz, and he said, "Well, I always got a good parking spot, right in front."

My mom, now calling herself Ann Ryan, soon became a local favorite, eventually performing on eleven radio and TV shows a week, as well as doing personal appearances on weekends. I have fond memories of sitting on Betty Clooney's lap while my mom was busy on camera. Betty's older sister Rosemary had moved to New York and stardom, breaking up their sister act and leaving young Betty behind to follow later.

Cincinnati was a great music town. In addition to the stars mentioned above, WLW was home to *Midwestern Hayride*, a rival at the time to Nashville's *Grand Ole Opry*. The city was also the home of King Records, one of the earliest independent record companies, owned by Syd Nathan, a short, stout, stereotypical record man who wore thick Coke-bottle glasses and chomped a big cigar. King started out as a "hillbilly" label, with acts like Merle Travis, Hank Penny, Cowboy Copas, the Delmore Brothers, Grandpa Jones, and Moon Mullican, before branching out into the rhythm-and-blues field, bringing fame to the likes of Bullmoose Jackson, Wynonie Harris, Hank Ballard, Little Willie John, and, most importantly, James Brown.

My earliest memories of music came courtesy of some 78 rpm records we had in the house. Besides my kiddie records, Walt Disney's *Dumbo* and *Song of the South*, with Br'er Fox, Br'er Bear, and that great tune "Zip-A-Dee-Doo-Dah," there were Vaughn Monroe's "Riders in the Sky"; "Wrap Your Troubles in Dreams," by Woody Herman, vocal by Mary Ann McCall; and my favorite, "The Frim Fram Sauce," by the King Cole Trio. Once I learned to use the record player, I played those over and over, Nat "King" Cole becoming a lifelong hero.

I was given a plastic ukulele, on which I picked out melodies and learned to play simple chords and sing easy songs.

We lived in Cincinnati from 1947 to 1951, when my dad, who also served as the union shop steward and was a by-the-book kind of guy, fell afoul of station management. Cincinnati wasn't much of a union town, and WLW, not being very union-friendly, fired my mother as a warning to him. But Daddy, who'd been a spoiled child, was stubborn and refused to change his ways, so they finally fired him, too.

Hearing of a job opening in Philadelphia, he headed east while we waited at our house at 1026 Sunset Avenue, up the street from St. William's, where I spent first grade. When that job failed to materialize, he kept on to New York and sent for us while he pounded the pavement, looking for work.

I was saddened that my mom had to sell the cool little Crosley station wagon WLW had given her, but it had to be. Now pregnant, she drove us in our light-green, two-door 1948 Buick Roadmaster all along the new Pennsylvania Turnpike, then up the New Jersey Turnpike, both of which were in the process of being completed.

For a while we lived in a midtown Manhattan hotel while my father picked up odd announcing jobs before landing a staff gig at NBC, where he would remain, thanks to a lifetime network announcers' contract he helped negotiate as a local board member of AFTRA, the radio and television performers' union.

Later that year, we moved to an apartment in Mamaroneck, a suburb north of the city, where I attended second grade and where my sister, Kathleen, was born on February 18, 1952. Daddy had little patience for children; the noise rattled him and set off his short temper, so my parents weren't getting along very well.

One afternoon, I was swinging on the swings in the playground when an attention-seeking girl my age kept purposely getting in the way. Annoyed, I called her a "fucking bitch," and an old Italian lady who was hanging clothes gasped and said, in her old-world accent, "Billy, I'ma tella you fadda." She did, and my father, embarrassed and enraged, came running out and dragged me by my arm into the house, where, in front of my mother, he put his hands around my throat and began to strangle me. My mother screamed, and, brought to his senses, he stopped. She threatened to leave him then but ultimately did not.

They thought a house with more room might be the answer to their problems, so we moved again, this time to a nice three-bedroom house farther north, in Hartsdale. It was red, with a white roof, on the corner of Poe Street and Stevenson Avenue. All the neighborhood streets were named for authors—Longfellow, Chaucer, Keats—hence the name Poets Corners. We moved in on Halloween of 1952.

The neighbors were mostly commuters, those men in the gray flannel suits, junior execs who took the train into Manhattan to work on Madison Avenue or in other white-collar occupations. It was right out of the TV show *Mad Men*: drinks in the bar car of the train, then one or two more at the bar across from the station, to take the edge off before heading home to the wife and kids. Daddy was not one of those. Other than the occasional beer on a hot day, he barely partook of alcoholic beverages.

My dad's hours were inconsistent. Like the other sixteen staff announcers, he was subject to be called to work at odd hours, so we never knew whether he was going to be home for dinner or sleeping all day after working the night shift, either at NBC's studios in the RCA Building at Rockefeller Center, their uptown studios in Harlem, or doing a "remote" broadcast from Birdland or some other nightclub.

Occasionally, my dad would take me to work. He sat in a soundproof booth and was handed a stack of scripts to read when the engineer or producer—one of whom was Sy Kravitz, father of future rock star Lenny—would point to him. In that era of "live" broadcasting, there was no "take two"; nothing was taped. You got it right the first time. Everything was timed to the second. As a result of this training, if you were to ask him what time it was, he'd look at his watch and say, "Oh, about thirteen and a half after." About.

On his breaks, there was the announcers' lounge, a smoke-filled room, dark with leather furniture and big men with big, deep voices. I'd hear them talking about the same things as normal men, ball games and such, but with these huge voices of God.

In addition to between-the-shows announcing, my father also did quiz shows like *Twenty One, Concentration*, and *Tic Tac Dough* for Barry/Enright Productions. Host Jack Barry would say, "And now, Bill McCord, who's our next contestant?" and he'd reply, "Well Jack, our next contestant is a housewife from Passaic, New Jersey! Meet Bessie Whoever!!" And that's how he earned his living and was able to send me to Catholic school, to make my mom happy.

She, a Catholic, mistakenly thought for years that she'd been automatically excommunicated for marrying a Protestant, but she was still determined that I get a Catholic education. In those days the public schools weren't nearly as bad as today, but they were still not up to parochial school standards.

Since I'd gone to second grade at Mamaroneck's public school, I was behind when I started third grade, two months into the semester, at Our Lady of Mt. Carmel, where the other kids had already been taught multiplication and long division. I managed to catch up somehow, under the strict discipline of the good sisters.

Part of that discipline consisted of our uniforms, which served to restrict the girls' competitive nature and ensure that the poorer girls wouldn't feel inferior to those whose parents could afford better clothes. The girls wore drab, monogrammed brown jumpers over tan blouses while we boys wore tan shirts, brown ties, brown corduroy pants, and green corduroy jackets.

I was the kind of kid who when school was out would leave the house early in the morning to play with my friends. I wasn't much into sports but loved baseball, so during the season we'd be up the street at a field some of the local fathers had turned into a rather bumpy and rocky diamond. We'd play all day, with a little time out for food at the home of whoever's mother would feed us.

I recall one afternoon walking quietly in the door and overhearing my mother say to a friend, "Oh, I don't worry about him; he comes home when he's hungry," and that's a pretty good description of how

I've conducted my life ever since. Come to think of it, this behavior, my yearning to be free, probably explains my lack of success when it comes to marriage. Finding a woman who'll put up with a man who comes and goes as he pleases isn't very easy.

Mt. Carmel was to be my school through eighth grade. That was the year Sister Mary Anita, fed up with the riot that would ensue each time she left the classroom, impeached our class president and installed me in a coup d'état because all the rough, blue-collar guys liked me and would be quiet if I asked them. She told my parents I had "leadership qualities."

Eighth grade was also the year a well-endowed new girl arrived too late to get a uniform, so she relied on her own personal fashion sense, which leaned toward tight skirts and sweaters, giving rise to all sorts of typical thirteen-year-old-boy comments regarding her name, which was, aptly, Sue Mellon.

In my fascination with girls, I was like any other boy my age, but it was in sixth grade at Our Lady of Mt. Carmel that I found my life's passion, a little thing called rock 'n' roll.

2
Hail, Hail, Rock 'n' Roll

One morning in late 1955 or early 1956, a classmate excitedly came into class and said, "Did you hear rock 'n' roll last night?" I asked what he was talking about, and he said, "Ten-ten WINS, man, Alan Freed! Rock 'n' roll!"

I tuned in the ancient Stromberg-Carlson radio on the nightstand next to my bed that night and had a life-changing experience. I no longer recall what songs Freed played that night. They might've been the Cleftones' "Little Girl of Mine," Shirley and Lee's "I Feel Good," or something by Frankie Lymon and the Teenagers, but I was hooked. As much as I loved music in general, this stuff really spoke to me, in that way that every new generation finds a sound they can call their own.

By now, my mom had tried her hand at getting work as a solo singer, appearing on *Arthur Godfrey's Talent Scouts*, where she won that week, singing the Doris Day hit "Secret Love," and was told by Godfrey that if he didn't already have too many girl singers he'd hire her as a regular. She and I won first prize on a radio show called *Live Like a Millionaire*, taking home a Roadmaster bike and one of RCA Victor's new 45 rpm record players. There is an acetate recording of my high-pitched, squeaky little seven-year-old voice singing "The Darktown Strutters Ball," with a gravelly sound that would make Louis Armstrong proud.

Among the records my mother brought home from time to time were albums by Frank Sinatra (*Songs for Young Lovers* and *Songs for Swingin' Lovers*, with his now-classic take on "I've Got You Under My Skin"); the soundtrack to *The Benny Goodman Story*; a compilation of Tommy Dorsey's forties hits; and, my favorite, Duke Ellington's *Ellington Uptown*, with his long version of "Take the 'A' Train," which my son, Charlie, has memorized and can sing along with today. Music had me in its grip.

Perhaps partially due to his odd working hours, my father didn't like to go out, preferring to stay home and watch ballgames or read his Zane Grey paperback Westerns, usually sitting in the bathroom. So I became my mother's designated date when she wanted to see a Broadway show. I think my first was *Damn Yankees*. She took me to so many—*West Side Story*, *My Fair Lady*, *Camelot*, and *Funny Girl* with that Streisand girl—and this furthered my education in the art of the theater, letting me see what makes one performer stand out over others. I got so good that I could pick who was going to be a star, as I did when we saw the Sammy Davis, Jr., vehicle *Golden Boy*. Out of the darkness, a white-hot spotlight hit a girl the color of Hershey's chocolate in a hot red dress—aimed directly at her astonishing derriere. She turned around, and it was Lola Falana. In that moment, anyone could see a star was being born.

My mom also took me to see movies and other shows. Two standouts were *High Society*, with Bing Crosby, Grace Kelly, Frank Sinatra, and Louis Armstrong, at Radio City Music Hall, and *The Girl Can't Help It*, with Jayne Mansfield and a slew of rock 'n' roll stars, all in Technicolor and CinemaScope, at the late and lamented Roxy at Fiftieth Street, near Seventh Avenue.

The five-thousand-seat Westchester County Center in White Plains had shows. There, we saw Nat "King" Cole, the Dick Clark *Caravan of Stars*, and Judy Garland. From our seats on the upper level, stage right, I could see Judy chugging what looked like a quart of vodka or gin in the wings as the orchestra played the overture. The moment she hit the stage, the largely gay crowd on the main floor rose and rushed the stage as one. It was the first time I'd ever seen an audience do that.

In the Bronx was a place called Freedomland, kind of a poor man's Disneyland that had weekly shows. We saw two volumes of the Motown Revue, featuring every Motown star you can name, from the Supremes, to the Temptations, to Smokey and the Miracles, to twelve-year-old Little Stevie Wonder, who played drums, organ, and his signature harmonica. My mom was most impressed that day with Kim Weston, a fine Motown singer who never really got her due.

But the Freedomland act that really blew me away was Count Basie. Holy Mother of God! The sound that rolled off that bandstand! It was thrilling beyond belief. One minute they were blasting your brains out, and the next, Basie took it down to a whisper, all the while swinging like mad, at whatever tempo or volume. Another great lesson tucked away for future use.

When a solo career failed to materialize, my mom decided to learn to sight-read music. That eventually led to a job with the Ray Charles Singers (the original Ray, not the more famous one), singing background on *The Perry Como Show* for several years and on Perry's hit records, like "Magic Moments" and "Catch a Falling Star." She also sang on Pat Boone's show and on her former boyfriend Frankie Laine's summer replacement show.

Sometimes I'd go with her to the Ziegfeld Theater on Sixth Avenue to watch the Como dress rehearsals on Saturday and stay for the show later that night. Song pluggers hung out by the stage door, in hopes of persuading Perry or one of the guest stars to sing the songs they published.

Today, for a young boy to be in that dressing room with all those half-naked singers and dancers might be considered child abuse, but to have all those beautiful women petting and kissing me as I sat on their laps was heaven.

Mom kept a brown leather autograph book for me, which I still have. It contains the signatures of some of the biggest stars of the day: Roy Rogers, Louis Armstrong, Tony Bennett, Jo Stafford, Gene Autry, Fats Domino, Liberace—you name them, they were all guests on the Como show.

My mother was in her glory, and everybody back in Bascom tuned in every week. I would be sent there each summer and was treated like the crown prince because they adored their Anna Rose. Those were some happy times. My Aunt Helen, the youngest in the family and my godmother, showed me what love was. It was written on her face every time I walked into the house. She'd sing, "Hey good lookin', whatcha got cookin'," and light up the room with that beautiful smile of hers. I'm not sure how her two boys took to the attention she showed me. Maybe they instinctively knew I was a lonely kid from a family that didn't get along and figured I needed what Aunt Helen gave me.

Still in sixth grade, I saved up my lawn-mowing and snow-shoveling money, went to Hunt's Music Shop in White Plains, and purchased my first three records of my own: "Blueberry Hill," by Fats Domino;

"Honky Tonk," by Bill Doggett; and "Priscilla," a local New York hit by Eddie Cooley and the Dimples. That year, 1956, Cooley cowrote a song that would earn well over a million dollars over the years, after Peggy Lee revived it a few years later, "Fever."

Those first three 45s are still in my shelves, which today contain a world-class collection. A few weeks later, I bought my first vocal group record, "Oh What a Nite" by the Dells. This subgenre wouldn't be named doo-wop until the 1970s, when a record collector named Wayne Stierle gave it that name and his friend, disc jockey Gus Gossert, used it on the radio. In the fifties, we just called it singing-group music.

I was one of several boys at my school who fell in love with these groups and even tried our hand at emulating that sound, often in the boys' room, to get the echo we heard on the records we loved. We weren't very good, but we had fun, singing easy songs like "Zoom Zoom Zoom" and "In the Still of the Nite." We even got up on the stage at Our Lady of Mt. Carmel and sang along with the Cleftones' "Little Girl of Mine" in hopes of impressing the girls. It was at one of those seventh-grade dances, the boys hugging the wall on one side of the room and the girls on the opposite side, that my friend Charlie and I got up the nerve to ask the prettiest girls in the class to dance, twice! We held them close, our heads filled with visions of romance, as the Heartbeats sang "A Thousand Miles Away" and Jesse Belvin crooned "Goodnight My Love."

These vocal groups had a big effect on my friends and me. In every way that counted to an early teen, these older guys epitomized for my generation what was cool, from the way they dressed to the way they carried themselves. Cool was important. I even coined a phrase: the eleventh commandment is, "Thou shalt be cool in all things at all times."

Having been born in 1944, I was among the last of a generation to whom debonair black style and black "cool" were influential in the extreme. The thing was to dress, dance, talk, and even walk like the hip, older black guys. The gap between us and those who followed, the ones born from 1946 on, was wide. They would become more influenced by the British and other role models. These were the Boomers, perhaps the most narcissistic and entitled generation in history. They were the "notice me" generation, driven by a need for attention and intent on having their way, no matter who objected.

Almost from birth, thanks largely to the teachings of Dr. Benjamin Spock, the Boomers were coddled and catered to. A booming postwar economy meant their parents had enough money to shower them with Hula Hoops, Slinkies, and other gimmicky toys. For the first time, there were phonograph records made just for kiddies, on labels like Golden Records, pressed up on special yellow vinyl for these special little tykes. When they entered their teens, the entire music industry changed, from an adult-oriented style of music to an adolescent one, to pander to and, some say, manipulate Boomer teen tastes.

From their clothing to their hairstyles to their drugs to their politics, everything about them cried out, "Me, me, pay attention to *me*!"

All this was alien to me. I had nothing in common with these people, which goes a long way toward explaining why I felt more comfortable among black people and listening to black music. Even the way black people approached drug use was cooler, although I never partook. A hippie Boomer might say, for all to hear, "Oooh, wow, let's all share this doobie," and pass it around, while a hip black dude would sidle up and whisper, "Hey man, I got some reefer. Wanna go outside?" I was too hip to be a hippie, I suppose.

Noticing my love of music, my parents offered me lessons, first on drums and piano and later on guitar. I banged away on my drum set in the den at the back of our house at 38 Poe Street, playing along with my favorite records, and tried to figure out the chords to my favorite songs on our piano.

Later generations now characterize the 1950s as a benign time, like something from the seventies sitcom *Happy Days*. Contrary to that Hollywood fantasy, fifties rock 'n' roll was dangerous music, a soundtrack for "hoods" and "greasers" who rumbled; smoked; drank; drove loud, scary cars; and cut up theater and school bus seats with switchblade knives. The Fonz, as portrayed by Henry Winkler from that sitcom, was a caricature, a harmless clown for primetime TV, compared to the real thing.

A "nice" kid foolish enough to wander into the haunt of the real hoods risked humiliation at best and a good ass-kicking at worst. It was a time of gangs and juvenile delinquents. The black leather jacket Marlon Brando wore in *The Wild One* was de rigueur in some circles, along with white T-shirts with a pack of Luckies rolled up in the sleeve and blue jeans held up by a Garrison belt with a sharpened buckle worn off to the side, providing a serious weapon when swung around its wearer's head. This "hood" image sold a lot of records in 1960, when it was used as the cover for an album called *The Paragons Meet the Jesters*, a compilation of songs by two doo-wop groups that had failed to sell several years prior. The image struck a chord among a newly post-teen working-class crowd, uncomfortable with the current changes in popular music and finding themselves nostalgic at an age when people tend to be moving forward in their tastes.

Toward the end of the fifties, the bad boys' costumes evolved from biker leather drag to something more urban: continental mohair suits with thin lapels; tight pants, pegged to fourteen inches at the ankle, the "high water" cuffs worn high enough to reveal colorful socks or black nylon hose; skinny tie; all topped off with a "stingy brim" hat and perhaps an umbrella with a sharpened tip for use as an additional weapon.

When I was in eighth grade in 1957, a new TV show came on after school, right before *The Mickey Mouse Club* with the lovely Annette Funicello, whom all the boys were in love with. The new show was *American Bandstand*.

The phenomenon of rock 'n' roll was in full swing, in New York especially. On radio, besides Alan Freed on WINS, WMCA at the left end of the dial was also programming the new music. Some of us learned of the black and ethnic stations at the right end of the dial, with boisterous, jive-talking black "personality" jocks, like Douglas "Jocko" Henderson, with his rap, appropriated from Baltimore's Maurice "Hot Rod" Hulbert ("Eee tiddy ock, GO, says Jock! I'm back on the scene with the record machine, sayin' ooh papa doo and how do you do!"). Jocko, the cool kids' fave, broadcast over WADO ("twelve eighty-o on your radio") and commuted from Philadelphia, where he also did a show. An enterprising fellow, Henderson grabbed everything he could, copping publishing or songwriting credits in addition to the payola that Freed and others took to play records. All this was, of course, unknown to us at the time. All we knew was that these were cool adults who liked our music.

Other black stations in the New York area were WLIB ("the voice of Liberty"), WWRL ("the sound of your world"), and Newark's WNJR, which catered to that city's more recent arrivals from the South.

I've often thought that one of the reasons rock 'n' roll caught on, besides its good dancing beat, was its racial ambiguity. Before any of us saw photos of these performers, none of us knew—or cared—if they were white or black. With the good and authentic rockers, their race wasn't important. Ronnie Spector once told me that when she first heard Frankie Lymon, she didn't know if he was a boy or a girl, black or white. Many black people bought Elvis's early records, thinking he was black.

Rock 'n' roll was served up on local television via Ted Steele's *Bandstand* on WOR Channel 9, Alan Freed's dance party on Channel 5, and *Jocko's Rocket Ship Show* featuring our favorite black vocal groups on Channel 13, all at 5:00 p.m., after *American Bandstand* went off the air.

The disc jockeys and hosts of these TV dance parties ranged, personality-wise, from jive-talking would-be hep cats, like Murray the K; to stiffs, like Ted Steele or Herb Shriner; to lames trying to act like teenagers and goofballs, like Clay Cole. Alan Freed was the Arthur Godfrey of our generation. We believed he was "on our side" and that he genuinely liked the music he played. Like Godfrey, he had a delivery that could sell anything. One product I recall was Snap Jack shoes. No laces, just a tongue that would snap open to allow your foot inside. I had a pair, in white buck.

Jocko was our favorite. His undisguised, utterly shameless, transparent insincerity was what made him seem so hip—that, and the fact that he played the best records. The day after he was thrown off the air, it was all we talked about. He had been peddling a cheap wine of the screw-off cap variety, called Hombre—and most likely imbibing a bit himself. "Yes sir, mommy-o, daddy-o. Get you some of that Hombre wine. It's really good shit." Boom! Dead air and another announcer came on to finish out the broadcast.

The most believable of them all was Dick Clark, who seemed like our older brother, friendly and amused at the crazy kids and their music, which he never judged. Dick was nonjudgmental long before that term became an annoying PC cliché. Dick seemed to actually like kids and treated the entertainers with respect, without fawning over them. The man knew how to walk that fine line.

The music was not always as hip as that on the black shows, but the kids were real, mostly working-class Catholic school kids from the South

Philly neighborhood around the studio, just being themselves. Watching them was like being a fly on the wall, which may have had something to do with the fact that a large portion of the viewership consisted of housewives. As long as *American Bandstand* was in Philadelphia, it remained genuine, with none of the narcissistic mugging for the camera that came into play once the show moved to Hollywood (I think it's significant that those later kids were Boomers). Plus, those Philly kids could really dance.

We knew the names of all the "regulars," those kids who danced every afternoon while Dick stood at his podium looking down and smiling benevolently. There were the super couples: Bob and Justine, Arlene and Kenny, and my dream girl, Franni Giordano, a Bridget Bardot lookalike in a tight skirt who was much too hot to have just one boyfriend, and almost too hot for fifties TV. I'm sure I wasn't the only thirteen-year-old boy who fantasized about running away to Philadelphia to meet this fourteen-year-old sexpot. Many years later, when I finally got to appear on *American Bandstand*, I cracked Dick up by saying during my on-camera interview, "Dick, I thought you said Franni Giordano was gonna be here." The next day, a messenger from Dick Clark Productions arrived at my house with an eight-by-ten photograph of Franni and Dick from 1958.

At this late date, I can't recall whether I first saw Chuck Berry on *Bandstand* or in the Alan Freed movie *Rock, Rock, Rock*. All I know is, once I saw Chuck, I wanted to be him.

I shoveled snow and mowed lawns to save up my thirty-five dollars to buy an electric guitar, a black and white Silvertone solid body from Sears. With no money for an amplifier, I plugged it into my mother's tape recorder and proceeded to learn Chuck's licks, those same licks that every young rocker from Eddie Cochran to Keith Richards would have in his arsenal.

From the beginning, I was interested in what had come before the new records I liked. White Plains had several record stores, two of which had listening booths or record players scattered about the store where you could hear your prospective purchases. There were also bins with the better-known artists' names on them, containing older songs by the acts as well as their latest offerings. That's how I managed to acquire every 45 by Frankie Lymon and the Teenagers. Frankie was a special hero to me and, as I discovered years later, also to many other New York singers of my generation. One year older than I was, Frankie was living proof that a kid my age could make it. Maybe I could make it, too.

Other shops had guys behind the counter who would suggest records and even play them for you. One such was Hunt's Music Shop. Working the counter there was a guy from my neighborhood named Kevin Falcone. Kevin, whose father, Frank, played trumpet in the NBC Symphony Orchestra under Toscanini as well as on *The Tonight Show* as an NBC staff musician, was the first hip guy I ever met. I marveled at how he could reach behind his back, without looking, and pick any record from the rack. Kevin could tell from what you asked for what you liked and suggest items to fit your taste.

In my case, he apparently saw something in me that led him to push the envelope, playing me songs that weren't on the radio, or even rock 'n' roll. Kevin turned me on to jazz and hip ballads like "Moody Mood for Love," by King Pleasure, or "To Be with You," by the Joe Cuba Sextet, a song that was a hipster favorite (back when "hipster" meant someone who was actually hip) and was played every night for years by disc jockey Symphony Sid.

Some years later, while working as a bartender at the 12-20 Club, a home base for my band, the Knight-Riders, Kevin stocked the jukebox with cool sides like Jimmy Smith's "Walk on the Wild Side," Dinah Washington's "Where Are You," Donald Byrd's "Cristo Redentor," or Horace Silver's "Song for My Father." As much as any living being, Kevin Falcone influenced what my own music would turn out to be like.

Meanwhile, Sister Mary Anita told my parents that I was one of the smartest in my eighth grade class, but I had a tendency to hang out with the rough guys. She suggested that, instead of going to high school with my friends, I'd be better off in private school. With my dad doing well with the extra income from the quiz shows and my mom's steady job on the Como show, they decided there was enough household money to send me to a place called Hackley School in Tarrytown, home of Washington Irving, creator of the literary characters Ichabod Crane and the Headless Horseman.

I hated the place from day one. I hated the preppy rich kids, with their plaid madras jackets, brown penny loafers, and paisley ties. They were such pitiful squares. Those who liked music at all were into that soulless folk crap that made me want to vomit. Luckily, I was befriended by a kid named Theo Vatis, whose father owned a Greek shipping line. A year older than me, Theo had spent the previous summer working on one of his dad's ships, where the sailors had taken him to a brothel, so he was, shall we say, a little more advanced.

At Hackley, our first class started at 8:20 a.m. and the last ended at 1:30 p.m. After lunch we had compulsory sports, which Theo and I both hated. So we came up with a scheme. Theo brought some girlie magazines and wine from home and we opened up shop under the school, where the ancient desks were stored. For twenty-five cents, we let boys come in and look at naked girls' pictures. For another quarter or a bus pass, they could drink wine from a paper cup. We let the kid who took attendance at sports in for free in exchange for marking us present while we snuck off to White Plains to hang out or go to the movies, which in those days was thirty-five cents for a double feature plus cartoons and a newsreel. For this activity, my caption in the yearbook read, "A young Al Capone."

Ninth grade at Hackley had been a total bust musically. I begged my parents to get me out of there, and for the remainder of my high school years I was allowed to go with my friends to Archbishop Stepinac High School in White Plains, where actors Alan Alda and Jon Voight had graduated before us.

I was already memorizing every detail on record labels. I knew the artists, the publishers, even the songwriters' credits in tiny print in parentheses under the song titles. I was an information junkie, so bad that my history teacher Father McAnn once said, in front of the whole class, "William, your mind is a veritable warehouse of useless knowledge," which is probably true to this day.

Word spread of a sophomore talent show, which I was intent upon entering. One problem: I had no band. So I grabbed two friends and taught one, named Henry Geoffrey, to play two songs on my drum set. Henry had never played drums before. My best friend, John Boland, was tone deaf, but his father had bought him a cheap guitar along with an amp, which I needed since I still didn't own one. John's musical ability was so poor that I had to tune his guitar and drill every note into him. But he had the right hair and that amp, so we worked with his limitations. I guess you could compare our ability to that of the punk bands of the 1980s.

Having been around show business my whole short life, I knew that you had to look right, so we went down to the army and navy store and bought cheap white jackets and metallic black shirts, topped off with white string ties like the one Chuck Berry wore on his album cover. With black slacks (remember the song? "B-b-b-b-black slacks make a cool daddy-o"), we were sharp.

We got a friend in the spotlight booth to use pink and purple gels to light us, and we learned two songs, "Come Dance with Me," by Eddie Quinteros, and the Isley Brothers' "Shout."

The school's music teacher got wind of us and, determined to see us fail, recruited several boys from the marching band to form a Dixieland outfit. Rounding out the contest was a talented classical pianist named Germano Romano, whose hands were insured for $100,000, due to his wizardry on the eighty-eight keys.

In all fairness, poor Germano deserved to win; he was no doubt the most skilled among the contestants. But in showbiz, flash always trumps talent, so we won 296 out of 298 votes, Germano racking up the remaining two. The Dixieland dudes got nothing but humiliation; as for the priest, he never spoke another word to the three of us for the remainder of our high school career.

3
Get a Job

Within walking distance of my house were two country clubs, Elmwood and Metropolis, where the bigger guys would caddy. Too scrawny to lug around two or even one bag of golf clubs for eighteen holes, I applied to Metropolis for a job as a busboy. My duties included serving the members at the pool as well as in the dining areas. Those rich girls and their mothers parading around in their bikinis didn't know this sixteen-year-old busboy was alive, but I sure got an eyeful.

It was at Metropolis that I first learned about the concept of intra-group bigotry, for Metropolis membership was restricted to Jews of German descent. Russian, Polish, Hungarian, and other Eastern European Jews were not welcome, and were relegated to Elmwood, down the street. There were no exceptions, and the Germans of Metropolis made no bones about their rejection of their fellow landsmen.

As a busboy, I was invisible and could overhear the mockery of the Elmwood "types" for the way they stuck to their Yiddishisms and for the delicatessen food they favored. The German Jews referred to themselves as Our Crowd. The bulk of them had immigrated to America some forty years before the mass influx of Jews from Eastern Europe, whom the Metropolis members considered "vulgar," *nouveau riche*, and "low-class." No matter how much money they made, the Germans never accepted their loud talk, flashy clothes, excess jewelry, and red Cadillacs.

They also preferred their help to be Irish, although there was an Italian waitress or two sprinkled in. One day, a rough-and-tumble Irish lesbian named Virginia grabbed me by my arm, saying, "You're coming with me, kid," and took me out to her bailiwick at the ninth-hole eating spot known as the halfway house. "You're the only one of these busboys that's worth a shit. I'm gonna reward you. You'll work like hell out here for three hours; then you can fuck off the rest of the day." Thus I learned the value of hard work and its rewards. The only thing I missed was ogling the teenage daughters of the members at the pool. Not that they'd ever give a second glance at a lowly busboy.

My second encounter with intra-group bigotry came one evening when I went to pick up my high school sweetheart Pam, who was widely regarded as the most beautiful girl in all of White Plains. Her family was a Southern Italian mixture of *calabrese* and *napolitano*. The father, who hated all teenage males, liked me because my mother was on television with that nice Italian boy Perry Como, and also because I had the sense to talk with him about Sinatra, whom he idolized.

So, as I waited in the living room that night for Pam to make her appearance, her father and I chatted about the ins and outs of the majesty that is Frank. Just then, the doorbell rang. It was a boy from up the street who was there to pick up Pam's younger sister, Rosalie, for a date. The father, recognizing the kid as a Sicilian, shouted, "Rosalie! What the hell were you thinking? Bringing this, this Sicilian into our home! Why don't you just bring home a *melanzane* while you're at it?"

The term *melanzane*, pronounced "mool-in-yahn" in Italian-American gutter dialect, means eggplant, and is a slur used to describe a black person. Everyone cringed as this poor kid stood there, practically in tears from humiliation.

Some years later, when I was living in the black community, I encountered a similar kind of intra-racial bigotry, based on hue. There was a ghetto saying that conveys it all: "If you're white, you're all right; if you're yellow, you're mellow; if you're brown, turn around; if you're black, get back." Along those same lines, blacks whose lineage in the North went back several generations invariably looked down on recent arrivals from the South, whom they considered too loud, ignorant, and uncouth.

After the murder of Dr. Martin Luther King, Jr., however, with the advent of Black Power, these color lines were reversed. In the neighborhood, I'd see light-skinned brothers and sisters constantly disparaged, even called "whitey," for not being "black enough."

Human nature is something we can't change, although those who think they know better never seem to tire of trying. People need someone beneath themselves to make them feel superior. They invent all kinds of reasons, the world over, fabricating divisions, caste systems, even where outsiders don't see the differences.

During my junior year, I was approached by two seniors, named Neil Pagano and Dennis Quinn, to join their band, the Pharoahs [sic]. Their singer, one Billy Vee, had left to join the Navy. Dennis, the drummer, had gone to Our Lady of Mt. Carmel, and the others were from Port Chester, where Neil's father ran a thriving real estate business. We rehearsed at his house, and his mother would cook us the most delicious Italian meals afterwards. I'll never forget her tiny meatballs, floating in a clear broth.

The first gig I played with the Pharoahs was in Port Chester at Saint Mary's Church, which had a huge auditorium with a full-sized proscenium stage. The bill was supposed to be Chuck Berry, Danny and the Juniors, a local band called the Orchids that featured the legendary Telecaster player Linc Chamberland, and the Pharoahs.

Chuck failed to show up, due to one of his periodic dust-ups with the law. We opened the show and went all out, closing with "Shout" and doing splits, during which a girl in front said, in her Puerto Rican accent, "Ooh, Billy, you got such nice underwears!" My trousers had split and we exited the stage to the sound of several hundred screaming girls.

The Pharoahs played all the church dances in Westchester County and became locally famous. At a place called Tie City downtown, we would buy fifty-cent ties and cheap cuff links and toss them to the girls in the audience to make them scream. Another trick was to remove my suit jacket and twirl it around my head, making them think I was going to throw it out into the crowd. At one church, Saint Eugene's in Yonkers, we caused such a riot that the priest pulled the plug and stopped the show, causing the angry kids to exit en masse.

One Sunday evening, as Ed Sullivan was announcing his next week's guests, I heard him say, right on network TV, "And next week, right here on our stage, from Port Chester, New York, the Pharoahs!" I thought I was hallucinating, but then the phone started ringing off the hook, people calling to ask if we really were going to be on *Ed Sullivan*. I called the other guys and no, we were not booked. Why would we be? We had no hit record. Sullivan had grown up in Port Chester, where every other family claimed he had grown up in their house, but that was the only connection anybody could think of. Ed was known for screwing up names, but this was too weird, even for him. We never figured out how it had happened.

Seeing that I was getting even more serious about a musical career, my mother took me to her voice coach, Myron "Pappy" Earnhardt, who in turn introduced me to a talent manager named Jim Gribble in his building at 1697 Broadway, above the Ed Sullivan (now David Letterman) Theater. Gribble's clients included the Earls, the Fiestas, the Passions, the Dubs, the Mystics, the Del-Satins, and, well, you get the picture. He had a guy named Stan Vincent working with the performers, and I wound up taking the train downtown several times a week after school, until one day a guy brought in a song, wanting some singers to record it.

Stan, a couple of guys from Gribble's stable, and I went into Regent Sound, where I sang lead and overdubbed the bass and falsetto parts. The song, entitled "January 1st, 1962," came out under the faux group name the Resolutions on studio guitarist Billy Mure's Valentine label and got some local airplay, partly due to my dad's AFTRA connection to DJ Peter Tripp, who played it a few times on his afternoon show. It also was played on the local Philly hour of *American Bandstand*, but never made it to the national segment.

On the strength of having a record out, I did the usual record hops, lip synching the song and signing autographs for kids who had no idea who I was. I also met some fellow performers. Tico and the Triumphs and Jo Ann Campbell, known as the "little blonde bombshell," come to mind. Jo Ann was especially nice to me, giving me several photos of herself and treating me like an equal. Many years later, I would have occasion to phone her at the Nashville home she shares with her husband, songwriter Troy Seals. When she heard my name, she gasped and told me that she sings along with my song "At This Moment" every day.

Gribble told me I should change my name so as not to be confused with my father, whose name was heard on radio and TV. I liked the sound of Vera, the last name of a girl I knew and, thinking a short name could fit in larger letters on a marquee, took it for my own. The only negative over the years has been people's tendency to mispronounce it "Veera," when it should rhyme with Yogi Berra.

About a month or so after my record came out, Jim Gribble dropped dead of a heart attack in his office one afternoon and I was left without a manager. One thing I'll never forget was the time I heard him yell from his office, "Where the hell are those goddamn Earls? I don't give two shits for anybody who's not fifteen minutes early." Ever since, I have always made it my business to arrive early, even to the most unimportant appointment.

Neil and Dennis went off to college, leaving the remaining Pharoahs to fumble along with new members. (In 2013, Neil would be elected mayor of Port Chester.) We were underage but managed to get into a nightclub called the O.P.G. (Old Post Grill) on the Port Chester side of the border with Greenwich, Connecticut. In those days, the drinking age was twenty-one in Connecticut and eighteen in New York, so border clubs did good business, as did the auto repair shops.

We played a New Year's Eve gig at the club, my first ever. At the stroke of midnight, 1962, girls stormed the stage to kiss the band. All of seventeen years old, I was passionately French-kissed by a twenty-one-year-old who told me at the end of the night she'd already been married and divorced three times. And yes, she knew how to kiss! Just as she was saying she wanted to take me back to her place to have her way with me, a body came flying through the air. I jumped up, landing on the poor guy's chest. The girl screamed and ran off, leaving me to spend the remainder of the night alone with thoughts of what might have been.

The O.P.G. also ran Sunday afternoon dances for teenagers, for which we played, along with a black organ trio called the Mighty Cravers, who were at least ten years older than I was. They took a liking to me and let me come up and sing with them, even inviting me to join them on some of their nighttime gigs. I guess they dug the novelty of a young white boy who sang in a vaguely black style.

One Sunday afternoon, after our set, I was called over to a table where three guys roughly my age were sitting. They introduced themselves as two of the Knight-Riders; the third was Phil Pepe, who was in my class at Stepinac and had told them about me. The one called Bob Power said he thought I was the coolest guy he'd ever seen and asked whether I'd be interested in joining their band to replace their singer, whom they were about to let go. The sales pitch was they had lots of nightclub work and were more established than we were. Plus they were making a lot more money than we did.

As it turned out, their main gig was at the 12-20 Club, where my band had already been working until the owner, Estelle Silverhardt, discovered I was underage. I had another month before I turned eighteen, so I worked a frat-house date at Yale with the Knight-Riders while their soon-to-be-history singer worked the 12-20 with the Pharoahs that night.

This singer, John Sweeney, claimed he'd written a song for me. He played it for us and we loved it. It was called "My Heart Cries." Bob Power got a local friend of the band to put up some money so we could record it. I taught the band a song I had written called "All My Love" for the B-side, and off we went to Dick Charles Studio to make a record.

Meanwhile, upon graduation from Stepinac, I took a job at Bandstand Music in Port Chester, which required me to take two buses. Bandstand was owned by Carl Erca, who'd played trumpet with Glenn Miller and who managed the Mighty Cravers. I played records for the customers. The two best sellers we had that summer were "Stop the Wedding," by Etta James, and Sam Cooke's two-sided smash "Havin' a Party" / "Bring It On Home to Me," with an unknown and uncredited Lou Rawls singing harmony.

Bandstand was also a one-stop distributor, so I had to deliver records, often driving as far away as Brooklyn or Bridgeport, Connecticut. Working until 3:00 a.m. with the band made this dangerous work, and I once fell asleep on the New England Thruway and scared the shit out of myself—so much that I've never again fallen asleep on the road.

At a gig at the RKO Keith's Theater in White Plains, we met Ted Daryll, who with his partner Greg Richards had written a song called "She Cried" that was on its way to becoming a hit for Jay and the Americans. Teddy's day gig was as receptionist at a small publishing company run by Gerry Teifer. Teddy introduced us, and Gerry offered to get our record to a label in exchange for the publishing on my song. We made the deal and he got us a release on Rust Records, a subsidiary of Laurie, the label famous for Dion and the Belmonts.

One night, before our record came out, a girl told us she'd heard it on the jukebox at a club called John's Paradise in the Bronx, which was impossible. We went down there and saw the song, which Sweeney claimed to have written, credited to "Etta and Harvey." I recognized the voices as Etta James and Harvey Fuqua of the Moonglows, one of my favorite groups. We informed the bosses at Laurie and they changed the credits in time for release.

The record came out and we were sent out to promote it. We did a TV show in Scranton, Pennsylvania, and "My Heart Cries" reached number one in Pittsburgh, thanks to heavy airplay by a jock named Mad Mike. It also did well in Connecticut. A couple of years later, I found out that my song "All My Love" had been a Top 10 hit in Texas and Louisiana during those days of regional records.

The Knight-Riders had, prior to my joining, made an instrumental for another label, so we had to come up with a name. My mother had told me to always use my name, rather than just a group name, to keep my name before the public, so on the spur of the moment we decided on Billy Vera and the Contrasts.

Estelle, the 12-20's owner, who was sort of a Margaret Dumont to our Marx Brothers, made us call her at the club every time we stopped for gas on the way back from Scranton, so she could give the customers a running commentary on our progress and, hopefully, keep them there until we arrived.

Her husband Al was a brute of a man who gave her seven sons and physically abused her, dipping into the till for money, which he gambled away at the track. Often, this heartsick woman would come onstage and sing "Can't Help Loving That Man of Mine" while we cruelly made fun of her behind her back, like something right out of a Marx Brothers movie.

The building that housed the 12-20 Club was a rat trap owned by Estelle's father, a slumlord who owned a string of similar buildings in New Rochelle. Upstairs were crummy, roach-infested apartments occupied mainly by the Chinese immigrants who worked at Tung Sing's, a restaurant down the street. These men worked like slaves, often for years, to save enough to bring their families to America. On their nights off, some would gamble in Chinatown, losing what little they'd earned.

One night, during a blizzard, our entire audience consisted of one of these lonely men. On our break, in broken English, he told me he'd played music back in China, so I asked him to go and get his instrument, which was a one-stringed Chinese banjo-type thing. He was thrilled to play onstage with us and promised to make us a real Chinese meal the next week, "not the crap they serve to white people at the restaurant." It was the best I've ever had.

People don't remember now, but before the coming of the Beatles, rock 'n' roll was a lower-class, blue-collar phenomenon. Our audience consisted of guys who worked in construction, pumped gas, or sold vacuum cleaners door-to-door, and girls who were beauticians, secretaries, or telephone operators. There were fights and brawls as often as not. The preppies from Scarsdale were more into Dixieland and folk music and only came to the clubs we played at when they felt like slumming. The British bands later made the music "safe" for these affluent young, taking it one more step up the socioeconomic ladder.

Most of the hottest chicks were hairdressers, and most of these were Italian. In the summer, when our bass player, Ronnie Hinds, and I would hang out at Rye Beach in Playland, you could see them in their bikinis, their hair wrapped tightly around beer cans so it would be straight when they came to the clubs to dance at night.

Ronnie loved to "play the role," as he put it. His main role was the King. The King had to do things that were "kingish." It was kingish to dress sharp, in a continental suit with narrow lapels and a skinny tie with a tie pin. Your shirt had to have a high collar and French cuffs, with just the right amount of cuff showing. No one had to tell you; if you were cool, you just knew. Your suit pants were form-fitting, pegged to fourteen inches at the ankle. You wore Italian heeled boots.

The hottest girls would dance, in their tight, short skirts. Not minis, just short . . . and tight enough to show off some of the greatest asses on the planet. It was also kingish to compete to see who could take the most girls out to the car on your breaks between sets. Over the course of a five-set night, two was cool. Three was kingish.

One evening, I was waiting in the kitchen for one of these club chicks to pick me up for a date. My mother was washing dishes when into our driveway pulled Carmela, an older woman of twenty-two who worked as a hairdresser. She was driving a white Thunderbird convertible with the top down. From the kitchen window, my mother could see her flaming red hair, done up in a large bouffant, with enough hairspray to prevent the wind from destroying its carefully crafted shape.

The look on my mother's face said it all. If Carmela came through that door, this was not going to end well. I think the word "chippie" emerged from her lips. I'm pretty sure I was out the door before these two formidable women could meet, and on my way to a night of certain lust.

I didn't even own a car yet. After our 1948 Buick Roadmaster grew too old, it had been replaced by a spanking new green-and-white 1955 Buick Century, followed three years later by a 1958 black Cadillac convertible with a white top and red leather upholstery, which my mother mostly drove to the city when she was working on *The Perry Como Show*. After my great-grandma died, my dad inherited her 1949 light-blue Plymouth coupe, in which I learned to drive. But mostly, my transportation was reliant on the kindness of friends, or girlfriends with cars.

The first car I owned was a used Alfa Romeo, a shiny gold convertible, a real lemon that lasted not much longer than a month. I traded it in for something more sensible, a used Volkswagen bus, with the idea of using it to carry the band equipment. This was before the hippies came along, so a VW bus was not yet a fashion statement, but merely utilitarian. It too broke down a little too often, so, remembering what my economics professor had said, that the most economical automobile to buy was a bottom-of-the-line Chevy with no extras, I went to the local Chevrolet dealer's and, for fifty-six dollars a month, bought a brand-new white 1965 Chevy Nova. The only extras were a radio and a side view mirror, which for some reason cost extra. It was a good, solid vehicle and lasted for three years, as per the great American tradition of planned obsolescence.

My parents, as so many parents do, urged me to go to college "to have something to fall back on." To humor them, I entered Fordham University, a Jesuit school in the Bronx, but didn't really apply myself. School had never interested me. I made it through freshman year, but two months into my sophomore year, with a record out and convinced that I was going to become a rock 'n' roll star in the next ten minutes, I took a leave of absence.

One young lay professor took me aside on my last day, handed me a small pile of his own Elvis records, and said, "You're not likely going to come back. But you've learned everything college had to teach you, which is how to find knowledge. What I'd like you to do is to never stop reading. Find an author you like, and read everything he wrote. Then find another and do the same thing. In this way, you will educate yourself." I took his advice and have never stopped reading.

One evening, I stopped by the 12-20 to pick up my amp. We had a gig at Jack 'n' Mac's, a bucket of blood on the other side of White Plains. A local tough guy, Butch Futia, carried my amp to the car for me and, to my surprise, got in. Butch was not the kind of guy you questioned about such things, but still, I asked where he wanted to go. "I'm going with you," was all he said.

The whole night, he stood by me, next to the bandstand. I thought it odd, but said nothing. Later, I was told that Sweeney had paid a guy from Yonkers to throw acid in my face, but the guy, knowing who Butch was, had wisely changed his mind.

White Plains was known for two things: some of the most beautiful Italian girls on the planet, and some real bad boys, with names like Babe Telesco, Sal Pelligrino, and Manny Santos. Babe, his brother, Gyp, and his father, Pep, were criminals to the core, but I loved Babe. As handsome as any movie star, he would fight until his opponent didn't get up, and if he liked you, he'd go through a wall for you. Every time he got out of jail, he'd come directly to the club and say, "When are you going to make it big, man, so I can take care of you and you can keep me out of jail?" Like it was my job to keep him out of prison. But that's criminal logic for you.

Babe was a lone wolf, never joined a mob, and always worked alone. He met his demise after robbing the wrong house one night in Yonkers. They got word to him that if he returned the merchandise, all would be forgiven. He declined the offer. Not long after, he was helping a friend carry some flammable liquid into the friend's beauty parlor when a lowlife named Richie flicked a lit cigarette into the container, causing it to explode in Babe's arms.

It took him two weeks to die, during which time Gyp snuck heroin into the hospital to ease his pain. The doctors said it was a miracle he had lived two days, much less two weeks. Only his incredible strength had kept him alive.

Of all the clubs we played in Westchester County, the greatest, bar none, was the Country House, later known as the Deercrest Inn, in Banksville, New York, just across the border from the wealthy town of Greenwich, Connecticut. We played there from 1963 until late 1967, when "Storybook Children" became a hit and I had to hit the road.

Patrons came from as far away as New Haven or the Bronx. Part of the attraction was the hit record acts that the owners, Mike and Maghee, with the help of our guitarist, Bobby Power, booked each Friday and Saturday. The club was home to the best bands in the area. When we first played there, the opposite band was the Furies, a terrific dance band whose entire repertoire consisted of James Brown and Bill Doggett songs. There were the Orchids, a seven-piece horn band led by the Telecaster genius Linc Chamberland. One of Linc's students, David Spinozza, had a band patterned after the Orchids. David went on to a career as a top studio guitarist. Later came my old friends Rex Garvin and the Mighty Cravers.

When British rock bands became the thing, the Country House crowd would have none of it. Soul, danceable soul, was their thing, and ninety percent of the record acts who appeared there were black, too. Many of those acts became friends, some for life. We played their music well and they appreciated us, as most house bands in nightclubs couldn't read music.

Seeing how well-dressed many of the better acts were, it was clear we needed to upgrade our stage clothes. We had already moved on from our cheap, thirty-five-dollar gray outfits, which we'd made fancier by adding black velvet collars, and were wearing sharp suits of black mohair, purchased at Paul Sargent's, a hip shop in Greenwich Village favored by the fashionable clotheshorses of the day.

The Isley Brothers befriended us after we backed them up so well, and we asked where they got their suits. They turned us on to F&F Clothiers on the Bowery in lower Manhattan. "That cat Sol will give you that same Paul Sargent's suit you paid $250 for and charge you only $125, and he'll make it from scratch. Fats Domino has three hundred suits a year made there."

So off we went, and Sol made us electric-blue mohairs, with bright red linings ("In the middle of your act, just flip open your jacket and watch the girls scream when they see that lining"). Bobby Power was the brains of the group, and he said, "You're the star of the band, the one people remember. You should have a selection of suits so you'll stand out even more," so I had five more suits made in bright colors: green, beige, brown, olive, and a red one you could see from a mile away. "You wanna be a star, you got to dress like a star," was the advice the old-timers gave me. I also had several black, monogrammed shirts custom-made.

The few acts that weren't nice stood out from the rest. Chubby Checker was a prick, the first truly nasty performer I ever met. He couldn't understand why his music wasn't viewed with the same reverence as that of, say, Jimi Hendrix, whom his envy fixated on for some reason. Instead of feeling grateful that people still paid money to see him, Chubby's ego caused him to believe it was racism that kept him from the kind of respect accorded to a Sinatra. He never understood that his dance hits, like "The Twist," were basically banal novelties.

Another nasty piece of work was Leslie Gore. A second-tier talent on the best day of her life, she acted as if she were the Queen of England, making no friends wherever she went. Tempting as it was to screw up the music for these two assholes, we were professionals and played as well for them as we did for the acts who were nice to us.

In addition to our club gigs in Westchester County and Connecticut, the Knight-Riders ventured into the city and the mob-owned clubs in midtown Manhattan. We played the famous Peppermint Lounge on Forty-Fifth Street, which Joey Dee and the Starlighters had turned from a sailor-and-hooker joint into a national phenomenon with a record called "The Peppermint Twist." Servicemen and prostitutes did the Twist, the Mashed Potatoes, and the Slop alongside Upper East Side swells in their gowns and tuxedos. Joey Dee made quickie exploitation flicks like *Hey, Let's Twist* and *Two Tickets to Paris*.

Next door was the Wagon Wheel. Bands weren't allowed to play both clubs, because one was owned by the Gambinos and the other by the Genovese crime family. Our main home base in that part of town was the Headliner, on Forty-Third Street, west of Broadway, so named because it was next to the *New York Times* building. One night, the Beatles even came in during their first trip to America.

A heavyset guy named Dino managed the place, with a bouncer named Sonny at the door. The floor plan was a backwards, upside-down L, with a long bar and a bandstand on the right in the rear. The stage faced a postage-stamp-sized dance floor and a group of tables to the left in back. At one time, a glass door, now blocked off, led to the lobby of the Times Square Hotel next door. Most of the bands that appeared there were of the Joey Dee or Louis Prima variety: loud, fast music to keep the suckers drinking cheap, watered-down booze at Times Square prices.

We played there on Mondays and Tuesdays, for fifteen dollars a man, so we could work our better-paying gigs in the suburbs on weekends. There was always action at the Headliner. One night, from the bandstand, I saw a guy pull a gun on Sonny at his post at the front door. There was a struggle and the guy fell to the ground, shot dead with his own gun. We knew enough to keep playing so the crowd wouldn't panic. New York City's Finest arrived, and Dino and Sonny did the Sicilian Shrug as the body was removed and life continued. Nothing to see here, folks, keep moving.

A singer named Sammy Ambrose used to sit in with the other band and do one song, then hop on the drums and play, or rather duplicate, the solo made famous by Count Basie's drummer, Sonny Payne. It went over well but always annoyed me, because he was doing nothing original.

So one night, my friend Pete Holman from the Mighty Cravers was subbing for our regular drummer when Sammy did his little routine. During our next set, I asked Pete, a wonderful drummer, if he felt like teaching Sammy a lesson and putting him in short pants. Pete smiled and gave me a tempo, then started playing softly on his high hat, subtle stuff you don't often hear. Then he played on the sides of his snare drum and on the rim, so quietly that people were forced to listen. Pete slowly raised the volume, playing with such dynamics and so many colors that the audience was on its feet when he finished . . . and Sammy Ambrose never again dared to set foot in the Headliner when we were playing.

I realized the folly of trying to follow something loud and fast with something louder and faster, as all the other bands did, ending their sets with some impossibly loud and fast song, to make it hard for the next band to follow. So I experimented by opening our set with the softest intro I knew, Ben E. King's "Stand by Me," allowing it to settle until I had the crowd's attention. Someone later told me that this was a tactic used by all the great debaters: when your opponent gets loud, answer with a whisper, forcing your audience to lean in and listen to what you have to say.

Another night, a Jewish gangster known as Moishe, or Morris Spokane, came in with a bunch of friends. He liked my style, gave me a large tip, and told the call girl who was at his table to take me home with her. This was no cheap streetwalker; she looked like a *Vogue* cover model. Her name was Rayna. After Spokane left, I felt sorry for her and told her she didn't have to go with me; I'd tell Moishe she was great if he asked. But she said she liked me and thus began a nice little fling. She would meet me at 4:00 a.m. closing time and take me to breakfast and to her place whenever we played in Times Square.

One night, after the loving was through, she began to cry in my arms and asked if I would be her boyfriend and live with her. She'd get us an apartment and I wouldn't have to work. She told me of how, back home in Australia, her father had molested her all through her childhood until she ran away at age twelve and wound up in New York, where she made her living this way. She was now seventeen and I was nineteen. I've often wondered whatever became of this exquisitely beautiful girl.

The prostitutes liked musicians. I treated those I met like human beings, talked to them, listened to them. They talked about the same things a lot of other girls talked about: clothes, hairdos, favorite songs, soap operas, etc. The ones I hung with liked to bring me gifts. It made them feel good to be able to take care of a guy they liked.

Rayna believed I had talent beyond the bedroom and encouraged me to try and do something with my songs. She even made a few calls on my behalf to her important contacts in the music business. So I guess you could say I owe my early success to a beautiful underage call girl.

Her gangster friend Moishe had a record company that had recorded one of the Headliner bands called Goldie and the Gingerbreads. Goldie would evolve into Genya Ravan of the band Ten Wheel Drive. We made some demos for Spokane, supervised by a songwriter named J. J. Jackson who'd one day have a hit record with "But It's Alright," but nothing came of our stuff. Just as well; best not to get involved business-wise with the mob.

Joey Dee fronted a club for the Gambinos called the Starlighter on Forty-Sixth Street, west of Broadway, and we were hired to play there the week of New Year's Eve 1965. Joey's band at the time consisted of three of the Rascals: Felix Cavaliere, Gene Cornish, and Eddie Brigati. Their drummer, Dino Dinelli, was working at the Metropole with another band.

Joey's opening act was a dwarf named Little Frankie, who did a sort of James Brown act in miniature. He was terrible but entertaining to the drunks in a carnival sideshow kind of way. Frankie couldn't hold his liquor and, when loaded, would go into the men's room and ask a total stranger at the urinal, "Have you ever gotten a blow job from someone who was standing up?"

On New Year's Eve, we were the opening band. Looking out into the crowd, I spotted mob guys from Little Italy, East Harlem, and Brooklyn scattered around the room with their wives. I prayed nobody would start anything, but twenty minutes into our first set, fists started flying, then chairs and tables, followed by bullets. It was like a Hopalong Cassidy movie. Panic ensued and we slipped out through a door at the back of the stage, through the dressing rooms, tripping over Felix and Eddie, and into the alley. The next day, the boss refused to pay us because we'd stopped playing.

I used to frequent a record store in the subway called Times Square Records, which catered to young guys who loved the sound of vocal groups. Some of the rarer items would be hanging on the wall, with "high" prices like five or ten dollars. Some of these sell for over a thousand bucks today. The owner was a Times Square denizen named Irving "Slim" Rose.

One day in late November 1963, I was alone in the store, except for Greasy Harold behind the counter. I was perusing the dollar bin and holding in my hand a record by Johnny Ace, the singer who had died in Texas from a bullet in the head while playing Russian roulette.

Just then, Slim came in, his face ashen, and said, "Did youse hear? Da president got shot in da head in Dallas! It's all over the radio!"

I dropped my Johnny Ace record and ran up to the street, where all was chaos. People were screaming and crying, staring blankly through the windows of those stores, the ones with the permanent "Going Out of Business" banners. The horrifying images were on a thousand TVs, up and down Broadway and the side streets. The nation would never be the same.

John F. Kennedy was a glamour boy who changed forever the way presidents were elected. Before JFK and his equally glamorous wife, Jackie, it didn't matter what a candidate looked like. Television wasn't such an important factor. Post-Kennedy, you could wager the winner would usually be the guy with the best haircut.

At the time, I was living in as close to poverty as I ever would, in a crummy one-room with no heat or water. My toilet was a bedpan purchased from a drug store. To keep out the winter cold and wind, I Scotch-taped my dry-cleaning plastic over the window. I took my showers upstairs, in the landlady's bathroom, with her criminal son's monkey perched on the railing, dropping monkey shit into the tub. People in the neighborhood told me that Lucky Luciano had hidden in that same room, back when he was avoiding the federal authorities, prior to his deportation to Italy.

I was coming out of that shower and sitting down at the kitchen table to keep warm for a while when the TV showed Jack Ruby firing his revolver into Lee Harvey Oswald's torso. The world was going mad, and it wasn't about to get any better.

A week or so later, I arrived at the Headliner early to find two mid-level mob guys sitting alone at the bar, hitting the sauce pretty good. I ordered a Coke, a few seats away, and overheard one of them say, "Well, I hear our friends in Chicago and New Orleans took care of that Irish fuck. They oughta whack his double-crossing brother while they're at it." This tidbit would not be the last I'd hear of this side of the story.

Farther north, at Seventy-Sixth and Broadway, was a club called the Lighthouse Café, where a group of older guys called the Jive Bombers played in the window. They'd had a 1957 hit called "Bad Boy" and had been old even then. They'd been on the first bill at the Apollo in 1934, when owner Frank Schiffman first opened the doors to black customers.

We played on a larger stage in the back, past the oblong bar, where one night a large black woman sitting next to me said, "My name's Odetta and I like the way you sing. Wanna come back to my place after you're done? I got some good stuff for you."

Thinking she meant sex, and not being interested, I said I had a girlfriend or some lame excuse. "No, baby," she explained, "I mean *stuff* stuff"—in other words, narcotics. I told her that wasn't my thing and she replied, "Honey, I know one when I see one." I had a good laugh at that, and still do when I remember being approached by the famous folk singer.

Another night at the Lighthouse, which was in a sketchy neighborhood aptly known as Needle Park, I saw two off-duty cops blow each other away in an argument of some kind that was all over the news the next day. The club was populated by every kind of society outsider—prostitutes, drag queens, dope dealers, you name it. But we were in showbiz, living the dream.

A couple of years after our record on Rust, we asked the company to give us back the master, so we could either press it up ourselves or take it to another record label. They declined but gave us the remaining two thousand copies in their warehouse to sell in the clubs. They also asked if I had any more songs as good as "All My Love" and introduced me to Larry Spier, who was now running their publishing arm, Just Music.

I played Spier a few songs, and he liked two of them well enough to pay for the band and me to make demos of them, giving me a thirty-five-dollar advance. One song in particular I thought would be good for this new girl singer, Dionne Warwick.

A couple of weeks went by and there was no word from Larry Spier. Then one morning he called to say he'd gotten a record on one of my songs, "Mean Old World," the one I'd had in mind for Warwick. Being a novice and filled with adolescent impatience, I'd expected a quicker response, so I gave him a snotty answer: "What? The B-side of a Joe Blow record?"

"No, the A-side . . . of Ricky Nelson's next record."

"Ricky Nelson! He's white," I rudely and stupidly replied.

"Listen, you ungrateful little putz. Ricky's going to do your song five weeks in a row on *The Adventures of Ozzie and Harriet*. Ricky sells records. You're virtually guaranteed a hit plus TV performances."

I felt like an asshole. Larry Spier was right, Ricky Nelson gave me my first chart record, and on the first song I ever presented to a publisher, no less. What an easy business! Or so I thought.

4
The Neon Lights
Are Bright

As late as 1965, when "Mean Old World" was on the charts, the music business was still a cottage industry. If you had a hit record, even a new kid like me, everybody on Broadway knew your name. The business was always looking for new blood. A Ricky Nelson record made it easy to get people to listen to my songs. The guys behind the desks were old, in their forties or fifties, and of another era. They knew from Sinatra and Tommy Dorsey. Even Eddie Fisher was new to these dudes . . . and his career was already over.

It was a good time to be young, as most record biz guys, realizing they didn't know squat about this new music, kept an open door to anybody under twenty-five, especially a kid like me who had a hit. I sold a few songs here and there before winding up at April-Blackwood Music, whose boss turned out to be our old friend Gerry Teifer.

April-Blackwood Music was the publishing arm of CBS/Columbia Records and was located at 1650 Broadway and Fifty-First Street, around the corner from the Winter Garden. Some people confuse it with the more famous Brill Building at 1619 Broadway. There was also 1697 Broadway, above the Ed Sullivan Theater, which was a low-rent version of the above two. All three buildings housed music publishers, independent record companies, and various publicists, booking agents, voice coaches, and other fringe characters. But most of us who were there at the time agree that 1650 was the cooler one. It was with great nostalgia that I performed at the nightclub Iridium, located in that same building, in 2014.

Also working at April-Blackwood, in the capacity of professional manager, was David Rosner, a classy guy who didn't seem like he belonged in the music business. It was David who got me my first record there, "It's Up to You," recorded by one Cindy Malone on Capitol. The song was later cut in England by the American transplant Madeline Bell. David, who lives in Los Angeles now, is still a friend and shows up at my big-band gigs in Hollywood these days.

Teifer, a Cincinnati expat who remembered my mother from WLW, was a friendly guy who called everybody "pardner." Gerry was an expert whistler who was often called upon to whistle on recording sessions. He took a couple of my songs, then gave me a job as a staff songwriter with my own little office next door to that of Chip Taylor, who was both a staff writer and an executive. Gerry said, "I want to put you with Chip, because you still need a little seasoning."

Chip, who was four years older than me and had also gone to Stepinac, had four more years of music biz experience under his belt. The first thing he said to me was, "You know, I'm jealous of you. I always wanted a Ricky Nelson record and here you are, just a new kid on the block, and you got one." That made me uncomfortable, wondering how I could work with someone who felt that way toward me. But then he said he knew my song "All My Love," and that it was one of his favorites, so I began to warm up to him. He played me a few of his tunes, including one called "Welcome Home," by Walter Jackson, a soulful thing that I loved immediately for its opening line, "We acted like children."

Chip, born James Wesley Voight, is one of the great songwriters. His way of writing lyrics borders on poetry, minus all the flowery bullshit that other songwriting "poets" employ. After graduating from Archbishop Stepinac High School in 1958, he and his buddies Ted Daryll and Greg Richards formed a band called the Town Three, playing local Westchester clubs. They recorded, under that name and as Wes Voight, for King Records before starting to walk Broadway peddling their songs, having some success, both together and separately.

Under Chip's wing, I learned some very valuable lessons in the craft of songwriting. One thing I remember was that a song is like a short story; it must have a beginning, a middle, and an end. In other words, it needs a setup, the main action, and a wrap-up. Another gem: don't just write trendy songs for the moment; write something you can picture people singing twenty years from now.

Not long after I arrived at April-Blackwood, Ted Daryll moved upstairs to write for Koppelman and Rubin, who had under contract Tim Hardin and the Lovin' Spoonful. Ted and I used to meet for lunch and head over to the Stage Deli or the Carnegie for a sandwich. One day, I got tired of waiting for him to come down to the second floor and went up to his office on the twelfth floor. There was Teddy and a bunch of other writers, looking out the window, across Fifty-First Street to the City Squire Hotel, with telescopes and binoculars. The City Squire was where many of the airline stewardesses used to stay. We'd see them sitting out on the deck by the swimming pool, lounging in their bikinis, and gaze at them for inspiration.

"Hey, check out room 426," said a guy named Reid Whitelaw. Apparently, these guys had scoped out the floor plan and could zero in on any room they wanted. "Holy shit, is that . . . could it really be . . . Damn! It is! That's Rex Fucking Harrison!" Indeed, there he was, Mr. *My Fair Lady*, *schtupping* some fair lady in room 426 in every position imaginable.

When the great actor had completed his acts of depravity, Reid grabbed the phone and called the hotel. "Give me Mr. Harrison in room 426 please." Sexy Rexy picked up and we all applauded as Reid said, in a faux upper-crust British accent, "Sterling performance, Mr. Harrison!" With that, Rex smiled, walked to the window, naked as a jaybird, and took an elaborate bow, to our standing ovation.

The first song Ted gave to Koppelman and Rubin was called "The Shadow of Your Love," a cross between the Righteous Brothers and Bob Dylan, if you can imagine. Teddy cut a great track and wanted me to sing over it. A talent manager friend of his and Chip's, Al Schwartz, somehow got in on the action and brought his client Gene McDaniels to the session, which featured the Cookies as backup singers. I was nervous, but Gene talked me through it, and I managed to come up with a good vocal.

The resulting record, with a demo of one of my songs on the B-side, came out on Cameo under the name the Blue-Eyed Soul featuring Billy Vera, a sort of takeoff on the Righteous Brothers. The Knight-Riders (now Blue-Eyed Soul) and I hit the road to Cleveland to do the *Upbeat*

TV show, driving all night, arriving at the hotel at daylight. As I lay in my bed, which was right below the hotel's showroom, for several hours I was serenaded by Ray Charles rehearsing his band on Gerald Wilson's chart for his hit "You Are My Sunshine." Not a bad lullaby.

On another TV show, we met a young act called the Five Stairsteps, who were managed by their drill sergeant father, a Chicago cop. They were produced by Curtis Mayfield for his Windy C label, distributed by Cameo. This nice family and I dug each other, and a few years later they revived "The Shadow of Your Love" before scoring with their biggest hit, "O-o-h Child."

Chip's office, which was right over the Fifty-First Street main entrance to 1650 Broadway, was much larger than mine, so we wrote in there. The first song we came up with, "Make Me Belong to You," became a summertime hit for Detroit soul singer Barbara Lewis. Van McCoy, another April-Blackwood writer, had composed her previous hit, "Baby I'm Yours," and had sung most of the background voices, which everyone thought was a girl group.

Barbara recorded for Atlantic Records, the great label that was or became home to many of my favorite acts: Ray Charles, the Drifters, the Coasters, Bobby Darin, LaVern Baker, Joe Turner, the Clovers, Wilson Pickett, Solomon Burke, and Aretha Franklin. Having a hit song on Atlantic gave us entrée to the legendary Jerry Wexler, the head honcho, the man who'd produced all of the above artists and more.

Chip and I decided to write a duet song, in hopes we could get a pair of Atlantic stars to record it. Chip suggested we write something based on the chord changes of a tune I sang with the band called "To Be with You," by the Joe Cuba Sextet. It ended up as "Storybook Children," and we made a demo of it with me and a girl named Suzanne who occasionally sang with the Knight-Riders.

Teifer got us an appointment to play it for Wexler. When we arrived, our demo in hand, he was all worked up over a song he'd just recorded in Muscle Shoals, Alabama, with Aretha Franklin, whom he'd just signed away from Columbia, where she'd suffered hitless for several years. The song, "I Never Loved a Man," was incredible. How were we supposed to follow that?

Jerry put our disc on his turntable, listened, and slammed his fist on his desk, proclaiming it "a fucking smash. Get rid of the girl and I'll put this out on Atlantic Records."

Holy moly! It was enough of a thrill to have my name in the tiny print as a songwriter on Atlantic, but to actually have my name as a singer on that legendary label would be a dream come true.

Meanwhile, at the Country House, we played two dance sets and backed up hit record acts for two shows a night. The top nightclub in the area, it also served as the university where we became experts in stagecraft, reading music, and backing up shows.

Our first weekend backing acts had been trial by fire. Friday night was Patti LaBelle and the Bluebelles, and Saturday was Little Anthony and the Imperials, two acts with some pretty difficult music. No ice-cream chord changes here; this stuff was complex. For example, Patti sang "Danny Boy" in D-flat and "You'll Never Walk Alone" in B-natural, not your usual rock 'n' roll keys. And Anthony's songs, like "Goin' Out of My Head" and "Hurt So Bad," by Teddy Randazzo, were also a different breed. But we passed the test with the knowledge that we could handle ourselves under any circumstances, and soon we became known as the best backup band around.

I had become friendly with Patti LaBelle and the Bluebelles. Bluebelle Nona Hendryx had a voice that I felt would blend with mine, so I called her in Philadelphia and asked if she'd like to make a record with me. She said of course and came up to New York; we cut "Storybook Children" and she sounded great. The group was already signed to Atlantic, so there'd be no contractual issues.

The other girls were all for the pairing, as they had no guitarist and they felt I could serve double duty, conducting their shows and singing our duet. Unfortunately, their manager, a Mr. Montegue, got into the act and, fearing Nona might leave the group if we had a hit, nixed the idea. Chip, Teddy, and I then auditioned some twenty girls, all of whom sounded more like they should be singing Broadway show tunes than what we had in mind.

As we were about to give up our search, Wexler called to say they'd signed Judy Clay, an adopted "cousin" of Dionne Warwick and a former member of the family gospel group the Drinkard Singers, and we should check her out. We made an appointment, and she walked into Chip's office looking about fourteen months pregnant and with a chip on her shoulder the size of Wyoming.

Judy was bitter because, although she'd sung lead with the Drinkards, she had yet to make a name for herself in secular music, as had Dionne, her sister Dee Dee, and their aunt, Cissy Houston. Also, unlike Nona, who was slender and attractive, Judy was neither. After she left, everyone said, "She sings great, but do you think you can handle that attitude?" I said yes, recognizing that beneath that gruff exterior was a scared little girl.

So we went into the studio and replaced Nona's vocals with Judy Clay. Wexler took the tape into another act's session and overdubbed a string section orchestrated by Ray Ellis, who'd arranged Billie Holiday's last great album on Columbia, among many others.

Unlike most records, which "break" in the outlying cities, ours caught on in New York first, rising to number three on the local pop charts and number one on the R&B stations. It spread slowly, first one city, then another, with as much as a month between each one. This prevented the record from going higher on the national charts than #54 pop and #20 R&B.

With a hit record came gigs. Judy was unable to tour, due to her new baby, so we hired a couple of girls to impersonate her. Before that, I went out with no partner, just Ronnie Hinds and a guitarist named Butch Mann, whom I knew from Ruby and the Romantics and who'd played on the record.

The first gig was in Buffalo, New York, well over four hundred miles away. I bought a used yellow Ford station wagon, roomy enough for the three of us plus their guitars. We left the Bronx at 8:00 a.m. and got to Buffalo in time for the job, played two shows, and drove back home, because there was no money for hotel rooms. I was paid $450, less the agent's commission of ten percent. Gas in those days was around thirty-five cents a gallon, so, after paying my sidemen fifty dollars each, I made a couple of bucks. Ah, the tinsel-and-glitter world of showbiz!

I had other songs recorded while at April-Blackwood: the Shirelles, a bunch of lesser-known acts, and Fats Domino, who was a special thrill, since I was a huge fan. Some years later, when I was working a show with Fats, arranger Leroy Kirkland introduced us by saying that Fats had recorded a song of mine. The Fat Man asked which one and I told him, "Make Me Belong to You." He replied that he had five daughters and that was their favorite of all his recordings.

I assumed he was blowing smoke, just to be nice, but after I moved to Los Angeles, my friend Paul Gayten, who was a New Orleans homeboy of Domino's, said, "No, if Antoine said it, he meant it. Fats isn't sophisticated enough to bullshit." The only thing I could figure was, his daughters were too young to remember his countless hits from the 1950s and they knew my song because by then they were old enough to be aware of what he was recording.

Often, Gerry Teifer would knock on the door and give the writers assignments. "Hey, pardner, the Drifters are recording next week," or, "Tony Bennett's coming up for a date; see if you can write something for him." In this way, we learned how to write for different types of singers. Following one such assignment for one of my favorite soul singers, Chuck Jackson, I came up with a song called "Don't Look Back." I based the middle section on the stop chorus in a record I liked by Little Junior Parker, "Driving Wheel," so Chuck could do a little preaching.

The Knight-Riders and I made the demo, but Chuck didn't record it. A short while later, second-in-command David Rosner got the tune to A&R man Ted Cooper at Epic Records. Cooper cut it with a new group he'd signed from New England called the Remains. The resulting single sounded little like my original intention, but I loved what they'd done with it, thinking I was finally going to get that really big hit I'd longed for. No such luck. The record died a sad death. The group went on tour with the Beatles, blowing people away, and broke up after one album, which became a collector's item.

In 1971, after my own career had gone down the tubes, I resumed my record collecting, as I've often done during slow periods. I was in a shop down in Greenwich Village when a skinny, long-haired guy behind the counter recognized me and said he knew where there was a stash of my Atlantic albums if I was interested. I thanked him, and he told me that his name was Lenny Kaye and he played guitar for a girl named Patti Smith. He knew of a store in Boston that was going out of business and had tons of 45s from the fifties . . . which excited me to the point where I hopped a train for Boston the next day in the middle of a snowstorm.

Almost as an afterthought, he brought up the fact that he'd produced a compilation of early garage band tracks called *Nuggets* and had used my Remains song, saying it was a cult fave among his crowd. I was flattered, but it still didn't make me any money.

Twenty years later, after "At This Moment" hit, I got a call one day from Cyndi Lauper's husband to say that Cyndi had recorded "Don't Look Back" and planned to release it as a duet with Joan Jett. I was excited, since I believed in the song and was happy it was finally going to get its due, but Cyndi's version never came out.

A couple of months later, someone sent me a promo CD from Robert Plant's forthcoming album, which included—what else?—"Don't Look Back." But when the album came out, my song, once again, was not incorporated. I was beginning to think this song was jinxed.

Cut to another twenty years later. Rhino Records put out an expanded box set of *Nuggets* that sold a ton of records and, two years after that, a Robert Plant box set. Finally, after forty years, "Don't Look Back" made me some serious money and came to be regarded, in certain circles, as a rock classic.

In 2012, a documentary was made about the Remains. The group's leader, Barry Tashian, invited me to a screening here in Los Angeles. The band was still sounding great, and during the Q&A after the movie, I was asked to stand up and take a bow. It was a proud moment of delayed vindication.

In January 1966, I married an older woman of twenty-two named Barbara Young. She, her sister Carole, and a model named Cathy Miller were regulars at the Country House, always showing up with two gay guys named Harold and Felton. Harold ran the black funeral home in Stamford, Connecticut, and was well off, always well dressed in an Ivy League style. His tasteful clothes came from the men's store that was his day gig, where, while measuring guys' slacks, he'd "accidentally" brush his hand against their crotch, to see if they might be open to what he was into. Harold and Felton used these three beautiful, light-skinned black girls as bait to attract straight guys, and often it worked to their benefit.

Barbara closely resembled Estelle Bennett, one of the Ronettes (minus the big hair). Estelle was the best looking of the group and Ronnie's sister. Barbara was a nice girl from a nice, middle-class family who lived in an integrated apartment building in Stamford, but our marriage was ill advised. I was a lonely kid who'd been in some trouble and probably would've married the first nice girl who wanted me.

Her parents accepted me with open arms, and we spent the first six months living with them in the close quarters of their two-bedroom apartment, sharing the second bedroom with Barbara's sister, Carole. My parents, although they had raised my sister and me without prejudice, were not happy that I had married so young, and worried that our interracial marriage might cause problems for us in the world outside of show business. But once they got to know Barbara and her family, they grew to love them.

Barbara was busy daytimes working as a hairdresser in a salon in the wealthy town of Old Greenwich, so my mother took me to see a new apartment building in Hartsdale. I rented a small one-bedroom and we moved in with no problem, other than one morning a month or so after we moved in, when I was stopped in the lobby by the woman who managed the building. In her nasal Queens voice that made Fran Drescher sound like Grace Kelly, she glared and asked me why I hadn't brought my "lovely" wife to look at the apartment before we rented it. It was her snarky way of letting me know that I had put one over on her and crossed the racial barrier. It was, thankfully, the only racial issue that ever came up during our two-year marriage.

Nine months later, on September 14, 1966, we became the parents of a beautiful daughter, who was the apple of everyone's eye and remains so to this day. I named her after a Maynard Ferguson record popular among hipsters, "Maria," from *West Side Story*. Maria could, in the vernacular of the time, "pass" for Italian. When she was little, black people put children like her on a pedestal, but later, during the Black Power era, her light skin was no longer such an asset, and she sometimes paid the price.

During this time, to support my family, I worked six nights a week with the band, got up each morning to take the train downtown to April-Blackwood to write songs, and on Saturdays I sold records at the

Boss Record Shop for a man named Charlie "Dr. Pill" Yates, a hep cat with big horn-rimmed glasses and a flat-top Afro.

On my first day, Charlie's orders were: a) if someone walked in asking for a record, I should figure out their taste and make sure they walked out with four more, and b) (and this is a direct quote) "Never correct them when they ask for the wrong artist or title. Black people don't like to be corrected. Your job is to figure out what they're asking for and give it to them." I became very good at gauging my customers' tastes and sold lots of records from behind that counter.

Black people weren't big album purchasers; they bought the song, not the artist. If your follow-up didn't move them, it sat in the warehouse. Other than jazz LPs, one album that sold like hotcakes was one by the rotund singer Billy Stewart. Originally entitled *Unbelievable*, this mixture of jazz and R&B by this unique vocalist was retitled *Summertime* after the song of that name became a hit single. The album version was longer, and all I had to do was put it on the turntable and those albums would fly out the door. I think every black household in town had at least one copy.

Every Saturday morning a steady customer, an old drunk named Roy, would stagger in and say, "Billy . . . play me a hot one," which translated to "Play me a blues." It was a weekly ritual with him. Well, one day I had no new blues records to sell him, but in a moment of inspiration I realized that it was the ritual that was important to this man. So I played him the flip side of a Jimmy Reed record he'd bought a few weeks earlier, and he walked out happy with his little 45 under his arm.

I was far too young to marry, having only recently discovered how much pretty girls like musicians. Learning to play an instrument is a lonely task, and few of us are prepared for the attention being onstage can bring from female audience members. I didn't have the willpower to say no when they began throwing themselves at me after the show. I knew what I was doing was wrong but was unable to stop. I made no attempt at self-justification. Eventually, I took a good, hard look at myself and came to the conclusion that the most honorable—or least dishonorable—thing was to end the marriage and hope my wife could find someone better than me.

My accountant, Sid Seidenberg, who also managed Gladys Knight and B. B. King, sent me to a guy named Jack Rabinowitz, saying he was "the toughest divorce attorney in New York." Upon hearing my story, Jack said, "Are you in love with someone else?" I said no, I had no desire to be married to anyone. "Then I'm gonna save you a lot of money," which was a joke, since I had very little. "Ask her what she wants and give it to her, then wait for the golden phone call, meaning she will eventually meet someone she wants to marry."

Seven years later, Barbara called one day to say the price for an uncontested divorce in Connecticut was about to be raised from seventy-five to one hundred dollars on January first. Translation: she'd finally met someone she wanted to marry.

Jack's sage—and gratis—advice enabled Barbara and me to remain friends until the day she died a few years ago, the victim of an SUV driver who ran a stop sign as she was walking to work one morning.

5
The Apollo Theater

Unlike "Storybook Children," which took weeks to chart nationally, our follow-up, "Country Girl-City Man," coming off a hit, got instant national airplay and reached a higher chart position, #36 pop and #41 R&B, although it sold less than half what the first record did.

In those days, R&B acts like us weren't signed to do an album first. You made a single, and if that sold, then you were allowed to make an album, the cost of which was recouped against the sales of your hit single. In this commonplace scheme, if your album or follow-up single failed to sell, it cost the record company nothing, since your hit single essentially paid for the album. It was no risk for the company.

My producers, Chip Taylor and Ted Daryll, booked Brooks Arthur's Century Sound. I wanted my friends Pete Holman on drums and Butch Mann, who'd joined me on guitar when his group, Ruby and the Romantics, stopped selling records. Jerry Wexler suggested studio regulars Paul Griffin on piano and guitarist Eric Gayle on Fender bass. The horn section included King Curtis and Memphian Charles Chalmers on saxes and Melvin Lastie, who'd played the classic cornet solo on Barbara George's New Orleans smash, "I Know (You Don't Love Me No More)."

Chip wrote a couple of songs with me and a couple with Ted. We filled out the rest of the album with recent R&B hits. The cover was a color photo portrait of Judy and me. At the Atlantic sales meeting, Wexler held up the cover and said, "I'm sending the first copy to Lester Maddox," the segregationist governor of Georgia from 1967 to 1971, who later served as lieutenant governor of that state under Jimmy Carter.

Colony Records on Broadway made a big window display of our album, which caused me endless embarrassment as I walked that thoroughfare, because every hooker on Broadway would call out, "Hey, there's that pretty Mr. Storybook Children! Love you, baby!" I eventually got used to it and joined in the banter with these hardworking girls, blowing kisses back and forth.

Before our photograph was widely seen, Judy and I got booked at the famed Apollo Theater on 125th Street in Harlem. It was the pinnacle of black showbiz. The Apollo was a seven-day-a-week, five-shows-a-day house, the first show starting at 10:00 a.m. on Friday. On Thursday night, after the previous week's last show, the new show would rehearse in the basement with the house band, led by Ruben Phillips.

Honi Coles, of the tap dance team Coles and Atkins, a longtime "class act" staple of black vaudeville, was the stage manager. He chose the running order and decided to put us on second, the worst spot on the bill. Opening acts were always flashy, choreographed acts to excite the crowd. The second act was either the worst or an unknown quantity. Each act was better than the last, doing roughly twelve to thirteen minutes each until the star, who did between twenty and thirty minutes, depending on the length of the show.

Honi said, "Harlem hasn't seen you two yet, so what I want you to do is this: Judy, you enter from stage right and Billy from stage left. Wait for her to take three steps onstage and then make your entrance, and watch what happens." These old pros knew show business inside and out, so there was no questioning his wisdom. In those days, those old-timers saw it as their duty to bring us youngsters along in the ways of stagecraft, down to simple, seemingly obvious things like how to make an entrance or an exit.

So, when we were up, I did as I'd been told and waited in the wings, one, two, three steps, then entered, stage left. Fifteen hundred people gasped at the sight of me. I could hear them saying, "That's him? That's him?" Our record was all over the radio and in half the homes in Harlem, but no one had expected to see this skinny little white boy singing in that voice.

There was a long history of popular white acts at the Apollo, performers like Louis Prima and Charlie Barnet in the 1940s, the Skyliners in the fifties, and the Rascals in the sixties.

What made Judy and me different and, if you will, daring was that we were an interracial, male/female act singing love songs, as opposed to cute little rhythm novelties.

There is no audience like a black audience, and you can multiply that tenfold for an Apollo crowd. You don't have to bullshit them with *American Idol*–type melismatic, over-the-top singing. A Jimmy Reed, with a vocal range of six notes, will draw greater applause than a dishonest performance by some six-octave diva. To win over a black audience, you merely need to stand up there and do it like you mean every word. To bask in the love of an Apollo crowd, to hear those shouts of approval and encouragement, is the most gratifying feeling any entertainer can feel.

We went over like gangbusters, and after the first show Honi came up to our dressing room and said, "I'm changing up the show. You two are going on right before the star, because ain't nobody gonna follow you two motherfuckers." Before lunchtime was over, all of Harlem was talking about "that white boy" who was singing with the black woman at the Apollo.

Tommy Hunt was the star that week. Tommy had been a member of the Flamingos before going out on his own, with hits like "Human" and Bacharach and David's "I Don't Know Just What to Do with Myself." He was a good-looking guy, and some said he pimped on the side. Two weeks after we closed, he relocated to the Netherlands, where he lives to this day. The other seven acts on the bill included the Radiants; the doomed Linda Jones, who died too young of diabetes; and Mable John, sister of Little Willie John; and several more. Mable was in our dressing room when she got the news that her brother had died in prison, where he was serving time for stabbing a man to death in a bar fight. After a couple of hit records, like "Your Good Thing (Is About to End)," she went on to become one of the Raelettes, singing backup for Ray Charles.

Backstage at the Apollo was a world unto itself. Two ex-cons, Ritchie and Spain, screened visitors and announced half-hour, fifteen minutes, and showtime, shouting, "All on." A light-skinned man named J. B. Horn, rumored to be related to Lena Horne, worked in the office, counting receipts and controlling all disbursements, subject to the signature of Bobby Schiffman or his father, Frank. Both Bobby and

Horn carried a pistol in a holster on their belts. Outside were the ushers, dressed in red uniforms with gray stripes and matching, brimless hats.

An ancient lady known only as Mom brought hot, home-cooked meals that she carried in a couple of canvas bags slung over her frail shoulders and sold to the entertainers and musicians for a mere dollar each. The bandleader, Ruben Phillips, had some side action going on, peddling various goods that "fell off the truck." I bought a tiny TV set with which to while away the long hours between shows.

There were other performers visiting the various dressing rooms, as well as friends, family, and girls. The stage door was guarded by a one-armed bouncer named Neil, who also worked throughout the theater. As you entered the stage door on 126th Street, you were greeted by a sign saying, "Please do not ask for passes for your friends. If your friends won't pay to see you, who will?" I never forgot those words of wisdom.

One afternoon, I looked out into the audience when the lights went up and spotted my mother-in-law, Betty Young. My marriage had ended by that time, but there she was, so proud of me. I loved that woman. A great cook, she made the best apple pie in the world and made me one each time I went to visit my daughter. When Barbara finally remarried seven years after our split, Betty said, "I don't care who she marries, you'll always be my son-in-law."

Judy and I became very popular in Harlem. When I walked down 125th Street, people would stop to shake my hand or put their arm around me. As a young Apollo customer, it had been one of my life's goals to stand on those sacred boards, the same stage on which every one of the greats in black entertainment, from Bill "Bojangles" Robinson, to Duke Ellington, to Billie Holiday, to Ray Charles had stood.

I had been in the audience the week that James Brown recorded his famous album, *Live at the Apollo*. It was the most exciting show I ever saw. My friend and I, the only white people there on a rainy night, got on the wrong line and someone offered to get our tickets for us. Naively, we gave him our money. No hip person would believe this, but the guy actually brought back our tickets. On top of that, a nice couple in front of us on line loaned us one of their umbrellas.

That album shocked the music business by reaching the pop Top 10. Every musician I knew bought one. Many of us memorized it, down to the spoken introduction, "Are you ready for STAR TIME?" In those last couple of years before the British Invasion, it gave us soul music fans hope that our music would prevail over the boring pap that much of radio fed us. But, to paraphrase what one music biz veteran told me at the time, preteen white girls, who buy the majority of records, don't find a sweaty, ugly black guy like James Brown sexy. Their fantasies are fueled by fluffy, harmless-looking, soft boys like the Beatles were in the beginning or Justin Bieber is today.

But James Brown made more hit records than anyone in the history of black music, selling millions of copies of songs that were virtually unknown to the vast majority of whites. Jimi Hendrix sold millions of albums to white hippies, while in Harlem he was mocked and laughed at, because you couldn't dance to a Hendrix song.

The thing I notice about many white critics who chronicle black music is that they never seem to get the importance of the dance. Otis Redding's song "Hard to Handle" is a terrific example, a record that held little appeal for black audiences. You couldn't dance to it. James Brown never lost that beat, the beat that pulled black people out of their seats and onto the floor. He never forgot where he came from . . . because he never left.

Judy had given birth to a son, Leo Gatewood, who grew up to make her proud, graduating from West Point and becoming an executive at various entertainment companies. I got to know Leo as a man, years later, after he came to see me with the Beaters one night.

Judy's pregnancy had prevented us from doing much touring during the run of "Storybook Children," just a gig at the Pittsburgh Arena, opening for the Association, along with the Esquires and a new group called Sly and the Family Stone. To my surprise, one audience member called out for me to sing "My Heart Cries," which had been a number one hit in that city six years earlier.

We did a gig in Detroit, at the Rooster Tail, and did our only televised appearance there, for DJ Robin Seymour. We were seen on no other television shows. Driving back from Pittsburgh, Butch and Ronnie wanted to stop for a drink at a bar, where we saw Peter Lawford and Minnie Pearl singing our song "Country Girl-City Man" on national TV. I later saw Tina Turner and Sammy Davis, Jr., do the song on another show; more recently, I heard it sung by Tina and Andy Williams on an old YouTube video. In New York, we taped the Clay Cole show, but they never aired our segment. All our songs met the same fate. "Storybook Children" was done by Nancy Sinatra and Lee Hazelwood. Later, when I had my solo hit, "With Pen in Hand," I never got to perform it on *The Ed Sullivan Show*, but Vicki Carr had that honor two years later. So much for the "liberal" media, who were not as liberal as they liked to think they were, "talkin' the talk but not walkin' the walk" when it really counted.

During our first week at the Apollo, I got a call backstage one day from Jerry Wexler, informing me that the distribution deal between Atlantic and Stax Records of Memphis had expired, and, as Judy was under contract to Stax, we could no longer record together. Jerry told me not to worry, he'd found a song on Bobby Goldsboro's *Honey* album that was another "fucking smash." He'd done some research and found it was not going to be Bobby's next single. He was sending me a copy, and if I liked it I should be ready to record it the morning after the conclusion of our Apollo gig. Otherwise, he would record it with Brook Benton or Percy Sledge.

Jerry was one of the great song men. In 1950, when he was a record reviewer for *Billboard* magazine, a record came across his desk, a cover by Harlem bandleader Erskine Hawkins of Pee Wee King's country song "Tennessee Waltz." Recognizing the tune's greatness, he thought it would be good for Patti Page and took the record to her manager, Jack Rael. Patti's version made her career.

I could tell Wex was hot for Goldsboro's song, so I was happy to see that it was a truly great, heartrending tune. He had Arif Mardin write a full orchestra arrangement, and at nine o'clock on Friday morning I was at Atlantic's studio to record it. This was Wexler's baby and he was not about to let Chip or Teddy get in the way, so they just sat there, happy to take their producer's credit on the record while Jerry was all over the studio like a whirling dervish.

After seven days, five shows a day, singing before that Apollo crowd, my approach to the song was in that soul mode, which was not what Jerry had in mind. He came into the booth and said, "You're singing too soulful, man. Do it more square, like Glen Campbell," which turned out to be the correct approach.

That was a Friday. By Monday, Wexler had vinyl pressings with typed labels overnighted to every Top 40 station in the country. That's how quickly an independent label like Atlantic could operate back then. Despite several other versions by bigger names on bigger labels, my version of "With Pen in Hand" turned out to be the hit, reaching #43 nationally.

Al Schwartz, by then my manager, brought to the session his friend Jilly Rizzo, who is best known as Frank Sinatra's good buddy. Forever after, Jilly would tell anyone who'd listen that "This kid, Billy Vera, after Frank, is the best phraser in the business."

The great soul star Jackie Wilson, who was dating my wife's sister Carole, stopped by backstage at the Apollo to say hello. He asked where I was headed next. I told him Columbus, Ohio, and then the Surf Supper Club at Revere Beach, outside of Boston.

"Oh, man, be careful up there," he warned. "Those gangsters will come backstage and tell the owner they're your manager and take fifteen percent of your pay." Well, I wasn't netting enough to give that much away, so I had to think of something.

Jackie knew all about gangsters. His manager, Nat Tarnopol, was no saint. One day, coming off tour, sick as a dog with the flu, Jackie called Carole and asked to come up to Stamford to get away, so he could avoid having to do Murray the K's TV show. He was a little tardy getting there, so Carole foolishly called Nat's office. The crafty Tarnopol asked her for the address and Nat, along with Johnny Roberts and another of his thugs, went up there, slapped Jackie around, and took him away to do the gig.

My father-in-law, Freddie, was infuriated, on the verge of getting his shotgun and shooting these white men who had invaded his home, but wisdom prevailed. Freddie Young was one of those Louisiana Creoles who referred to both blacks and whites as "them." His family owned land in St. Francisville, an oddly-shaped Creole enclave, said to be "two miles long and two yards wide," in the eastern part of the state.

I told Al what Jackie had said about Boston and he sent me over to Jilly's joint. Jilly, who lived above his club, showed me around. "See this table? That's Frank's table. Nobody sits there but Frank. Now let's take a walk, kid."

As we walked east on Fifty-Third Street toward Broadway, he told me, "If anybody bothers you up there, you mention Mr. X; he's from there. If they still bother you, mention Mr. Y; he's from here. If they don't stop, mention my name. If that don't work, call this number." He handed me a scrap of paper with a phone number in pencil. At this point, a smallish guy, about five foot six, with a neck the size of my thigh, materialized from the wall. "This here's Little Joe; he bodyguards Frank. Joe, if Billy calls you, you go wherever he says and do whatever he needs."

As the Italian comedian Pat Cooper quipped, "Revere Beach is so Italian, there's a Chinese restaurant there called the China Roma. Their most popular dish is egg foo yung Parmesan."

Fortunately, the Surf's owner's son, who was maybe ten years older than me, thought I was the cat's meow and took me under his wing, so I had no worries in Boston. Back in New York, I'd sometimes run into Little Joe, always driving a Volkswagen bus, on the West Side, where he apparently hung out. He always waved and called my name.

After rehearsal with the house horn section at the Surf, my guys and I went over to the boardwalk, where there were the typical games of chance. There was the basketball toss, which nobody could make, while the guy behind the counter had no trouble at all. Another scam was a dart game. You'd toss darts at little circles of paper on the other side of which were numbers, representing the amount of money you'd "won" or lost.

I wound up losing forty-five dollars, and the others lost even more. I have never again gambled on anything involving dollars.

Back at the Surf, the son schooled us, saying that his father had put him to work on all those boardwalk hustles as a kid. He explained that the basketball hoop was set at an angle that made it impossible for the mark to get it in without it banging against the ceiling.

As for the dart toss, here's how it went. You weren't shown the first numbers, the ones where you supposedly won money. Psychologically, most people won't question a win. Then, once you were hooked from piling up some wins, you suddenly began to lose. He'd show you those, to build up your trust. There'd then be a few more "wins," interspersed among the greater losses, until you gave up, inevitably having lost. The lesson? Never trust a carny.

Clive Davis, who was then running Columbia Records, invited Chip and me, along with Gerry Teifer and David Rosner, to lunch in the executive dining room at Black Rock, Columbia's new building on Fifty-Second Street. As you'll recall, April-Blackwood Music was in the same CBS corporate family as Columbia. I was seated at the right hand of God, and as we dined with the gold silverware and the good china, he who thought he was God spoke, in that phony British dialect often affected by those wishing to deny their Brooklyn roots. "Billy, it would be an honor and a pleasure to have you as an artist on Columbia Records." With all the naïveté and foolish honesty of a twenty-three-year-old, I answered, "Thank you, Mr. Davis, but I'm under contract to Atlantic Records, the label I've always dreamed of being on. Ray Charles, the Drifters, Bobby Darin, Joe Turner, the Coasters. Why would I want to be anywhere else?"

With that faux pas, all meaningful conversation ceased. The Great Man's neck and ears turned bright red. Showing magnificent control of his temper, he proceeded to pontificate about how, with Columbia's "superior distribution and advertising capability," I would have sold far more records than I had on Atlantic. I countered by reminding him that he'd recorded "With Pen in Hand" with Jerry Vale two weeks before I had, and yet his record hadn't come out until two weeks after mine. Atlantic had the ability to move swiftly.

At that point, the meeting was essentially over, and to this day Clive has never spoken another word to me, other than a short, terse rejection note I received after sending him a demo of "At This Moment" intended for Whitney Houston.

A third Billy Vera and Judy Clay single, "When Do We Go," had been released, but when the Stax deal ended, Atlantic ceased promoting it, concentrating on "With Pen in Hand," which was rising up the charts. Judy and I were booked at the Apollo again in July, this time with Wilson Pickett as the headliner. Honi Coles put us on right before his spot.

Pickett was hot; his record of "I'm in Love" was burning up the radio, so the place was packed every night and most afternoons as well. One night a little girl in the front row yelled out for me to sing "With Pen in Hand." I was thrown for a moment, as I was onstage with Judy; even if I had rehearsed it with the band, what would I do with her? I never expected an Apollo audience to go for a country/pop song like that. Then again, Ray Charles's career had blossomed once he recorded all those country tunes like "I Can't Stop Loving You" and "Born to Lose." I explained that we hadn't rehearsed it, apologized to the little girl, and went on with our portion of the show. Another lesson learned. As the Boy Scouts say, be prepared.

During our run at the Apollo, Al Schwartz got me a booking on *The Dick Cavett Show*. The network sent a limo to ferry me to and from the theater between shows. The way it worked at the Apollo was, as I said, five shows a day, with a rotten movie in between whose function it was to clear the house for the next show. For the price of one ticket you could stay all day, as some winos and junkies did, to stay warm in winter and to enjoy the air conditioning in the summer heat.

Those winos and junkies could be a rowdy bunch. I remember one time going to see Nina Simone at the Apollo. She was the headliner, and when the M.C. announced her and she regally entered stage right, those bums up in the balcony were making a little too much noise for Miss Simone, who was not known for taking any shit.

Nina sat at the piano in silence for a beat, glaring up toward the noisy balcony, then began playing some classical piece, giving those boys the evil eye until they settled down. Only then did she deign to begin her act.

In the makeup chair at the Cavett show, comedian Louis Nye warned me, "You probably won't end up going on today, kid. That bitch Gypsy Rose Lee never stops talking." He was right; the famed former stripper blabbed right through my segment, so they had me back the next day, when I got to sing "With Pen in Hand" and another song and chat with Dick. The limo got me back uptown in time for our next show. Looking at that tape today, I cringe to see how shy I was during the interview portion of my appearance. I guess Cavett, a snobbish intellectual who seemed to enjoy looking down his nose at those he considered his inferiors, must've taken pity on me, because he treated me generously.

Another TV appearance was *The Joe Franklin Show*, a staple of local New York television for many years. Joe, known as "the world's oldest amateur," knew more about pre-1940 showbiz than just about anybody, and little about anything after World War II. A likable, friendly guy who loved entertainers, Joe approached all his guests as if they were stars, whether they were Frank Sinatra or some schlub who sang on weekends at a New Jersey bowling alley.

Atlantic's chief of publicity, Bob Rolantz, got me the booking. When I asked what time the show went on, he said 11:00 a.m. I said, "So I should be there around nine thirty or ten?"

"Nah, Joe doesn't show up until the last minute."

Thinking Bob was exaggerating, I got there at ten and waited around by myself until Joe arrived around five minutes before air time, quickly changing from one rumpled suit to another just as rumpled. He did his own makeup, dabbing it on in blobs, and walked nonchalantly to the set just in time to go on the air, live, no tape.

Due to union rules, acts couldn't perform live or even lip synch to their records, so what viewers saw while your record played was you and Joe chatting or shots of your album cover and photos of yourself. The other guests that day were several scruffy Brits just arrived in the States who called themselves Fleetwood Mac. This was the original, all-male iteration of the group, back when they were still a blues band.

Their song sounded like the legendary bluesman Elmore James, complete with Elmore's trademark slide guitar lick. I mentioned this to the guys and their eyes lit up. Joe said, "Yeah, talk about that when we come back from commercial," relieved that there would be conversation, even if it was about a realm of showbiz he knew nothing about. Gotham is not a blues town, and I doubt there were six viewers, black or white, who had any idea who Elmore James was. But this was the beauty of Joe Franklin. He was eclectic, before anybody knew what the word meant.

At the time, Al Schwartz was married to Donna McKechnie, who'd been lead dancer on the TV show *Hullabaloo* and is today one of the great stars of cabaret. Donna taught me how to move and stand properly on a stage, with my legs slightly spread, because "You'll look more confident that way. Women like that." She later would set Broadway on fire when she originated the role of Cassie in *A Chorus Line*. After years away from seeing Broadway shows, my mom took me to see the show. I was surprised and happy to see Donna on that stage in all her glory, now recognized as the finest dancer in the business.

One of Al's other clients, in addition to Gene McDaniels and Timi Yuro, was Clyde McPhatter. Clyde's time as a star had passed, but, as a Harlem homeboy, he could still headline at the Apollo. Clyde had become a hopeless lush. The Knight-Riders and I had backed him one night at the Country House. Luckily, I knew all his songs, for after rehearsing two forty-minute shows, at showtime, he called none of the tunes we'd rehearsed and we somehow got through it.

One afternoon, Al got a call from Bobby Shiffman, saying, "Come get your boy. Clyde's locked himself in his dressing room and won't come out." Schwartz hopped in a cab and headed uptown.

Clyde was sitting at the dressing table, his toupee ajar and blood dripping down his forehead. Apparently, he had introduced his latest release by saying something to the effect of "And here's my newest recording, 'Crying Won't Help You Now,' and I just wanna say crying won't help none of you niggers up in the third balcony." With that, a wine bottle came flying down with unfailing accuracy, hitting McPhatter square on his head and knocking his wig loose, bringing to an ignominious end one of the great careers in rhythm and blues.

Wednesday night was the Apollo's traditional amateur night, and it was always a sold-out weekly event. All of Harlem came out dressed in their finest. In the box seats sat the drag queens, all dolled up in tight, sexy dresses and huge, high wigs. They'd sit there, making risqué remarks to any male singer they fancied, and I got my share, in my custom-tailored mohair suits of many colors. It was smart to have enough suits to change with each show, five times a day. I witnessed one poor vocal group, in town with their first hit record and only one outfit. Those little girls who sat all day in the front row were merciless. "Can't you afford another suit, baby?"

On one especially memorable Wednesday, I wore my red one, with a custom-made black monogrammed Jackie Wilson shirt, no tie and open at the collar, and my black suede shoes with my black silk socks. You had to have black silk socks. Those drag queens, and all the women in the joint, were digging the view.

As usual, we opened with "Country Girl-City Man," followed by either "When Do We Go" or "Let It Be Me," closing with that Harlem favorite, "Storybook Children." We got a standing ovation I thought would never end. We exited stage right, and, when they refused to stop clapping and yelling, "More, more," Honi Coles told us to "get back out there and take it from letter B," that is, to repeat the second half of the song.

We had stopped the show! When they finally let us off, waiting backstage was Judy's "aunt," Cissy Houston, with little four-year-old Whitney in her arms. Cissy had tears running down her cheeks. It may be difficult for some to comprehend today, but Judy and I represented an important moment in race relations, sadly, one of the last before the assassination of Dr. Martin Luther King, Jr., that April. Up until that time, integration had been a goal among many, if not most, black people. With the murder of Dr. King, attitudes began to change. The feeling was, "If Whitey doesn't want us, then why bother trying?"

After our exit that night, as I walked up to our dressing room, across the hall from the star's, I heard Pickett yelling at his bandleader, "Get out there and play an instrumental. How the fuck am I supposed to follow that shit?" Wilson Pickett, the greatest screamer in the business, bar none, afraid to follow little old us? That was crazy. Pickett was an exceptional performer, one who could follow anybody. His insecurity led him to an irrational fear of following anyone who was good, to the point of refusing bookings on shows with acts he saw as competition. I've always felt it was better to follow a good act. When you follow a lousy one, you have to work that much harder to put your audience back in a good mood. A good act primes them for you. Crazy old Pickett apparently didn't see it that way.

He could be nasty when he drank. I saw him punch out his drummer right onstage one time. To protect themselves, his band started him smoking pot, which had a calming effect. Unfortunately, he graduated to cocaine, which made him really nuts and really mean.

After the show that night, I went out front to watch the amateurs from the back of the theater. Stars were sometimes born on amateur night.

One famous example was a little raggedy girl from Yonkers named Ella Fitzgerald who was discovered and asked to join Chick Webb's band.

This particular night, not long after the tragic airplane crash that took Otis Redding's life, a big lumbering guy walked out onstage. He was awkward, like Otis, and had a big square head like Otis. Honi Coles asked him his name and he said, "Dave, David Redding." The crowd booed at the audacity of this man.

"And what are you going to sing for us tonight, David Redding?" Honi continued, turning to the audience with a broad wink.

"I'm gonna sing 'Try a Little Tenderness,'" this poor fool replied in a thick southern drawl.

Now the crowd had blood in their eyes. They were ready to murder him. There were a few boos from the balcony. Porto Rico, the long, tall gentleman whose life's work it was to chase offending performers off the stage by shooting a blank pistol at them, was gearing up to do his thing.

Well, young David Redding went on to sing "Try a Little Tenderness," Otis's signature song, but he sang it nothing like Otis. He sang it his way. He was himself, which is the secret to success with the Apollo's or any sophisticated audience. And there was no more sophisticated audience than the Apollo Theater's. That bunch had seen it all, every black entertainer, and some select white ones, from the magnificent to the stinko. They were demanding; you didn't dare walk on that stage, those sacred boards, half-stepping. You gave it your all, and if you did, they took you to their hearts. But if you insulted them with a poor or uninspired performance, they let you know, and in no uncertain terms. Many a mediocre act never recovered from the takedown they received at the hands of an Apollo crowd. I've seen more than one hopeful exit with tears in their eyes. Young David Redding never made the big time but went home that night, I am sure, a proud young man, for, although they were slow to warm to him, by the time he finished his song, the audience was roaring their approval.

Stax had Judy record a duet with William Bell called "Private Number," which became a hit for them, further frustrating her because what she really wanted was to become a star on her own, not to be connected with a partner in the public mind. But it was never to be.

Stax guitarist and producer Steve Cropper told me Judy's frustration fueled her anger, making her difficult to deal with, and a year later the Memphis company let her contract lapse. She returned to Atlantic, as Jerry Wexler commented, "with her tail between her legs."

But before that, I had an album to make on the coattails of my solo hit. My producers, Chip and Teddy, had been called up to serve in their Air Force Reserve unit in Newburgh, New York, rendering them of little use in the making of the album. We all wrote some songs and again chose some known material to fill out the album. I knew Leroy Kirkland from my friends Ruby and the Romantics and asked him to write some of the charts, and Chip's partner Al Gorgoni wrote the remainder, as Arif Mardin was tied up on another project.

In short, my producers were distracted but unwilling to let anyone take over, and the album showed it. It was a nice enough record, but nothing spectacular. I, who had never mixed a record before, was given the responsibility of mixing it. Fortunately, Atlantic had a good engineer, Jerome Gaspar, to do the heavy lifting. The single, the Otis Redding / Jerry Butler tune "I've Been Loving You Too Long," made no impact.

The same fate befell two more singles. One of these, "The Bible Salesman," which Chip and I wrote for the Maysles Brothers' documentary film *Salesman*, was pretty good, one of our cleverest lyrics. We cut it at Chips Moman's American Studio in Memphis. I got to work with those great players, Tommy Cogbill, Reggie Young, Gene Chrisman, Bobby Emmons, and Bobby Wood, who'd played on so many hits, including Dusty Springfield's classic album *Dusty in Memphis*.

By the time Judy returned to Atlantic, we were both in need of a hit, so Wexler recommended we head down to Muscle Shoals, Alabama, his latest favored recording spot. Chip and I quickly wrote a song, "Reaching for the Moon," and I picked three more to fill out the date. We also chose songs for a solo date for me. Judy met us down there.

Muscle Shoals was a relaxing place to record. The house musicians, Barry Beckett, Jimmy Johnson, David Hood, and Roger Hawkins, with the addition of Eddie Hinton on lead guitar, were wonderful and had played on tons of hits. "Reaching for the Moon" came out great.

Trumpeter Gene "Bowlegs" Miller brought his horn section down from Memphis and added some cool licks. To this day, Chip says that, when he goes to England, more people ask about this song than any of his many bigger hits.

The next day I recorded alone. In need of a fourth song, Chip and I wrote something overnight called "J.W.'s Dream," a very weird item, mostly written by Chip. It became my last Atlantic single and died a merciful death. The flip side, which I wrote alone, "I've Never Been Loved (Like This Before)," might have been more accessible but never got heard. It was covered by a couple of other artists who had no more luck with it than I did.

Jerry Wexler and Tom Dowd flew down to do a date with Judy and asked me to stay an extra day to smooth things over, should she be in one of her moods. Relishing the opportunity to work alongside these giants, I agreed and suggested she record an Allen Toussaint tune called "Greatest Love," which wound up becoming a minor chart hit for her, the only solo chart record of her entire career. I also got her to record a song of Chip's and mine called "Before Her Time," which is still in the vaults, unreleased.

Back in New York, Jerry had Arif write strings for "Reaching for the Moon." The record came out beautifully, and Atlantic took out a full-page ad in the trade papers to play off our astronauts' recent moon landing. It was pick of the week on virtually every R&B station in the country, and the Apollo invited us back at the same salary—$2,400 a week—that we'd made when we had our hits, a good indication that we were still popular in Harlem.

But Judy refused, saying, "My cousin Dionne gets a raise every time she plays the Apollo."

"Your cousin Dionne has several more hit records each time she returns," I replied, trying to talk some sense into her.

But she couldn't hear the logic. This would have been a great way to reintroduce the act and kick off the record in a big way. But my thickheaded partner was adamant, and Billy Vera and Judy Clay would not be playing the Apollo again. Wexler, sensing he had a smash on his hands, was furious. "Fuck her," he said, and dropped her from the label.

Judy Clay and I remained friendly, and every few years she'd call me to say, "Hey Billy, you know, duets is getting popular again. We ought to do something." But it was not to be. She moved back home to Fayetteville, North Carolina, where she sang in the church the rest of her life.

6
Oh, No!
It's the Seventies!

As 1970 loomed, Gerry Teifer and David Rosner had moved on, to be replaced by Neil Anderson and, taking over David's corner office, Tony Orlando. Yes, that Tony Orlando.

Tony, who'd had a pair of hits, "Halfway to Paradise" and "Bless You," in the early sixties, had bottomed out by this time. He told me he'd been reduced to playing bowling alleys in New Jersey and he and his wife were eating scrambled eggs for dinner when he decided to use his hail-fellow-well-met, backslapping personality to look for work behind the scenes. He'd put on an enormous amount of weight and had no interest in performing anymore.

He earned extra cash making demos for songwriters, one of which, "Make Believe," became a Top 30 hit in 1969 when anonymously issued under the group name Wind (one wag called it "Breaking Wind"). The following year, with background singers Telma Hopkins and Joyce Vincent, he recorded "Candida" and "Knock Three Times," both big hits, under the *nom du disc* Dawn. Irwin Levine and L. Russell Brown, who'd written the latter, asked me to replace Tony on the road, but I wasn't interested, still hoping to score again with my own material. I asked Tony why he didn't do the road himself, and he said the memories of those scrambled eggs and bowling alleys were too painful to risk going through it again. But, three years later, when Larry and Irwin's "Yellow Ribbon" song became one of the most recorded tunes of all time, he went on a diet and returned successfully to live performing.

I did a few demos for other songwriters myself. One of these was perhaps the worst song Elvis Presley ever recorded, a piece of drivel called "Rubberneckin'," which wound up in the movie *Change of Habit* and had a second life over forty years later on the British charts. Dave "Baby" Cortez, of "Happy Organ" fame, played piano on the demo.

The funny thing about that session was that Colonel Parker paid everyone with checks that had Elvis's photo on them, assuming a good number of people wouldn't cash them and would keep them as souvenirs. I needed the thirty-five bucks at the time but wish I had that check now.

A friend of mine named Jonny Meadow worked for Hill and Range Music, the company that handled the publishing interests of Elvis and the Colonel. Part of his job was to deliver demos to the studio for Elvis's consideration. He explained how Presley came to record so much garbage during those years when he rarely recorded anything from outside publishers.

Hill and Range songwriters, like most, were paid advances, which were recouped if and when royalties accrued. The demos of writers who were in the red were placed on top of the piles Jonny brought for Elvis's consideration. If Elvis chose those songs, any income would be charged against the writers' accounts, costing the company nothing.

Meanwhile, the business was changing, and for staff songwriters, even the big ones like Goffin and King, Mann and Weil, and Sedaka and Greenfield, getting songs cut was becoming difficult, as it seemed every recording artist wanted to write his or her own songs and was encouraged to do so by the record labels, who often had side deals with the artists for publishing. Albums were filled with crappy, often pretentious tunes by would-be artistes while many professional songwriters wondered what was next and how they were going to pay the rent.

I had a few things cut, by acts like former R&B singer, now jazz vocalist Margie Day, or P. J. Proby, a talented American who became successful in England; and Zombies lead singer Colin Blunstone made a wonderful record of one of my best songs, "Don't Try to Explain," under the pseudonym Neil MacArthur; but for me, things were starting to look bleak, and I was only halfway through my twenties.

Chip was now distracted by our pretty receptionist, which resulted in a huge song for him, "Angel of the Morning," which he originally intended for my sister, Kathy, to sing. Kathy was sixteen and had already made one single for Chip's Rainy Day Records, using the family name, McCord. But Chip's partner, Al Gorgoni, felt they owed it to their other artist, Evie Sands, a terrific, Jackie Wilson–inspired singer who had the worst luck imaginable. We called her "hard-luck Evie." The first song Chip and Al recorded by her, on Leiber and Stoller's Blue Cat label, was Trade Martin's "Take Me for a Little While," followed by Chip and Al's "I Can't Let Go," both good records that were dead on arrival, only to become big moneymaking tunes when revived by Vanilla Fudge and the Hollies, respectively. The latter tune sold even more when Linda Ronstadt revived it in the seventies.

A label switch to Cameo resulted in several more flops for poor Evie. The wonderful original version of "Angel of the Morning" that she cut with Chip and Al was just starting to get airplay when Cameo's new owner, accountant Allen Klein, decided to shut down operations. Merrilee Rush, an unknown singer from Seattle, made a smash out of the song, which has since become a standard that, along with his "Wild Thing," has supported Chip in high style to this day.

I suppose I should tell you how that latter song came to be. One night, as I was getting ready to leave the office for a Knight-Riders gig in Stamford, Chip said that Gerry Granahan was recording this group, the Wild Ones, at nine o'clock the next morning and didn't have enough songs, so anything we wrote would get on the date. I said, "I can't stay, because I have a gig and the band can't work without the singer," plus I needed the fifteen smackers. He tried to persuade me, but I couldn't let the guys down and went down to Grand Central Station to catch my train.

The next morning, Chip hadn't come up with anything, so he went in the studio and virtually wrote the thing while the tape was running. The group cut it, sounding nothing like Chip's demo. The record came and went without notice.

A year later, another record of the song, by a British group called the Troggs, came in and we took a listen. It sounded like the demo, and I could immediately tell it had the makings of a number one hit. What no one could foresee was that it would go on to be recorded by tons of acts, including Jimi Hendrix, earning Chip a fortune over the years.

Speaking of Hendrix, Jimi was playing in the Isley Brothers' band when I met him at the Country House. During their act, Ronnie Isley would sing T-Bone Walker's blues classic "Call It Stormy Monday" and bring Hendrix down front. Jimi's solo was excellent, and he'd do all the clichéd bluesman tricks, like playing with his teeth, under his leg, behind his head, that T-Bone Walker and all who followed him had also done.

At the bar, Jimi and I struck up a conversation, and I found him to be a friendly, low-key guy. Some time later, I ran into him again, when we were both playing a gig at the Café Wha in Greenwich Village, during which he told me he had a record deal and the company was going to send him to England, to become a star over there first, before bringing him back to the States. He was wearing his hair in a Beatle cut to get ready for the trip. I'd heard stories like this a dozen times from sidemen and, not seeing anything that special in him, forgot about it. Boy, was I wrong.

Ted Daryll had moved on to an A&R job at RCA Victor, where he recorded several of my songs plus two he and I wrote for Peggy March. I even got to play guitar on a full-orchestra date backing her. After the session, Teddy and I and a couple of other guys went over to Sardi's, the famous theater district restaurant. We were beginning to grow our hair a bit longer and dressing a bit more "down" than before, so the maître d' was about to deny us entrance when Mr. Sardi happened upon the scene, mistaking us for the Rolling Stones, who were in town for a Madison Square Garden gig.

We were swiftly whisked upstairs, where a table in the center of the room was cleared and set for us. When the table adjacent was too noisy, we were asked if we'd like the party removed elsewhere. We laughed all night, enjoying how it felt to be big shots. I remember eating venison for the first time that night.

Chip seemed disheartened after Evie's "Angel of the Morning" flopped. Al Schwartz, like Chip, was spending too much time at the racetrack and I was feeling neglected, so when Ted's friend Murri Barber came along with some big ideas for my career, I thought it best to see where that might lead.

Murri had connections with Creed Taylor, the record producer who had taken jazz into the mainstream with hits like Jimmy Smith's "Walk on the Wild Side," Stan Getz's "Desafinado," and "Girl from Ipanema," sung by Astrud Gilberto. Creed had heard my song "Good Morning Blues," the B-side of "With Pen in Hand," and wanted to record it with

George Benson, who'd done a couple of successful albums for A&M Records under Creed's supervision. So I met with Creed, who expressed interest in recording me for his new label, CTI.

I felt some new blood might be helpful to my career, and Murri and I talked about bringing my sister Kathy into the deal. She was writing some good songs, looked great, and had a nice commercial voice. Murri came up with an idea to form a four-way publishing company, me, himself, Kathy, and Creed, which would publish all new material recorded on CTI. At least, that's how Murri presented it to me. With that enticement, I was ready to join up.

Jerry Wexler said he hated to see me leave Atlantic. Both he and Leiber and Stoller had wanted to produce me, he said, but I was under contract to Chip as long as I was on Atlantic, and that had tied his hands. Now, reluctantly, he gave me a release.

By this time, Atlantic was split into two camps, Wexler's and Ahmet Ertegun's. Seeing the future, Ahmet concentrated on the label's white rock acts, like Sonny and Cher; Buffalo Springfield; and Crosby, Stills and Nash, while Jerry stuck with the R&B he loved. Ironically, the one rock act Wexler signed, Led Zeppelin, wound up being the label's biggest.

The two barely spoke to each other, and, with the company's sale to Warner Bros., Ahmet was secretly making plans to move Jerry out. To be fair, Wex hadn't kept up with the times, and the acts that interested him, like Dr. John, Doug Sahm, and Willie Nelson, were, in his own words, "drowning in an ocean of red ink." Add to this the fact that black/white relations were at an all-time low. Like so many others, Jerry couldn't understand why his well-meaning efforts might be resented by people who wanted to make their own decisions and their own way in the world.

Creed Taylor wanted to begin our relationship by recording my sister, as I didn't have enough material yet. So they went into Rudy Van Gelder's studio across the Hudson River in Englewood Cliffs, New Jersey, and made a terrific album: all but two songs written by Kathy; one Beatles' number, "She's Leaving Home"; and one Kathy wrote with me, "Velvet Smile." The album, *Kathy McCord*, eventually became a cult record outside the United States and was recently reissued as half of a two-CD set by Ace Records in the UK.

I suppose I should have asked myself why a big shot like Creed Taylor would want to be partners in a publishing company with the three of us. But Murri had a way of making outlandish things sound plausible, and I wanted to believe it. Creed eventually claimed he'd made no such agreement, and I decided not to sign with him in the end.

My Knight-Riders pal Ronnie Hinds was still playing bass with me. I'd been living with Barbara Lee, one of the Chiffons, and playing guitar for them, but after a year and a half, I felt the need to go home and live for maybe six months at my mother's house, until I figured out the rest of my life. Those six months turned into nine years. With Ronnie and a drummer named Dennis Carpenter, I managed to get small-time gigs as a trio. Any popularity I had from my Atlantic days had dried up.

Sometimes, when not working with my own trio, I'd go play with my friends Rex Garvin and the Mighty Cravers. I played on some of their records, too. They worked a different circuit, mostly the black clubs in the Bronx and Harlem, like Small's Paradise and the venerable Club Barron, where on Tuesday nights French tourists would be bused uptown from their ship to see "real, live Negroes in their own habitat," or the Gold Lounge in the Theresa Hotel, by day a hangout for winos, who'd be shuffled out at 6:00 p.m. so the staff could clean up for the nighttime crowd of pimps, whores, hustlers, and other sporting-life types. The Gold Lounge was known among the cognoscenti as the cocaine clearinghouse of the East Coast, with a direct phone line in the office to the police precinct in case of a raid. To go to the bathroom, you had to be buzzed in by the bartender, as that was where much of the drug-dealing action took place. Comedian Slappy White would fly in from LA to pick up a stash for his buddy Redd Foxx, from time to time.

As people knew me in Harlem, I was accepted as part of the furniture. People looked differently at the other white guys who came in, pegging them immediately as either cops or chumps looking for women.

On rare occasions, I'd play with the Cravers at white clubs, where we were expected to remain in the dressing room, hidden offstage, away from the customers. The guys acted like they didn't care, bringing their own gin in briefcases, like executives. But I knew it had to hurt. I remember conducting for the fifties doo-wop group the Channels at a New Jersey country club where we were housed in the basement between shows. Lead singer Earl Lewis was a proud man, used to being idolized by the white blue-collar guys who make up the majority of fans of this music. By this time I had begun to see myself on the black side of things, and this insult infuriated me, although I wasn't about to start any trouble that could interfere with the guys getting paid for this gig or booked for future ones. But I had to do something, if only to assuage my own resentment. I spotted a few boxes of Coca-Cola glasses and decided to "liberate" a couple dozen for my personal use at home. The Channels thought this was hilarious. My big moment of rebellion.

The early seventies saw a major oldies revival. Richard Nader's vision had given new life to old rockers in concerts at Madison Square Garden, and clubs began booking the less expensive oldies acts to bring in customers on off nights. The success of movies like *American Graffiti* helped create a vogue for fifties nostalgia, and entertainers who hadn't made much money in their heyday and had ended up working at menial jobs were happy to be back in showbiz.

Having idolized rock 'n' roll stars in my teens, it came as a surprise when I discovered that few had made much money during their glory days. Fred Parris, lead singer of the Five Satins, set me straight one night. Most groups would have one or, at best, two hits. Since their audience was made up of teenagers, there was no nightclub work. Their fans were too young to go to clubs, so the only work available to fifties acts was at stage shows put on by disc jockeys, who expected them to work cheaply or for free in return for airplay. Quid pro quo. Aside from those, there were the chitlin' circuit theaters: the Howard in Washington, the Royal in Baltimore, the Uptown in Philadelphia, the Regal in Chicago, and the Apollo. That covered five weeks, which you could do maybe twice over the course of a year. Hardly enough to make you rich, much less earn a decent living. Once the hits stopped, the fickle R&B audience had no interest in laying down their hard-earned money to see you, and the bookings stopped coming. So this oldies revival was a boon to guys who'd wound up bagging groceries for a living.

For my little trio, a typical week might be: Monday night, a Mafia joint in New Jersey, backing an oldies act and competing for the crowd's attention with a topless go-go dancer in a cage above the stage; Tuesday would find us playing in a cop and fireman's bar in the Bronx, fending off requests for "Stairway to Heaven" or "Colour My World"; Wednesday, sitting in rush-hour traffic on the Long Island Expressway to work at a polyester singles bar in some town called Islip; Thursday at a Port Chester dive called Rapson's that attracted rich hippie kids from Connecticut. At Rapson's, we were usually joined by my old friend Kevin Falcone on conga drum. Murri talked Laurie Records into paying for the four of us to record our parody of the fifties hit "Little Darlin'" with a comic recitation I'd been doing in the clubs. We called ourselves the Imperial Gents for that record because it sounded like a fifties street-gang name.

Soon the hippies began following us around to these other clubs, some of which did not exactly welcome them with open arms, but they were gentle and sweet kids and bothered no one, so the working-class types soon accepted them and their odd-looking garments and hairstyles.

They liked hearing me announce the names of the artists who had originated songs they knew only in cover versions by acts like the Rolling Stones or the Grateful Dead. I liked having them around. They were loyal fans.

The girls were very loving, and free about sharing the love. Other men might have taken advantage of their innocence, but I felt protective and did my best to treat them kindly. The kids would offer to share their pot with the band and me, but I've never been into drugs or alcohol, so I always declined. It never fails to surprise civilians when I say that, because most people assume that musicians are all drunks or stoners. In those times it was especially true, and I was often the only sober person in the bands I played in. To this day, I am asked why and how I never used. I tell them I never met anyone on drugs or booze I wanted to be like.

I came from a family where the females were alcoholics and unable to confront this horrible disease head-on and take the steps toward recovery. It is accepted as fact today that there is a genetic component to substance addiction, as well as a connection to sugar, as alcohol turns to sugar in the body. If so, I suspect I may have inherited this gene, since I've always had a craving for sugar. My poison of choice is Pepsi-Cola. I call it the nectar of the gods.

Addiction doesn't have to be a lifetime sentence. I have seen a number of those I love overcome it, thanks to programs like Alcoholics

Anonymous. These lucky ones are living productive lives today. My mother was what is called a "functional alcoholic," one who can do her work but when not working will often go off the deep end. When I was a kid, one beer or half a martini would cause her face to get red, and I knew there'd be an argument if my father happened to come home for dinner that night.

At a party, the few my family was invited to, she'd start out the night lively and fun. Then, with more booze, she'd become guilt-ridden, blaming herself for putting her career before us kids. At stage three, she'd turn belligerent. If my father didn't get her out of there by that time, things could get ugly, really ugly.

The drinking got worse after she was let go from *The Perry Como Show* at age forty. That was the policy then. God forbid the public should have to look at a woman over forty on television. For the next thirteen years, she puttered around the house, buying and redoing antiques or making her garden beautiful. And drinking.

When she turned fifty-three, she learned enough piano to accompany herself and got jobs singing in restaurants. One in particular was the Town Tavern in Bronxville, a wealthy Westchester town where the customers fed her ego for the next decade, until she contracted the terminal cancer that took four years to kill her. She never touched a drop on the nights she worked but would get sloshed on her two nights off, and it was hard to be around. She went to her grave never admitting her addiction.

My trio performed under different names, mostly for our own inside jokes and amusement. We called ourselves the Crabs, just so we could advertise, "Catch the Crabs here, every Thursday night!" We came up with an idea to call ourselves the Boogie-Men and took denim jackets, cut off the sleeves, and got the name embroidered on patches on the back, like the Hell's Angels. It was a cheap uniform that fit in with the oldies revival. We later worked as the Billy Vera Band, for those who still remembered me.

Ronnie married Bernie, a Stamford girl he met at Rapson's and to whom he's still married today, forty years later. He was replaced by Eddie Garr, about whom the less said the better.

Unable to get my sister or me a record deal, but never giving up, Murri came up with a scheme for me. He convinced an old record man,

Doug Moody, who with his father Wally, onetime head of EMI Records in London, owned the old Del-Fi Records Studio in Hollywood, to give me six weeks of free studio time to make an album.

After leaving April-Blackwood, I'd started writing more unusual, less overtly commercial songs, aiming, in my own way, for what the FM radio crowd was buying. Doug booked us rooms at the Lido Apartments in the bowels of Hollywood, populated by old-time, has-been actors, actresses, and vaudevillians. It was a bit seedy but clean. They took messages, and it was walking distance to the studio on the corner of Selma and Vine.

We laid down tracks in this comfortable, warm-sounding studio, where Ritchie Valens had cut "La Bamba," and I brought in Elaine Hill, an old girlfriend from the Headliner days, and her friend Patti Brooks to sing background on a couple of songs and Elaine's husband, Ray Lignowski, to play some tenor sax. Ray was one of the great, unknown rock 'n' roll saxophonists. Although he couldn't read a note of music, other players, including King Curtis, used to come to hear him play at the Wagon Wheel on Forty-Fifth Street, where his band, the Jewels, held forth.

The finished album, crude in that way that people liked their music in the early seventies, came out pretty good. It was different. Murri took it to jazz saxophonist Curtis Amy, who was working for Lou Adler's Ode Records in Los Angeles. Curtis connected with what I was doing and played it for his boss, who jumped on a plane for New York and booked the Nola Studio on Fifty-Seventh Street so he could hear me alone at the piano doing my songs.

After I finished, Lou put his arm around me and said I was exactly what he was looking for. He'd just had an enormous success producing one of the biggest albums of all time, *Tapestry*, with Carole King, and he saw me as a male counterpart, someone who was respected within the industry but whom no one had figured out how to make happen. He told me to call him collect when he got back to LA, which I did.

He spoke with me every day for over a week, sometimes for over an hour, filling my head with what I wanted to hear. He said, "I have a big ego, and what would serve that ego is to make you as big a star as I did

Carole." This was the man I'd been looking for my whole life. Then one day he told me to have Murri call him to discuss the details of the deal.

Murri Barber was a man with what most psychologists would diagnose as delusions of grandeur. Murri thought in big terms, often confusing, as he had with Creed Taylor, how he wished things were with what was more likely to occur. So I got uncharacteristically stern with him and insisted he cool it with the big demands, as if he were negotiating on behalf of a major star. I said, "Whatever the deal is, take it, within reason. Do not argue. No hocking or hondling. Do not play the big shot. Lou Adler is a man who can take me where I want to go, so, whatever the price, I'm willing to pay it."

Two days later, as Lou had instructed, I called, and his secretary, who was by now my new best friend, answered and said cheerfully, "Hi Billy, I'll put you right through." The uncomfortable sound in her voice when she came back on and said he'd be right with me did not bode well. Up until now, he had always picked up immediately. She kept coming back every five minutes as I held the line until finally she told me he'd left the office for the day. I could hear the despair in her voice. This woman liked me and felt compassion for me.

I smelled a rat and called Murri, demanding that he tell me what he'd asked for. He hemmed and hawed, making like he'd been reasonable with Lou. But I knew Murri and I knew he'd fucked up, big time. I was never again able to get Lou Adler on the phone. This man whose enormous ego made him want to build me into his male Carole King and I have never had a conversation to this very day. Years later, when the Beaters and I were recording our album at the Roxy, the Sunset Strip club that Lou co-owned, I spotted him from the stage, standing in the doorway, watching me. But that was it. I have no idea if he even remembered me, eight years later.

I fell into a deep depression, one that I would struggle with for years, not that I recognized it as such. This man, Murri Barber, for all his good intentions, had ruined my life and my career, the one thing that mattered to me above all else.

My daughter, Maria, and actress Angie Dickinson at my star ceremony. (AUTHOR'S COLLECTION)

My dad, his stepmom, Alva, his dad, Quinn, and sister, Louise. (AUTHOR'S COLLECTION)

My mom, age nineteen. (PHOTO BY MAURICE SEYMOUR)

Family Christmas. (AUTHOR'S COLLECTION)

Daddy at work. (AUTHOR'S COLLECTION)

Kathy and me at our childhood home. (AUTHOR'S COLLECTION)

Mom with puppet Ollie and Perry Como. (AUTHOR'S COLLECTION)

Rockin' at the 12-20 Club. (AUTHOR'S COLLECTION)

RIGHT: Publicity shot.
(PHOTO BY MAURICE SEYMOUR)

BOTTOM: The Knight-Riders.
(PHOTO BY MAURICE SEYMOUR)

Billy Vera and Judy Clay, Atlantic Records publicity shot. (PHOTO BY STEPHEN PALEY)

Billy and Judy at the Apollo Theater. (AUTHOR'S COLLECTION)

Apollo Theater marquee, May 1968. (AUTHOR'S COLLECTION)

Apollo newspaper ad, May 1968.
(AUTHOR'S COLLECTION)

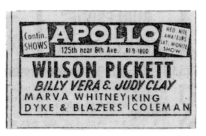

Apollo newspaper ad, July 1968.
(AUTHOR'S COLLECTION)

ABOVE: The Beaters play the Whisky.
(AUTHOR'S COLLECTION)

RIGHT: My sister, Kat McCord.
(AUTHOR'S COLLECTION)

7
Darkness Falls

It was back to the clubs, scrounging for a living, rooming at my mother's house. My sister was living in Woodstock with Michael Lang, the brains behind the Woodstock Festival. She befriended the many talented musicians who'd relocated there and was highly thought of among that crowd. These guys were happy to record songs with her and try to help her out. As much as anyone her age, she was "of" that generation and perfectly in her element living in Woodstock.

The oldies revival was now in full swing and we were gigging six or seven nights a week. At some of the more boring club gigs we played, when things got dull at the end of the night, to conserve our energy we'd play the old doo-wop rock-a-ballad chord changes and play "stump the band," having the audience request fifties classics, like "In the Still of the Nite" and "Earth Angel," to kill time. Some nights we'd do this for forty-five minutes straight as there were so many songs that fit the pattern. At one club on the Van Wyck Expressway, which packed them in during the week with topless dancers, we got hired for the weekends because the young owner was a fan of mine.

At first, we played to tables and chairs, as the pervs who came on weeknights to gawk at bare breasts had no interest in music and were home with their families on the weekend. One night, we were doing our "stump the band" routine for a lone table of six who loved it and asked me to come over after the set. They were a bit older, the first generation of Alan Freed fans, Italians who'd lived on the border of a black neighborhood in lower Manhattan in the early 1950s. They still fondly remembered the old days and liked hearing the songs from their teenage years, like "Work with Me Annie," by the Midnighters, and "Gee," by the Crows.

They began bringing in their friends, and soon the place was packed every weekend. We still played our wide variety of clubs during the week, only now some of those were bringing in the less expensive old groups, like the Harptones or the Chantels, to spice up their off nights. An agent named Neal Hollender, another fan, offered to get us gigs and we were soon working every night, sometimes augmenting the trio with a horn section for theater shows.

One of the groups I often played with, during both the 1960s and the early seventies, was the Coasters. I learned my comic timing from watching their shows while playing behind them. They were brilliant comic actors. Earl "Speedo" Carroll was a man I considered a national treasure. To see him, and that beautiful rubber face, was to watch one of the world's great clowns in action.

Lead singer Carl Gardner was another friend. Like the other three, Carl was a heavy drinker. One night, after rehearsal, he and I were sitting at the bar and he said, "Come with me, my boy." He led me to the office, which also served as a storeroom and dressing room for the musicians and entertainers, including the topless dancer who shook her goodies in a cage above the bar.

He went right to the go-go girl's makeup case and drew out her panties and one of her G-strings, ran his fingers across the section that rested on her sweet parts, and put them to his nose and sniffed. Just then there was a knock on the door. It was Speedo, yelling "Gardner! You in there sniffing the dancer's drawers again?" Apparently, Carl was known within the group for this kind of behavior. Later, during their show, every time a bit of choreography caused him to turn toward the band, he would lift his fingers to his nose, causing me to crack up laughing.

Larry Marshak of *Rock Magazine* booked me with an expanded band to back his first show at the Academy of Music on Fourteenth Street. Unlike the Richard Nader shows at Madison Square Garden, with big names like Chuck Berry and the Shirelles, Marshak's featured hard-core doo-wop, like the Cleftones and the Nutmegs. Working-class New York was ecstatic and the shows were sell-outs. We would eventually play thirteen of these.

Randy Irwin, who managed the Shirelles, called one day to ask if I'd be interested in being their conductor and guitarist. The group is best remembered for their many hit records, including "Soldier Boy," "Mama Said," and "Will You Love Me Tomorrow." I took the job, having done the same for the Chiffons, only the Shirelles, being the top of the girl-group heap, worked more often and for more money. I still had to rehearse lousy club bands that could barely read music, some of whom had no idea who the Shirelles were, but I always managed to make it work somehow.

At the time, the girls' act consisted of contemporary tunes with a couple of their own hits sprinkled in. Recalling some long-ago advice from Jackie Wilson—"If you ever get a hit, kid, make sure you do it every show. That's the only reason they're paying their little two dollars to see you"—it occurred to me that the Shirelles should be doing all their biggest hits. Entertainers can get tired of doing the same old hits and want to do new things to show that they're still "relevant." I somehow convinced the Shirelles to add things they'd dropped years before, like "Boys," "Thing of the Past," and even "I Met Him on Sunday," which their grateful fans loved them even more for doing.

I was still able to play with my own band when not working with the girls. The Shirelles occasionally hit the road, like two weeks in Miami or one-nighters here and there, and I went along with them.

The only other male who traveled with the group was Ronnie Evans, a flamboyantly gay guy of forty-five who'd been with the girls for thirteen years. Before that, he'd worked for Pearl Bailey. His part of her act was to sit in the front row until the finale, when Pearl would ask if anyone wanted to "come up and dance with Pearlie Mae." Ronnie would jump up and they'd do a spectacular choreographed routine that brought down the house.

For the Shirelles, he served as M.C., bodyguard, and general major-domo, running errands, having their gowns cleaned, etc. Ronnie had personality plus and often kept the show alive when the girls were tired.

I was only twenty-seven and, although I'd been around plenty of gay people in show business, felt a little nervous when told I had to room with Ronnie. What I failed to realize was that, just like straight people, gay guys have their own preferences and tastes. Some like blondes; others prefer redheads. What Ronnie Evans liked was Spanish-looking black guys, so as it turned out I had nothing to worry about.

On one low-paying gig in the South, we had to take the Greyhound bus. Ronnie was his usual entertaining self, always "on," chatting up the old ladies or nodding out in the seat next to me, when who should step onto the bus but a young Marine—a Spanish-looking black Marine. Ronnie perked up and elbowed me, saying in a stage whisper, "Look, Billy Bet [his pet name for me], there's my meat!"

I said, "Man, that's a fucking Marine. How you gonna pull that?"

"You just watch and learn, baby," and with that, he sauntered up to the front of the bus and struck up a conversation with the young man. At the next stop, in Richmond, Virginia, we had a twenty-minute layover. The two of them entered the men's room, and nineteen minutes later, out they came, Ronnie snapping his fingers, winking broadly, and saying, "Don't you ever doubt your grandmother, honey."

Ronnie got an extra kick out of "turning" or "pulling" a straight person and freely named quite a few of the big-name R&B stars he had "pulled" over his years in show business. Out of respect for people's privacy, I shall name none of these for you.

I was surprised to find out that, in all their years of fame, the Shirelles had never performed west of the Mississippi. Randy felt it was important to establish the real group on the West Coast, to discourage any more fake Shirelles. So we did an oldies tour of California, playing arenas in Los Angeles, San Diego, Sacramento, and Oakland, with a bunch of LA acts that included Bobby "Rockin' Robin" Day, Shirley "Oop Shoop" Gunter, her brother Cornell's West Coast Coasters, Bill Haley, and the great blues shouter Big Joe Turner. The tour bus picked Joe up at his home in South Central, and he climbed aboard carrying a gigantic jug containing some alcoholic concoction that he and his old pal Haley proceeded to imbibe until their faces turned cherry red.

Joe and Bill were old friends, from the time in the fifties when Haley covered Joe's big hit, "Shake, Rattle and Roll." Many ignorant people think white acts covering R&B hits is some kind of racist plot to "appropriate" music that "belongs" to blacks. Bullshit, I say. If that were true, then why not criticize Ray Charles for singing country-and-western songs or Leontyne Price for singing Italian opera or Nat "King" Cole for "appropriating" the "Jewish" songs of Irving Berlin and George

Gershwin? Songs don't "belong" to any one group. Songs are meant to be sung, by anyone who wishes to sing them. End of sermon.

I have asked this question of a number of black artists and songwriters over the years: "How do you feel about white singers recording your songs?" Most were happy and grateful, especially those who wrote the tunes, as they profited from the cover versions, often greatly, as when Elvis revived Lloyd Price's "Lawdy Miss Clawdy" or the McGuire Sisters sold three million copies of "Sincerely," written by Harvey Fuqua of the Moonglows. Johnny Otis expressed great pleasure over Georgia Gibbs's cover of "Dance with Me Henry," or at least over the windfall royalties he received.

The Shirelles were booked for the first time in Las Vegas, in the lounge at the Sahara Hotel, where Louis Prima and Keely Smith had made their big success. The girls were given rooms in the hotel and Ronnie Evans and I were put up in a clean but modest two-bedroom apartment across the street. We were there for several weeks and I was pretty bored, since I don't gamble and most of the good-looking women were either hookers or there with rich sugar daddies. Ronnie, on the other hand, had no problem hooking up with a chef from the hotel next door, who, he exclaimed, was gifted with "the dick of death."

On our first night off, Ronnie was all set for his big date with his culinary Romeo. He spent the day cooking his special West Indian gumbo and chattered nonstop about his expectations. I made plans to go out with guys from the house band to catch Harry Belafonte's show and come back after 2:00 a.m.

I arrived on schedule to find Ronnie pacing the floor in a huff. At first he didn't want to talk about it, but when he could no longer contain himself, he related the following:

"Well, I cooked for the bitch, we ate, played around a little. Then I went into the bathroom to powder my pussy. And when I walked in the room she was laying on her back with her legs stuck up in the air!"

Confused, I said, "Wasn't that the plan?"

"No, fool," he replied, "I wanted to be the woman!!"

I had to bite my lip to keep from laughing, although to my friend Ronnie it was no laughing matter.

During the first part of our engagement, Sonny and Cher were headlining in the main room. Ronnie always made friends with the housekeepers, to keep up with the latest gossip, like how Diana Ross didn't like the color of her dressing room, so she had a hissy fit and threw her plate of spaghetti against the wall so the hotel would have to repaint it.

This one morning, one of the cleaning ladies, giddy with excitement, said, "Chile, we went in to clean the dressing room this morning and Miss Cher's things were all gone! Not one bobby pin was left. The bitch done gone back to LA!" That night, Johnny Mathis and Erroll Garner came in three days early to cover for the big celebrity breakup, soon to be celebrated in the *National Enquirer*.

Ronnie quickly developed a huge crush and dragged me in between shows so he could gaze upon Johnny Mae, whom he was convinced he could "pull" if he only got the chance to meet him. Alas, Ronnie never got the chance at his dreamboat.

Another night at the Sahara, I came offstage and went downstairs to wait for Ronnie while the girls changed into their street clothes so he could take their gowns to the dry cleaner's in the morning.

A smallish guy, with a loud plaid sport jacket, a pencil-thin moustache, and a noticeable lump under his armpit, said to me, "You're the guitar player, right?" I nodded yes and he continued, "You know, my wife is up in the room, crying." Now I was on the verge of giving a shit, but I began to look around for a beer bottle to hit this joker with, in case things got ugly. "She's crying because you pinched her in the casino."

"Listen, man," a beer bottle now within easy reach, "that's not my style."

"You calling my wife a liar?"

I said, "No, but here in Vegas, wives sometimes feel neglected when their man is spending too much time at the tables. She was probably just trying to get your attention."

He wasn't going for it. Just then, down the stairs comes Ronnie Evans, with three crinoline gowns slung over his shoulder, dressed in a black jumpsuit complete with mirrors worthy of Little Richard. I said, "Ronnie, this dude thinks I pinched his wife in the casino," to which Ronnie replied, "Oh palease, chile, my friend Billy Bet was with me."

Now the chump doesn't know what to think. He looks at Ronnie and calls him a queer or something, causing Ronnie to jump up in the guy's face and say, "Listen, motherfucker, there's two things in this world I like to do, fight and suck dicks . . . and before we're through here, I'm gonna do one or both with you. And if you got any ideas about pulling out that piece you got under your jacket, I'll shove it so far up your ass it'll take an army of doctors to get it out."

With that, the dude's eyes started to roll around in his head and he turned and walked out, wondering what had just happened. I knew Ronnie could fight. He was strong as a bull and I'd seen him beat up three guys at once when they'd tried to bother the girls.

As he was fond of saying, "When you grow up a sissy in Harlem, baby, you better know how to fight."

During a two-week Shirelles engagement at a hotel in Miami, I met a college student from Jamaica, Queens, who was vacationing with her girlfriend. We stayed in touch, and when I got back home, we evolved into friends with benefits.

After graduation, Liz, a middle child of thirteen, opted to teach at the junior high school she'd attended, to give something back. In the intervening years, the school had become run down, with metal detectors at the entrances.

Her first day, she told the class, "All of you who want to learn, come sit in front. Those who do not, sit in the back and keep quiet, and anyone who picks on the kids who want to learn can look forward to an ass-whupping from me. And if you don't like it, send your mama and I'll kick her ass, too. I sat in those same seats you're sitting in now and I'm here because I care." Liz was a tough-love advocate.

"Furthermore, only proper English will be spoken in my classroom. I don't care what those white teachers have been telling you, that it's okay to speak Ghetto. I grew up around here and can speak Ghetto as well as any of you, but if I went to France, how far do you think I'd get if I couldn't speak French? If you can't speak proper English when you cross that river into Manhattan, you'll be sweeping floors or washing dishes for the rest of your life."

Too tough, you say? By the end of the year, those seventh graders, who'd been reading at third grade level, were up to grade level, thanks to Liz and her tough love . . . and those kids adored her, even the hard-core ones.

Liz was a wonderful teacher, but not all teachers are good ones. When my daughter, Maria, was around ten, her teacher went around the classroom, asking each kid what his or her ethnicity was, in some sort of misguided diversity exercise, before there was such a term. One kid said, "I'm Irish," another said "I'm Italian," etc., and when it got to Maria, she said, "Well, my mom is black and my daddy is white."

The idiot teacher replied, "Maria, that makes you black."

"Why should I have to choose?" shot back my smart little girl.

I'd like to believe the experience taught that ignorant teacher a lesson, but I doubt it. We got her out of that school as soon as possible.

When concert promoter Richard Nader convinced Dion and the Belmonts to reunite after many years apart for one show in 1972, it was the talk of the town and tickets sold out in three hours. To New Yorkers of a certain age, Dion was the Sinatra of his generation, and to have him back singing with the Belmonts, even for one night, was a major coup. Neither Dion nor the group was pleased with the band Nader normally used on his shows, and one of their demands was that he hire us to play for them, which we were only too happy to do.

The night of the performance, when Richard announced the act, there was a roar and stamping of feet the likes of which I've never heard, before or since. You could actually feel the floor of Madison Square Garden shake. The crowd went wild after and even during each number, starting with "I Wonder Why," right on through "That's My Desire" and "Runaround Sue," all of which ended up on an album for Dion's label, Warner Bros., that has remained in print ever since.

At one Academy of Music show in 1973, the featured act was Ronnie Spector, fresh from escaping the clutches of her husband Phil and back living at her mother's in Washington Heights. She needed to make money, so she hired two girls and called them the Ronettes. Her cousin Nedra had become a born-again Christian and no longer wanted to do the old act, which was rather sexy, and I had no idea yet why her sister Estelle wasn't invited.

After rehearsal, Ronnie approached me to say that she was going to be working again, she'd heard I was the best conductor in New York, and she wanted me to work for her. I said I was working for the Shirelles, but when they weren't working I'd be happy to cover for her until she found someone. In an aside, I also mentioned that I'd once had a crush on her sister Estelle. Ronnie was the personality and the sexpot, but Estelle was the real beauty of the group, with a face made for modeling.

Ronnie asked me to dinner and we wound up hanging out until dawn. This was a girl who wasn't used to being told no. I hadn't intended it, but by saying I'd had a crush on Estelle, I'd been inadvertently using one of the age-old pimp's plays. It wasn't on purpose, I promise. At any rate, it had the same effect: she wanted me, at least partly out of competition with her sister, and was determined to have me, as both her conductor and her boyfriend. She went into full seduction mode. I don't recall whether we slept together that night or the next, but we were quickly involved.

Often, I stayed at her mom's apartment or she came to my mother's house. She charmed my mom with flattery to spare, the kind that only comes from a supreme narcissist who wants what she can't have immediately.

You must remember that, to my generation of New York boys, the Ronettes were the number one sex symbols of their time, right up there with Marilyn Monroe, Sophia Loren, and the rest. So to be Ronnie Spector's first boyfriend after she left her husband was a BFD, a Big Fucking Deal. In the eyes of the guys, I was now a man among men. Had they only known what madness was to come . . .

All this is nothing Ronnie herself hasn't revealed in her own book, so I'm not telling tales out of school.

As one might imagine, living with Phil Spector would drive any woman to take pills, and Ronnie was on tranquilizers at the time we met. On top of that, she was also on the sauce, a lethal combination. I quickly ascertained that it would be wise to bring Mama Bennett along on gigs, as there was always someone willing to bring Ronnie a Coke laced with vodka, so we couldn't smell the alcohol.

One night, after a gig, we all stopped off in Harlem at Wells Chicken and Waffles for a bite to eat. I'd hired a bass player for that gig. Ronnie's little girl cousin was there and snuck her a vodka and Coke. Before long, the telltale signs appeared: the puffy face, the unfocused eyes . . . and then, plop, she fell face down into her food. Looking around to see if anyone had noticed, I pulled her up, wiped her face, gave one of the girls money to pay the check, and said quietly, "We're going to walk her out of here, before anybody notices, so everybody, be cool." Harlem is a gossipy little town and I didn't want all of uptown talking the next morning about how homegirl fell smack into her waffles.

Another time, up in Boston at a mob-owned club near Fenway Park I'd worked at several times with the Shirelles and the Channels, I was struggling with a worse-than-usual lame house band, trying to get them to make the notes on the paper sound like music, while looking over my shoulder to make sure the girls were okay, when I turned and . . . no Ronnie! The lights went out and someone grabbed my arm, leading me to the office where Ronnie sat, all puffy-faced and out of it. I knew at a glance some asshole had gotten her a drink and she'd fallen off the stage.

The gangster who owned the place said to me, "Good thing I know you and like you. Otherwise, that broad would have two broken kneecaps right now. You go back to the hotel and find me an act to finish out the week, then get this dumb bitch out of town in the morning."

I did as I was told and dialed that phone until I got ahold of Gary Bonds, who was happy to come up and replace us.

One day, Estelle, who wanted to be in the group again, asked me to intercede with Ronnie. I said, "You should be in the group; you're a Ronette. Let me talk to your sister." But Ronnie wanted no part of Estelle; she would've had to pay her more than the pittance she was paying the two pretend Ronettes.

With her drinking, Ronnie couldn't be trusted with her own money, so I had to take it all, paying the girls, the hotel, gas, agents, and other expenses, then giving the remainder to her mother when we got home. I doubt she had ever paid for so much as a hot dog in her life. Although one of the great performers onstage, offstage, the girl was utterly helpless.

The final straw for me came in Florida, when the booze and tranquilizers combined yet again to make Ronnie fall down onstage. I had gotten a call from Steve Cropper, who'd left Stax Records and opened his own studio and label in Memphis and wanted to record me. I'd had enough of Ronnie's dysfunction and gave her mother the money, keeping enough for a plane ticket to Memphis, where I stayed at Cropper's house. I am happy to report that Ronnie eventually found the help she needed and, as far as I know, is sober today.

Steve loved to fish and, with his royalties from songs like "Knock on Wood," "In the Midnight Hour," and "Dock of the Bay," had a private pond built and stocked for that purpose. The first day I was there, we fished and his wife cooked up the most delicious catfish I've ever had, one I'd caught!

Finally relaxed after my ordeal as conductor, guitarist, and de facto manager of Ronnie Ronette, I went with Steve to the studio the next morning, where he was recording Jerry Lee Lewis, another crazy person. On one song, "Jack Daniels Old #7," Cropper asked me to sing harmony with the Killer, which was a real thrill. It became the single from the album.

Steve and I wrote a couple of songs, and, as I had on Atlantic, I chose an album's worth of tunes I liked by other people. Unfortunately, the house band was not up to the standards of Steve's group at Stax, Booker T. and the M.G.'s, and the album, deservedly, never came out. Just one lone single, a song I wrote called "Big Chief," made a little noise in New Orleans at Mardi Gras time. The B-side was a tune Steve and I wrote called "Hold On," the sort of thing Percy Mayfield used to write for Ray Charles.

Back in New York, the Nutmegs were on one of the Academy of Music shows. I liked their doo-wop classic "Story Untold" and the way they sang a cappella, so I asked Randy Irwin to help me get funding to record the group in that style for a label he'd been working with. Up in New Haven, the Nutmegs' hometown, was a studio owned by Tom Sokira, who'd recorded that city's groups in the fifties, including the Five Satins' classic, "In the Still of the Nite." He even had the same original microphones.

We recorded the guys at Tom's, I got one of the Rapson's hippies named Tommy Hammang, who used to be a Times Square Records collector, to take the beautiful cover photo of the guys surrounded by a bunch of little kids from the projects, and the album came out. At the recording session, the Nutmegs' bass singer, a wild and crazy guy who called himself Black Mack McNeil, wore Bermuda shorts all year round, and shaved only one side of his face, had brought to the studio a little guy named Jimmy Becton. Jimmy had played me a really cool song called "Why Can't It Be Real" on this odd, organ-like instrument he'd brought with him.

I loved the sound of it, and him, and brought some musician friends up to New Haven to record Jimmy, who sounded a bit like Joe Tex. My pal Pete Holman came to play drums, and I had a guy named Warren play trombone, an unusual instrument for an R&B record. I sent the tape to Cropper, who agreed to put it out on his label, TMI. He loved Pete's drum sound. Although distributed by RCA Victor, TMI was not funded to promote, so none of their records went anywhere. They were soon out of business, and Steve moved to LA.

I loved that record and have often thought that if I had brought it to Jerry Wexler it could have been a hit on Atlantic. It was Jerry's kind of sound: Southern, honest, and real. But my self-confidence was so low at that point that I couldn't bring myself to go to my old contacts.

After Memphis, it was back to my little trio in New York. One gig stands out among the many. Noted bon vivant George Plimpton threw a party for five hundred of his closest friends on a large yacht docked off Manhattan's East River. Plimpton was pals with Atlantic cofounder Ahmet Ertegun, and all four acts that night were Atlantic alumni. As we approached the boat, I heard an alto sax that sounded like Hank Crawford, who'd played in Ray Charles's band and was now a jazz star on his own.

Following the sound, I spotted what I found out was the New York Rock 'n' Roll Ensemble. The sax player was Dave Sanborn, and standing at the edge of the stage was my sister Kat. "What are you doing here, little sis?"

"I'm going out with Sanborn," she replied. Just as I had for pretty girls, Kat had a weakness for musicians. She wound up singing on one of David's albums. I got to talk with him and found out that, in addition to Hank, he loved the playing of Junior Walker and Louis Jordan, so we had in common our taste in horn blowers.

The other two Atlantic acts performing that night were drummer Elvin Jones, who'd played on John Coltrane's jazz classics, and the Drifters, whom we were to accompany after playing our own set. While we were on, Elvin came up to me and said, "Man, I like what you cats are doing. Think I could sit in for a few numbers?" Duh, as the kids say, who wouldn't want to play with the great Elvin Jones? The dude had no trouble playing our funky style of R&B.

During the Drifters' show, Ertegun interrupted to present the group with a plaque that said, "To the all-time greatest Atlantic group." Given that, besides the Coasters and the Clovers, the label's luminaries included

Led Zeppelin; Crosby, Stills, Nash and Young; and the Rolling Stones, that was the highest praise, and well deserved, if you ask me.

During this period, for fun, I often spent my off nights playing with the Mighty Cravers. Drummer Pete Holman, who'd played on the album I made with Judy Clay, was an especially close friend. We'd often talk on the phone late at night after our respective gigs about all kinds of things.

One afternoon, Pete and I thought we'd head to the Apollo, where Richard Pryor was headlining in the wake of his breakthrough album, *That Nigger's Crazy.*

Outside the theater, waiting on line, we spotted an old pimp we knew and hadn't seen in some time. We struck up a conversation as we waited for the doors to open and he told us he'd moved up to Bridgeport, Connecticut, and become a minister at one of those little storefront Baptist churches.

We remarked that this was quite a switch from his former profession and he replied, "Man, I'm making more bread than I ever made pimping. Plus, I never pay for food; those good sisters feed me every night; and I'm getting more pussy than I ever got as a pimp." That, and he didn't have to worry about being arrested, either.

The Apollo was packed, and after two lackluster opening acts—the Stylistics, no two of whom sang in tune with each other, and Billy Paul, who did his hit "Me and Mrs. Jones"—an offstage announcer spoke:

"Ladies and gentlemen, will you please give a warm Apollo Theater welcome to the star of our show, Richard Pryor!"

Nothing, no Richard.

"Uh, will you please welcome . . . Richard Pryor!"

Still no Pryor. Mild titters from the hipper audience members, knowing that jokes come in threes.

"Um, ladies and gentlemen, please . . . Mr. Richard Pryor!!"

From behind the curtain, stage right, we saw the bulging eyes and rubber face of Richard, looking scared out of his wits. He said, in a frightened, little-boy voice, "Hi y'all. Hope I'm funny . . . 'cause I hear you Apollo niggers are . . . CRAZY!"

The place went wild. He had them in the palm of his hand from that moment, and did the most incredible comedy act I've ever seen.

8
Polyester Rules

For me and for many others, the 1970s was a cultural desert. So much had changed, especially the music. And let's not even talk about the sartorial styles—the polyester, the muttonchops, the big hair and shoulder pads for women. People dressed like clowns—the long collars, the puffy sleeves, the bell-bottoms, the weird fabric designs. Nehru suits. Yuck. And on the other side of the coin were the leftover hippies, still wearing their fringe and sandals. It was as if a mass psychosis had descended upon us.

Musically, I couldn't figure out how to fit in. It was no world for a blue-eyed soul singer. I couldn't put on tight spandex and turn into a heavy metal guy. I had no interest in morphing into some wimpy singer/songwriter, and, like all the musicians I knew, I loathed disco and wasn't about to whore myself out trying to enter that market, especially after seeing many of my R&B friends make fools of themselves in the attempt.

My life during that era was about survival. I put together my first horn band, and it was fun, sort of. But, as the only sober cat, it was lonely at work. I had nothing in common with the other musicians; they'd come into work talking about how fucked up they'd gotten the night before. That was no basis for conversation, so I hung out with the girls who wanted to sleep with the singer, and that in itself turned into a kind of addiction, taking my attention away from writing songs and trying to get ahead. I was in my thirties now and there was little time left to make my mark.

I wrote a song called "Back Door Man" about a doomed affair: a guy in love with a married woman who was selfishly using him to fill the void in her marriage. It sounded like a hit to me, so I got Ted Daryll and we went into a studio and recorded it. We got a guy named Bob Reno, who was a fan of mine, to put it out on his label, Midland International. Bob had been having success lately with disco acts like Silver Convention and Carol Douglas, as well as a hit with a kid from the TV sitcom *Welcome Back Kotter*, John Travolta. Not exactly the hippest roster or where I'd like to be, but beggars can't be choosers, any port in a storm, or any other cliché that fits. Reno put out the single, and it faded quickly.

A number of players came in and out of that band before we finally settled in as a group of seriously committed guys, one of whom was Tommy Wolk, a wonderful musician whose main instrument was the Fender bass, but who also excelled on guitar and keyboards and could even make an accordion sound hip. He was a major asset and a good guy.

Unlike previous bands, I no longer had to be a slave to six-nights-a-week, dead-end club dates. These guys were happy to play a few nights, so we could concentrate on things with a future, although we did play the occasional two-week hotel gig.

One of these was the Ramada Inn in Stamford, Connecticut. Fans from my Country House days would show up, along with younger people. The manager was a guy named Pete Ceruzzi, who'd been in the Casinos, the group who'd hit with "Then You Can Tell Me Goodbye," so he liked and understood musicians.

It was the kind of job where, on weekends, you had to play at least one disco tune per set, to appease the cretins who wanted that stuff, but Pete also let us play what we wanted because he liked me. At the time, there was a fad for disco remakes of old tunes, like Frankie Avalon's disco version of his fifties hit "Venus," or Esther Phillips's disco retread of "What a Difference a Day Makes." To amuse myself and the band on slow nights, I'd say to the audience, "I wonder what it might sound like if Georgie Jessel did a disco remake of his famous song, 'My Mother's Eyes,'" and go into a ridiculous version that nobody got the humor of, other than Pete and the band, who laughed until tears ran down their cheeks. Picture me doing an imitation of Jessel saying things like, "Come on everybody, get down, get down with Georgie," in that Lower East Side voice of his.

One week, there was a nostalgia revue playing at the local theater, and the cast—Milton Berle, Dick Haymes, maybe Margaret Whiting, and who else but Georgie Jessel—were all staying at the hotel. As was my habit, I came in early one evening to find an old guy at the bar talking with the bartender, who saw me and said, "There's the kid who does Jessel."

"You do Jessel?"

"Yeah," I said, and went into a very good imitation of the Toastmaster General of the United States, as he was known. Just then, walking down the hall, there he was, all five foot one of him, Georgie Jessel. It was a setup. He walks up to me and says in that unmistakable voice, "Kid, you sounded so much like me, I thought my voice got here before I did."

Later that night, after their show, the whole cast came in, old Georgie hitting on waitresses one-third his age, trying to impress them with lines like "See this ring, sweetheart? It was a gift from General MacArthur," whom undoubtedly the waitress had never heard of. I did my Jessel routine while Berle sat there, glaring because Jessel was getting the attention he thought was his due.

Some time later, we were playing a two-week gig at another Ramada Inn in New Jersey, one of the lowest points of my career. To understand this kind of a gig, picture yourself playing to three customers, all traveling businessmen who hate you because the waitresses are more interested in you than in them. You get the idea.

On one such night, after the set, the waitress came over and said, "The guy at that table over there would like to buy you a drink." I walked over and saw the outstretched hand of this guy with a large head and crazy eyes, his wife at the table—big, flaming red hair, dressed in one of those seventies denim jumpsuits with rhinestones up and down one leg. He shook my hand and said, "L. Russell Brown. I wrote 'Tie a Yellow Ribbon Round the Ole Oak Tree.' Call me Larry."

"How nice for you," I thought.

"Vera, I've been watching you. You're one of the greatest singers and entertainers I've ever seen. You're a great songwriter. Everybody in the business knows it. Everybody respects you. But you never make any money. Me, I make a lot of money, but nobody respects me." I thought I was listening to Rodney Dangerfield. "I have an idea. We should write together. I could show you how to make money, and you can teach me how to get respect."

Well, that sounded pretty good to me, and I began spending a lot of afternoons and my evenings off at Larry Brown's house in New Jersey.

He was a very energetic guy, and we wrote a lot of songs, not all of them good, sometimes as many as three in one day. Lesson number one: Don't expect to write "Stardust" every time out.

The more I got to know him, the more I liked him. He was crazy as a loon, surrounded by a wacky wife and three daughters. Half Jewish and half Sicilian, his was the last white family to move out of the Seth-Borden Housing Projects in Newark. He'd been jailed at age ten and in 1958, in his teens, decided to become a rock 'n' roller. After he'd been turned down by every record man on Broadway, someone suggested he go up to Harlem and seek out a guy named Bobby Robinson, who had a record shop on 125th Street. Robinson, with his brother Danny, also owned a number of record labels over the years, starting with Red Robin in 1951 and a local group of junior high school kids called the Mello-Moods singing a Frank Loesser tune, "Where Are You (Now That I Need You)" that made the Top 10.

After Red Robin came Fury, with Louis Lymon and the Teenchords, Gladys Knight and the Pips, and a huge hit with Wilbert Harrison's "Kansas City." Bobby's other labels included Whirlin' Disc, Enjoy, and Fire, and artists like Elmore James, King Curtis, and the Channels. He kept his ear to the ground and was always on top of every Harlem trend, right up into the rap era with Grandmaster Flash and Kool Moe Dee.

Bobby was operating Fury when Larry and his partner made their way uptown to play their songs. Robinson, who'd made his fortune in black music, thought these two white boys reminded him enough of the Everly Brothers to take a shot with them and they made a record as the Duals, which sank like a stone.

A few years went by and Larry hooked up with hit songwriter/producer and fellow Jersey boy Bob Crewe, cowriter of "Silhouettes" and numerous Four Seasons hits. On staff with Crewe's organization, Larry wrote "Sock It to Me" for Mitch Ryder and "C'mon Marianne" for the Seasons, among others. In the seventies, he hit the big time with numerous hits for Tony Orlando and Dawn: "Knock Three Times," "Yellow Ribbon," and more. The guy knew how to make a buck in the songwriting racket.

"I don't consider myself a songwriter," he's always claimed. "I'm a song combiner," by which he means he takes bits and pieces of hits and puts them together, much like John Lennon, who once quipped, "The greatest songwriters are the cleverest thieves," among whom he considered himself.

Like many people who are good at one thing, Larry wanted to try his luck at something else. He wanted to be a record producer, like his mentor, Bob Crewe. So he got a gig to produce a Juno award–winning Canadian group called the Good Brothers. We set about writing songs for the siblings and took them to Nashville to the studio of pedal steel guitar wizard Pete Drake. Pete contracted an A-team of Music City's finest session pickers, including Pig Robbins and Reggie Young, along with my drummer, Ben Beckley, and my bassist, Tommy Wolk, and me joining in on rhythm guitar.

The first day, I was nervous among this august company and had the opening lick on one song, a simple lick I'd played a hundred times, but I kept blowing it, until Pete, in his understated Southern manner, quietly said, "Boy, maybe you ought to take off your gloves before you try that again." Haw, haw, everybody laughed, but I was no rube and realized I was being tested, so I retorted, "Pete, I can stick a drumstick up my ass and run it across those strings of yours and sound better than you."

Everybody, including Pete, guffawed and I was now a member of the club. Next take, I played my lick flawlessly. By the time the album was finished, Pete was trying to get Larry, Tommy, and me to move to Nashville and be with him.

By 1976, soul music as we knew it was over and done with. It seemed the only soulful music was being done by the country artists known as the Outlaws, Waylon and Willie and that crowd. Larry felt my brand of soulful crooning would be right at home backed by a combination of my musicians and those Nashville guys.

Knowing I was still signed to Midland (now Midsong), Larry talked Bob Reno into letting me do an album at Pete's Place, so we wrote some more tunes, and that November we again made the trek to Tennessee.

Being a novice behind the glass and with a head overflowing with ideas, Larry had a tendency to overproduce, and things got a little too busy behind my singing. I was in the habit of putting myself in the hands of a producer instead of taking charge of my own music like successful artists do, so I kept my mouth shut.

One night we went to a local Italian restaurant in Nashville owned by a guy from New Jersey. After dinner, Larry asked how I'd rate the joint. Referring to my favorite pizzeria back home, Johnny's in Mt. Vernon, I said, "It ain't Johnny's, but it ain't bad." This gave Larry an idea, and we went back to our hotel and wrote "She Ain't Johnnie," about a guy who returns to his hometown, looking for an old girlfriend named Johnnie. Like a peeping Tom, he spies her in her backyard, hanging clothes with curlers in her hair, and, after all the women he's been with since, he realizes that even she ain't Johnnie, but she ain't bad.

The next morning, with no time to overthink the song, Larry let the musicians figure out for themselves what to do with it. It turned out to be the best thing on the album, but for some reason, Reno chose not to release it as a single. Years later, on the heels of "At This Moment," "She Ain't Johnnie" found its way out and wound up on the country charts.

The album, *Out of the Darkness*, came out and, like everything I did that decade, sold nothing. As part of my renegotiated deal, thanks to Larry's salesmanship, Reno leased a car for me, a 1977 Mercedes-Benz 450 SEL, the best car on the road at that time. My friend and piano player, Joe Renda, drove a Mercedes and suggested it, his logic being that Mercedes weren't that well known yet in America; the bad guys thought of them as nothing more than big Volkswagens, and the cops were less likely to stop you in a car like that. Plus, a Mercedes was far classier than the usual gaudy red Cadillacs favored by New Yorkers who'd made good. I loved that car; it made me feel like a winner, even though I was not selling records. I still have it.

Not long after I got my Benz, I stopped at a red light on a hill near my mother's house, and some stupid drunk rear-ended me going about forty miles an hour, smashing his front end and, amazingly, leaving not a dent on my car. Two Greenburgh cops happened to see the accident. They knew me from the clubs and from my neighbor, a cop I'd occasionally helped out when he got into situations, and they grabbed the drunk, offering to toss him over the side of the hill. I said my car and I were unhurt and there was no need for anything so extreme, so they just arrested him and took him off to the station.

Only once did I make the charts during that decade, and that was when R&B singers Sam Dees and Bettye Swann cut a revival of "Storybook Children" in 1976. It did nothing to raise my profile, my bank balance, or my spirits.

The one bright spot was a regular gig at the Siding, a club alongside the railroad tracks in the upscale Northern Westchester town of Pleasantville, home of *Reader's Digest*. For most of my adult life, other than a couple of those Rapson's hippie girls, I'd predominantly been dating black women, feeling more comfortable in a black environment, but here was something different. I'd lived in the black world so long that I had begun to see these white girls from well-to-do families as exotic.

One night at the Siding, I spotted a classy-looking girl at a front table with a guy and another couple. Her body language told me she was with but not *with* the guy. The way she looked around like she owned the room and played with her hair told me she thought she was hot shit . . . and she was. I asked around about her and was told her name was Nina and that she had previously worked there as a waitress.

I couldn't get her out of my mind, and the next time my band played there Nina and I met and hung out. She told me the guy had been her boyfriend and went into vivid detail about breaking up with him and how he'd taken it hard, seeming to almost enjoy telling me how deeply he'd suffered, as if she were turned on by the power she had over him.

A few days later, I began a song, writing from what I perceived as the guy's point of view, putting myself in his shoes. But I was unable to finish it. Normally, when I can't finish a song, I toss it, feeling that if it can't keep my attention long enough to complete it, it must not be that good. This time, though, I put it away in my mother's piano bench.

Nina and I quickly became an item. Our relationship was highly intense, both emotionally and sexually. She was twenty years old and in college, very intelligent, with a low, sexy voice almost like a young Lauren Bacall. She exuded class and oozed sex. My mother was charmed when I took Nina to see her sing at the Town Tavern in Bronxville.

She lived with her parents, a pair of psychologists, in a sort of ultra-left-wing collective community of apartments in Pleasantville. They didn't object to me staying overnight in Nina's room when she wasn't spending nights with me at my mother's. One morning, as we lay in her bed, she confessed she was "head over heels in love" with me. Before long, I was obsessed with her, more than with anyone before in my life. I finally had someone who made me feel like a winner.

I was still occasionally playing with the Shirelles. Randy Irwin got his people to back two albums, which we recorded at RCA Victor's studios in Manhattan, one with the group doing updates of their old hits, and the other of Shirley alone doing contemporary songs under the pseudonym Lady Rose. Tommy, Ben, and I played all the instruments, and Shirley cut three of my songs.

At one of these sessions, on August 16, 1977, on a bathroom break, I walked down the hall, past the mastering labs, and heard Elvis's voice coming out of each room. Normally, you'd hear various RCA artists, John Denver, Perry Como, or Dolly Parton, coming from these rooms as the engineers prepared the tapes for release. I said to myself, "It's not Elvis's birthday. I wonder why they're mastering Elvis in every room today."

We finished the day's recording, then left to go home. On the car radio, all anybody was talking about was that Elvis had just died at age forty-two. That's how fast RCA was on it, knowing that, with his passing, demand for his music would be through the roof. They were right: within two weeks there were eighteen Elvis albums in *Billboard*'s top 100.

One of my three tunes that Shirley recorded had been written one day at Larry Brown's. He'd gotten a gig to produce Nancy Sinatra and had three songs but needed a fourth to round out the session. He said, "I have to go pick up my wife at the beauty parlor. See if you can start something while I'm gone and we'll finish it when I get back."

I started banging on his guitar, trying to think of what to write for Nancy, coming up with lines like "when I see your laughing face," alluding to her dad's old hit "Nancy with the Laughing Face," from when she was born, or "I love my daddy but it really doesn't matter what my daddy might say," obviously referring to her father, Frank. By the time Larry got back the song was completed. He loved it, declaring it "a definite number one smash. It makes the hair on my arm stand up."

Fortunately, as things would turn out, Nancy's friend, music publisher Al Gallico, hated my song, so she refused to record it, pissing Larry off, as he felt this was the only hit he had for the date. He told me I had to do something with this song, "if only to prove me right and Gallico wrong."

Inspired by Larry's faith in the tune, I enlisted Crazy Joe, who also played with a country band up in Connecticut that had a girl singer named Marion who had a nice voice. She also had an unfortunate habit of reading lyrics off a card, which should've warned me she was too lazy to learn songs.

We took her in the studio and made a little record of her singing "I Really Got the Feeling," but she didn't learn it properly, so every place we took the record, the answer we got was "Love the song; hate the girl," over and over.

The last person on my list was Charlie Koppelman, whom Michael Lang had talked into doing an album with my sister, which ended up on Koppelman's tax shelter label. Dolly Parton recorded one of Kat's songs, which made me proud of my little sister and earned her a few bucks, too.

I played the record for Charlie and, like the others, he said "Love the song; hate the girl . . . but"—and this was the first time I'd gotten a "but"—"we're recording Dolly next week. Give me the song for her and I guarantee it'll be the single." This was a big deal, as Dolly was just coming off her big pop breakthrough of "Here You Come Again" and was the media darling of the year.

Not trusting the man, I said, "Put it in writing, Charlie, and give me some money." He had his girl write me a letter of intent and a check and I left. Nina was with me, and in the elevator she grabbed the envelope and looked at the check. "Holy fuck, baby! He gave you twenty-five hundred dollars!" Now that was a lot of money in 1978, and a fortune to me, a thirty-three-year-old grown man still living at his mother's house, like some cliché of your typical loser musician. We had dinner at a nice East Side Italian restaurant, and then went home to celebrate in bed. There are few things sexier to a woman than when her man makes a big score.

A few weeks later, the phone rang. It was one of Dolly's assistants saying that Dolly wanted to meet the guy who'd written the song. She was on tour, and the only date that was possible for me to make was in Maryland. It would have been foolish not to take the opportunity, so I made plans to go. Maria's mom said it would be okay to bring her with me, so off we went on our father/daughter adventure.

We were invited to hang out in Dolly's elaborate bus, done up in full-on country music star mode.

Everything you've ever heard about Dolly Parton is true; she's as nice as they come. She brought us with her into the wings as she was about to go onstage. Maria, being only twelve, was chattering away, so I told her Dolly had to prepare to go on, but Dolly would have none of it. She put her arm around my child and said, "Honey, you stay right here with me until I hit the stage." Just as down to earth as you'd want her to be.

Over the ensuing years, we'd run into each other, and she was always the same. One time in particular is worth telling. Some years later, I was doing a biopic about the Judds and Dolly was scheduled to appear, as herself, in a scene where she presents an award to the mother-and-daughter duo. I was standing around, chatting with a few of the other actors, including one especially pretentious actress.

I remarked, to no one in particular, "Boy, do you guys think there's anyone in this auditorium who's not going to go home tonight and say, 'Honey, I saw Dolly Parton today'? You can just feel the electricity." The pretentious actress said, "Well, yes, she has all the externals, but I prefer to work from the inside out."

Just then, as if on cue, here came Dolly. Spotting me, she ran over and hugged me, saying, "Well, as I live and breathe, Billy Vera! How the heck are you, baby?" The actress blushed and the rest of us rolled our eyes. Busted!

The band now included Tommy; Ben; Bill Walker, who played bass and sax; Crazy Joe; and a Scarsdale rich kid named John Leventhal, a terrific pedal steel and guitar player, a James Burton freak who would one day marry Rosanne Cash. It was a hot little band, with no addicts and guys who actually liked each other.

A couple of those Rapson's hippies, dope dealers now on the lam from the Feds, were hiding out on the island of St. Croix in the U.S. Virgin Islands. They owned a small hotel called the Strand (six rooms and a performance space on the second floor) on the "wrong" side of the island in Frederiksted, where the tourists rarely ventured, so it made the perfect hideout. They would hire their favorite bands, for six weeks at a time, to play for them and their friends. In the middle of a cold New York winter, these were welcome gigs, despite the low pay.

The first time we played there, Nina came down to join me for one week of bliss. The place was paradise and so romantic, too.

When I got home, though, I sensed something different. She was less attentive, growing distant, and I started to get insecure, not the most attractive quality to a woman. In time, as gently as she knew how, she ended it. To say I was devastated is a gross understatement. For the first time in my life, I was crushed, crying day and night. I felt I was losing it.

What I did lose was thirty pounds, and I was slender to begin with. My mother, worried stiff, sent me to our family doctor, who recommended a therapist named Shirley Schecter. I'd never been in therapy before, but I was willing to try anything. She put me on a drug called Elavil, to even me out, so therapy could begin in earnest. At first, rather than looking to discover what was wrong with me, my only goal was to get Nina back.

I was still able to write songs. I finished the song I'd begun when we met, now knowing how it should end, and wrote another, perhaps the first purely autobiographical song of my life. "Here Comes the Dawn Again" perfectly captured that small window of time in which the affair is over but you haven't yet accepted it, so you're in the bargaining stage, which is where I was.

My mind was messed up. I was half insane with grief. At night I would drive up to a position on a rise above her parents' place and gaze toward her bedroom window, just looking at the light. It was too high to actually see her. Like all discarded lovers, I talked incessantly about my pain. Only friendship, I'm sure, kept my friends from disowning me.

In the midst of my suffering, one day I drove up to see her mother, whining to her, hoping for sympathy—stupidly, as it turned out. At this insensitive woman's hands, I got a taste of the first real prejudice directed at me in my life. Not belonging to any one ethnic group had saved me this humiliation in the past. Anywhere I went, I was never the enemy, never the black kid walking through the Irish neighborhood or the Irish kid sneaking home through the Italian part of town. But all of a sudden, here was Nina's mother, who'd always been pleasant to me in the past, saying, in the most condescending tone of superiority you can imagine,

"Well, I'm sure you're a decent fellow, but truthfully, we'd rather see her with one of her own kind." If I hadn't been in the heartbroken state I was in, the proper response would've been, "Fuck you, you pretentious, snotty-ass bitch," but I didn't have it in me at the time. The irony was that Nina's sister was married to a gentile.

To take my mind off my suffering, a friend of Tommy's hooked me up at radio station WBAI, to host a show featuring the music I loved, old rhythm and blues. A far-left-wing station, their idea of the blues was some old geezer in overalls with a piece of straw hanging from his mouth, playing an out-of-tune guitar, mumbling lyrics about the downtrodden. Their taste in jazz was equally ludicrous.

I somehow managed to convince them to let me play music that black people had actually listened to and purchased during the 1940s and early fifties, acts like Louis Jordan, Wynonie Harris, Joe Turner, Little Esther, etc. The first day I was on the air, a call came in from some clothing store saying there was an old black gentleman there, tears running down his face because the songs I was playing took him back to his youth. I was a hit. There was an audience for this music, and within a few years that audience would grow to the point where there was a hit Broadway show, *Five Guys Named Moe*, featuring the songs of Louis Jordan.

Before too long, Johnny Leventhal's Scarsdale girlfriend, Amy, brought around her friend Michelle, who was practically a clone of Nina—twenty years old, college student, Jewish, beautiful, hot in bed. She even drove the same kind of car, a Volvo. I latched onto her and we had a sweet little interlude for the rest of that summer of 1978, alleviating my pain. Thanks to Michelle, I wrote another song that would eventually make the charts a decade later, "Between Like and Love."

One day, a random phone call came from my old manager Al Schwartz. He had relocated to LA after welching on some gambling debts owed to the wrong people. Even Jilly couldn't get him out of it this time, but thanks to Jilly's influence, Al was at least alive, under orders never to set foot in New York again.

Al said, "I'll be straight with you. I'm broke and I need to make a deal. You're the only major talent I know who hasn't made it yet. Send me a tape and I'll get you a record deal." With nothing to lose, I mailed him a tape with "At This Moment" and "Here Comes the Dawn Again," the two tunes inspired by Nina.

Dolly's album came out that summer and was selling well. The band and I did a return engagement in St. Croix. It was during this trip that, thanks to a leaky air conditioner in our room, I was bitten by a mosquito and contracted dengue fever, a mild form of malaria common to the tropics. It drained my energy and I'd lean against the wall between songs and go to my room and lie down on my breaks.

With Michelle back in Scarsdale, I found myself still pining over Nina, especially during my more feverish moments. Schwartz tracked me down at one of the only telephones on our side of the island with a deal.

It was not a record deal, but a publishing deal with Eddie Silvers, another former New York guy who was now running Warner Bros. Music, one of the biggest publishing companies in the world. Eddie wanted me to fly out, to make sure I was still alive, since he didn't quite trust Al's say-so. I said I'd have to wait until the St. Croix gig was concluded. He told me to come straight from there. Schwartz was obviously desperate to make the deal quickly.

When the gig was over, I hopped on a plane to LA to meet with Eddie. He gathered his staff and had me play "At This Moment" on the piano. When I turned around, this longtime music exec was crying like a child and the staff sat in stunned silence. It was the first inkling I had that this song might be a winner.

The deal was neither great nor terrible: $15,000 a year for three years. I would copublish, and Al took a chunk of my advance that I felt was a bit excessive, but it was time to quit New York and start a new life in a new place. I'd long felt I might do well in LA, and here was a chance to give it a shot.

I had a few more local Westchester gigs with the band and one as house band for an oldies show at the venerable Howard Theater in Washington, DC, backing some of my favorite old doo-wop groups. I tried to get Tommy Wolk to come with me to LA, but he was afraid. As things turned out, he eventually did quite well, reinventing himself as T-Bone Wolk and becoming an important part of Hall and Oates, contributing greatly to their success.

On January 9, 1979, with everything I owned except my record collection packed in a light-blue 1972 Mercedes my friend Julio had found and fixed up for me, I prepared to leave my childhood home for a new life. Nina came by my mom's house to see me off, promising to keep in touch, which she did (whether out of caring for me or secretly in love with the idea that I was someone who adored her and would go to the ends of the earth for her is anybody's guess). At any rate, with one last hug from her and my mom, I drove off to an unknown future.

9
California, Here I Am

My cross-country trip was strategically planned with stops at the homes of friends and family, so I wouldn't have to pay for lodging. First was Washington, DC, where I spent the night with a girl I'd met in St. Croix; then Atlanta, where my sister was living, trying to get her singing career back on track with her old Woodstock friend, bassist Harvey Brooks, who was working at a studio in town.

From Atlanta, I drove sixteen hours nonstop along Interstate 10 to Dallas, to stay with my Aunt Louise, my father's sister. Every twenty minutes, it seemed, my Dolly Parton record came on the radio, making me feel I was back in show business for real. It was another long drive to my next stop, New Mexico, where I had to pay for a cheap motel. From there, it was one last all-day drive to LA.

I'd made plans with my old friend from the Headliner, Elaine Hill, to rent a room and bath at her house. She and Ray had recently divorced. Elaine got the house and needed the rent to help with the mortgage. She'd been singing in a disco group, sometimes on the road, and hanging out with the gay disco crowd, including members of the Village People. She was one of those women whom gay men referred to as a "fag hag," but she was also the kind of person who fantasizes that she can turn a gay guy straight once he realizes how awesome she is. Some years later, I ran into her ex-husband, Ray, now working in the audio department at CBS, and he told me she had died of AIDS.

At thirty-four years of age, I thought I was getting too old to think about becoming a rock star and decided to spend the next stage of my life, perhaps even the rest of my life, writing songs. Several days a week, I conscientiously showed up at Warner Bros., where I banged out chords on a small piano in a tiny, windowless room until a song came out.

I ran into Chuck Fiore, who'd played bass in my band back in Westchester before moving to LA with his seventeen-year-old girlfriend, Wendy. Chuck, who'd been in town three years, introduced me to some musicians who I used on demos of my new songs. He also invited me to come out to Venice Beach on the weekend, where he was playing with some guys. Since I had nothing better to do, I went and sat in with them.

Some of us got friendly, and one night at the movies in Westwood we passed a bunch of UCLA girls who lit up our eyes. One guy's wife had dumped him, Wendy had by now moved on from Chuck, and I hadn't met any girls yet, so we said, "Let's start a band, so we can meet girls," which struck all of us as a genius plan. Soon after, Beau Segal, the drummer, found the love of his life, Nancy, who advised us, "Since none of you have a girl, you should call yourselves the Beaters," and the name has stuck ever since.

Later, after our first hit, "I Can Take Care of Myself," some rock writer saw a connection between that title and our name, the Beaters, surmising we were making some masturbatory inside joke. To tell the truth, it hadn't occurred to me until that moment that there was any connection between the song's title and the group name. When asked, we'd say it meant "If you don't like our music, we'll beat it into you," or any number of other "meanings." But Nancy's quip was the real genesis of our name.

Chuck reminded me that I'd always wanted a horn band, like the one Ray Charles had in the 1950s on Atlantic. I'd been listening lately to Bob Wills and thought the addition of a pedal steel might be a cool and unique addition, too. Chuck knew some terrific musicians, some of whom are still with me after all these years, and we held rehearsals, mainly old R&B tunes that hadn't been done to death by other bands.

Our first paying gig, for six dollars apiece, was in April 1979 at a club called Shenanigan's in Hermosa Beach. Al Schwartz came and suggested we do some of my songs. We rehearsed some more, and Al brought two famous groupies, one of whom was Ringo Starr's girlfriend, Nancy Andrews, to judge whether we could appeal to that type of hip woman, the opinion makers. We could and did, resulting in my first Hollywood fling, with a gorgeous model/actress with the unlikely name of Garrie Kelly.

More gigs at more clubs came our way, and we were soon the darlings of the beach crowd, but Al said we needed to be seen in Hollywood to make any real impact. So he booked us at a club called Pippy's, operated by some mob guys from Boston and a hangout for top studio musicians and coke dealers. One night Little Esther Phillips came up and sang "Fever" with us while drumming legend Earl Palmer stood in front of the bandstand, digging the goings-on. The next morning, I wrote a tune for Esther called "Corner of the Night" and took it to her house. She loved it but had no record deal at the time.

Another night at Pippy's, Jimmy Witherspoon, the great blues singer, came in. A couple of drunks at the bar were making noise and Spoon grabbed one by his shirt and said, "I came to hear this man sing, you understand, sucker?" The chump quieted down politely.

That summer, I was homesick and booked a couple of gigs back there to finance a trip. I got to see old friends, one of whom was a woman I knew slightly from St. Croix. She was living in a nice older building in White Plains above a venerable old French restaurant called Le Gai Penguin. She invited me to lunch there, saying her roommate was a fan of mine who used to come to see me sing when she was an underage model. Intrigued, I went.

The roommate turned out to be a girl named Za Za de Saint Phalle, one of the great blonde beauties I've ever seen. She was from an old-money banking family, and her aunt was the famous French artist and sculptor Niki de Saint Phalle. I immediately remembered her dancing at the front of the bandstand some years before. During lunch, you'd have to have been blind not to see the heat developing between us. At one point, I excused myself to use the men's room. When I emerged, our eyes met, and in an instant we were in a passionate kiss. The rest of my stay was like that, an immediate bonding the likes of which I had never experienced. Za Za brought me home to meet her mother and a couple of siblings, and this very wealthy family took me to their hearts. I introduced her to my mother, who fell in love with her right away.

Za Za introduced me to the concept of understated old money, which is quite different from *nouveau riche* Scarsdale money. Old money feels no need to make a vulgar display of who they are and what they can buy. Old money is quiet money. Cars don't have to be new and shiny, cuffs can be frayed, changes in fashion are subtle. From Za Za, I learned to avoid the gauche and gaudy and lean toward the tasteful classics, the things that last.

When I got back to LA, we were on the phone every night for two hours or more. She came up with an idea: "People never really know each other until they're under the same roof. How about I come spend two weeks with you, then you come spend two weeks at my place, so we can be sure this is real?" That sounded like a good, solid, logical plan, so she came out to visit and all was swell. She was beautiful and charming, and anyone could see she was madly in love with me. We even looked at apartments.

Several weeks later, I went back East to stay with her. At twenty-seven, her modeling career was over, and, with no need for an income, she worked at a small boutique, mainly to occupy her time. I spent the days while she worked visiting my friends. But, after her work day was over, I began to notice that she would have enough white wine to get a little buzz on, which, given my mother's drinking, made me more than a little nervous.

After returning to LA, I became more aware that she was tipsy when she called at night. Knowing how unpleasant my mom could be when she was drunk, I told Za Za I needed to take a step back. "But Daddy says he'll send us on a two-year honeymoon when we're married." I explained about my mother, and Za Za assured me that she "used to have a problem" but no longer did, despite the mounting evidence to the contrary.

My decision to step back hurt Za Za deeply, and she went to stay with her sister in Michigan for a few months. Later she revealed that while there she had had a miscarriage in the shower one morning. I am not proud to admit that I was relieved. Maybe if I'd known what I know today about alcoholism, I would have been able to steer her to Alcoholics Anonymous and we could have had a life together, but it was not to be.

We continued to see each other from time to time when I was home for visits. She truly loved me, perhaps the only woman who ever has loved me that deeply, and waited five years for me to change my mind.

Eventually, she married her former boyfriend, and they are still together over twenty-five years later.

Chuck, our drummer Beau, Beau's sister Rebecca, Danny Robinson, and I were among the first to eat at Maurice's Snack 'n' Chat, a newly opened soul food restaurant on Pico Boulevard operated by Maurice Prince, a large black lady who had worked in the homes of movie stars like Loretta Young, John Garfield, and Peter Bogdanovich when he was with Cybill Shepherd, and in the U.S.O. during World War II. Her customers were few at first. Some nights our little group were the only ones, watching TV with her, listening to her stories about old-time showbiz, and eating her fabulous fried chicken and peach cobbler.

Danny, an agent at the Agency for the Performing Arts, was the son of Bud and Cece Robinson, the former dance team who'd opened for all the big stars from Sinatra on down. Bud managed Doc Severinsen for twenty years. Soon, Doc, Ed McMahon, and other luminaries started coming, and Maurice's became the new "in" place to eat. But Maurice always found room for her "starting crew," as she called us. One piece of memorabilia she gave me that I'll always treasure is an eight-by-ten glossy of Pha (pronounced Faye) Terrell, the male singer with Kansas City's Andy Kirk Orchestra who made a big hit in 1936 of "Until the Real Thing Comes Along," singing in a falsetto voice that has been a big part of rhythm-and-blues singing ever since.

One night at Maurice's it was so crowded that, on my way to the men's room, I tripped over Suzanne Pleshette's foot. Maurice, who was in her cups, said, rather loudly, "Billy Vera, why'd you step on that lady's foot?"

A man overheard and asked if my name was Billy Vera. I said yes and he said, "I hear you have the best band in LA. My name is Matt Kramer and I run the Monday night Hoot Night at the Troubadour. Would you like to play there?"

The Troubadour is a legendary club on Santa Monica Boulevard in West Hollywood, where in the 1970s acts like Linda Ronstadt, the Eagles, and Elton John had appeared. I was familiar with Hoot Night, which tended to feature folkies, one of the few music styles that hurts my ears, performing twenty-minute sets. Diplomatically, I said it didn't make much sense to bring in a ten-piece band to set up and play for

115

twenty minutes, and Matt said, "What if I put you on at midnight and you can play as long as you like?"

Now, this did make sense. The money would be nothing to speak of, but it was a chance to be seen in Hollywood by the in-crowd of club goers, more opinion makers.

I told Schwartz, and he added, "No advertising, no flyers up and down Laurel Canyon. Let them find you, word of mouth. In six weeks you'll know if you've got something people want." He was right, except that after only two weeks there were lines around the block by eleven thirty. We were a hit, the hottest band in town, and would remain so for all of 1980.

After the show one Monday night, Jon Voight and his acting coach, David Proval, came up to the dressing room. Jon was Chip Taylor's brother and we'd known each other back in my April-Blackwood days, before Jon had his breakthrough role in *Midnight Cowboy*. Now he had just won an Academy Award for *Coming Home* and was as hot as it gets. Schwartz was writing a movie with Jon called *Lookin' to Get Out*, and both Jon and David were around Al's apartment a lot. The script was based loosely on Al's own troubles with his gambling debts. In the movie, Jon and Burt Young try to escape the mobsters to whom they owe money.

That night, after the show, Jon got all serious on me, saying how he'd never seen a singer work the way I did, "from the inside out. This is how we work out in David's class. You should come. You need to come." I had no eyes to be an actor and told Jon as much, but he was persuasive, saying that if they could get me to do what I do without a song to sing or a guitar and a microphone to hide behind, I'd have the makings of a great actor.

He said "Most singers manipulate their audience, deciding for them what they should feel. This type of singer makes them laugh, cry, or become sexually aroused. You just lay your emotions out there, allowing them to feel what comes organically. You're doing something important onstage."

I don't know how "important" it was, but I agreed to go to one class, mostly to humor him. The first two guys I saw onstage that first night were Chris Mulkey and Rocky Echevarria, later known as Steven Bauer. These guys were awesome, no-bullshit actors, doing something real and true up there. That night, I met another great actress, Jude Narita, and we became friends. I decided to stick around.

I began to see that these actors were doing something not unlike what I'd been working at on my own: the notion that, as a performer, I have two obligations: a) to the words, the author's intent, and, to a lesser extent, b) to what's going on inside me, Billy, rather than just the character. So, if I'm singing a comical song, I have an obligation to be funny, but what if my best friend died today? Do I not also have an obligation to acknowledge those feelings, at least within myself, while not wallowing in self-pity, baring all in front of my audience? This was also the basis of Proval's work; the crashing together of these two obligations becomes bigger than either one by itself. Over the next few years, I would slowly learn to do this within an acting role, and it would also increase the truth in my work on the musical stage.

Some tremendous actors passed through David's class, many unknown but also others, like Andy Garcia, who have gone on to successful careers. David, who'd been in Martin Scorsese's *Mean Streets*, would wind up on *The Sopranos*. Eventually, I would be asked to be in some plays, and in time TV and movie parts would come my way, but that was in the future for now.

One of the plays I did was called *High Tide* and was directed by the actor Steven Keats. Steven took five actors with different styles of working and managed to make us into a cohesive cast.

I played a sleazy dope dealer who gets to seduce Melanie Griffith. She was replaced when she was hired for the sexy movie *Body Double*. One morning, shortly after she left the play, I walked out my door and there was a honey wagon with Melanie's name on the door. Just then, she popped out and, seeing me, exclaimed, "Billy! What are you doing here?" Small world, this Hollywood.

For my character, I took a green eye pencil and drew a fake prison tattoo of a cross between my left thumb and forefinger, like the gangbangers do. The show was theater in the round, so there was audience on all sides of us, very close in the tiny theater. One night during the two-month run of the play, I heard a guy whisper to his date, "See that tattoo on his hand? That guy really is a gangbanger." It's the actor's job to make them believe, so I guess my little bit of eye pencil did the trick.

Steven Keats, who continued to be one of my greatest supporters, had one of those careers that started out at the top and slid downward. Eventually, he committed suicide, a tragic loss to the world of theater.

In 1984, a year after I had worked with Steven in *High Tide*, I was cast in the West Coast premiere of the Sam Shepard play *Geography of a Horse Dreamer*, in the title role of a guy who is able to dream the winners of horse races. I spent ninety-five percent of the play chained to a bed, held prisoner by three bad guys who force me to dream winners for them.

Over the course of the play, under tremendous pressure, I slowly lose my mind, taking on an Irish dialect, until I can no longer dream horses and switch to Irish wolfhounds, ultimately coming to believe I am one of these dogs. In the final moments, my two brothers break in and blast the bad guys with shotguns, rescuing me.

Aside from the Irish accent, for which I was coached by one of my roadies from that country, I had to convey the proper emotions from one position, chained to a bed. It was quite challenging, but rewarding as well.

As Billy and the Beaters became better known around town, all kinds of musicians wanted to be part of it, including some big names. Steve Goodman, best known for his song "City of New Orleans," came in one night and wound up recording Larry Brown's and my song "Millie, Make Some Chili," before his untimely passing. When our steel player, Steve Fishell, moved to Nashville, Jeff "Skunk" Baxter asked to be a Beater, so we let him in.

Skunk, besides his tenure with Steely Dan and the Doobie Brothers, was a top studio musician, a real pro who was wise in the politics of that side of the business. When he first saw us at the Troubadour, part of my act was making fun of celebrities. Celebs are easy targets, given an abundance of opportunities to make fools of themselves in public, and my wisecracks got me a lot of cheap laughs.

Diplomatically, Jeff cautioned, "That material is really funny; the audience loves it. But Hollywood is a small town and you need to have everyone on your side. You're right, these celebrities you mock are assholes, but you can't just come out and say it. You don't need enemies. Whenever anyone asks me what I think of so-and-so, I say, 'He's great!'"

It seemed phony to me, but eventually I saw the wisdom of keeping my opinions about people to myself, although I did miss this great source of easy laughs.

Others wanted to sit in with us, but I didn't want this thing of ours to turn into a jam session. I wanted to showcase what we were doing, so when one of our roadies told me Cher wanted to jam one night, I told him to "Please inform Miss Cher that the Beaters do not jam." Another night, local hipster Art Fein brought the great bluesman Roy Brown in, so I just had to break my rule and get him up to sing his R&B classic "Good Rockin' Tonight."

The only other singer I ever allowed onstage was Rickie Lee Jones. After she won her Grammy, she started coming in each week. One night I spotted her, just standing in front of me, looking up with longing in her eyes, and I extended my hand to help her onstage. We sang the old Everly Brothers song "All I Have to Do Is Dream" for nine weeks straight. I felt a special connection with this vulnerable girl, so it just felt right to have her up there with us.

Another night, a girl with the odd name Little Itch climbed onstage, uninvited, drunkenly whining that "You let Rickie Lee sing; you should let me, too. I deserve it." Chuck Fiore, deciding he would decide whether or not she deserved to be on our stage, grabbed her under her arm and tossed her off the stage before I could remove her more gently. Unfortunately, this all happened the night Schwartz had brought David Braun, the high-powered attorney for Bob Dylan, Neil Diamond, and Robbie Robertson, to see us.

Later, Braun told Al, "He sings and writes great, has great stage presence, all the makings of a star, except for one thing: that killer instinct. There's no way Dylan, Neil, or Robbie would ever allow anyone to stand in front of them onstage." I've since wondered if he was right. Almost every big star I've known, male or female, would stick a knife in anyone who stood between them and something they wanted.

So many strange things happened during that year at the Troubadour. Part of my stage patter was to say, "I don't want a record deal; I just wanna meet Tuesday Weld; and bring me cash, no checks, in a brown paper bag." After the show one night, a William Morris agent approached me, saying, "I know Tuesday Weld. I could introduce her to you, but you wouldn't like her now; her ass got too big. But my wife, she looks just like a young Tuesday. You'd love her." Was this guy willing to pimp out his wife to get me to sign with his agency? This was my first up-close view of the ugly, demented side of Hollywood. Some time later, I ran into the agent and his wife at a screening of the Blake Edwards movie *Victor/Victoria*. He was right about one thing: his wife did look like a younger, even better-looking Tuesday Weld.

The guys in the band were three to four years younger than me, so they'd come up during a period when music was played at one volume: loud. With Ray Charles as my hero, I was used to hearing certain dynamics, songs played with loud sections and soft ones to heighten the dramatic effect. It took some doing to teach guys schooled in the Stax/Volt style of playing at one volume to get them to play with the subtlety I was looking for. But, once they got it, it put us ahead of every other band in town and gave me the freedom to write songs that were nuanced and more sophisticated than what other bands were doing.

It didn't hurt that we had soloists like Jerry Peterson, Lon Price, and, later, Ricky Hirsch, who could outplay any other rock musicians in LA. Remembering the words of the old-timers who schooled me, "If you ain't different, you ain't shit," I encouraged the guys to find their own voices on their instruments, so they'd be identifiable to listeners.

Over time, an esprit de corps developed within the band, a fearlessness that came from knowing we could follow anybody. The guys always played with a defiance that set fire to any stage they stood on. Bands who went on after the Beaters did so at their own risk, and many went home after such confrontations with their tails between their legs. I'd tell the guys, "You are the best. Never forget that," and that instilled in them a certain pride that being a Beater means you are part of something special, a cut above. You are the Yankees and every song is a home run.

After the Beaters got known around Hollywood, other horn bands sprang up in our wake. Most had good, solid musicians who could play, but in all those bands there was something missing. Ask the guys and they'll say we had better songs and a better singer, but it was more than that. We had a vision and a sound of our own.

A Beater gig was never just another job. We had a saying, a motto: "We're the Beaters and we don't give a fuck." One might misconstrue those words to mean that we approach our music uncaringly, when just the opposite is true (reminding me of an old Dizzy Gillespie quote when someone asked if he played "serious" music: "Serious music? Do you think I'm kidding up there?"). In the beginning, our rehearsals were few. Arrangements were conceived organically, onstage, under fire. Later, with the more complex songs, things had to be worked out without an audience present.

What we did not "give a fuck" about was the competition, secure in the knowledge that we could and would wipe the floor with all comers. When it came time to play, the band that didn't give a fuck was as serious as a pair of brass knuckles.

Performing weekly before a real listening audience that was there to see us, not just some anonymous "Live Band Tonight," I was able to get my performing chops in shape. In addition to my work in Proval's class, Al gave me tips from his years in show business. One important one was, "You're one of the great performers. You don't have to do what everybody else does. They have to start with a peppy tune and end with a rousing, up-tempo one. You can do anything you want. If you want to close with a ballad, do it. If you want to sing ten ballads in a row, do it. They love you and will love anything you do. Trust that." So I began ending shows with "Here Comes the Dawn Again," a twelve-minute opus of heartbreak, and he was right. They begged for more.

But instead of the obligatory encore, we just left them wanting more, just as the old-timers had taught me. I instructed the announcers to never, ever beg the audience to "Bring 'em back. Come on, you can do better than that." It's so embarrassing to watch a band return to the stage to tepid applause.

Throughout 1980, I'd look out in the crowd and spot A&R guys from record companies, digging, smiling, and tapping their feet. They'd been making the rounds of the other clubs, looking for the Next Big

Thing, which usually meant a group that sounded like what was already on the charts. At the time, they were all looking for bands that looked and sounded like the Knack, a good band who'd had a big hit with "My Sharona." With four saxophones and a pedal steel, we were anything but what they were looking for. But, over the course of that year, after all those sound-alikes flopped, labels began looking for something different, and different was what we had, in spades.

One week, toward the end of 1980, everything changed. There were three offers from record companies, two majors and Alfa, a label out of Japan that had recently opened offices in LA. I talked with Lorne Saifer, Alfa's head of A&R, and it was clear that he got it. He said, "I talked to the guys from other labels, and they thought the songs were too good to be self-generated. I knew you'd written them and that's why I wanted you. It was the songs. You're one of the few real songwriters in bands today." I also knew that, as the first act signed to the label, we'd get the big push and have the best shot at having a hit.

Al felt that the Beaters were better onstage, playing to an enthusiastic crowd, than we were in studio, so he talked Lorne into letting us make a live album. After all, hadn't James Brown's Apollo album been his first pop breakthrough? It was risky, but, to their credit, Alfa went along with the idea. We booked three nights at the Roxy on the Sunset Strip, set to record and video the event, with Skunk producing. He had a name in Japan, and the company felt his name on the label would help sell records.

The gifted art director Roland Young designed a nice, clever cover, with photos by the fine photographer Mark Hanauer, but Al wasn't satisfied. He wanted something bolder. He picked up a Billy and the Beaters button, Roland's simple design of plain white letters on a black background, threw it on the floor, and said, "Look at that. See how it jumps up at you? That'll pop from the racks at the other end of the store." He was right again; it was beautiful and arresting in its simplicity, a classic design that looks as fresh and new today as it did in 1981.

As contracts were being prepared, Alfa Records made it clear that they were in no way interested in signing a band. They reasoned, as do many record people, why deal with ten egos when you only need to deal with one? We have the singer and the songwriter. The others are easily replaceable. They were adamant and unmovable on this point, and so, for purposes of morale, I gave the entire advance to the band, split evenly among them. But Alfa's non-negotiable demand would plant the seeds of a rift that would bite us in the ass later on.

10
Back on the Charts

Nineteen eighty-one would prove to be a busy, game-changing year. On January 15–17, we recorded our album at the Roxy before a sold-out crowd of fans who had stood by us and were now thrilled to see their faith come to fruition. As the recording shows, this was one of the great bands of the era.

At the Troubadour, we had been wearing Hawaiian shirts as a sort of cheap uniform, but Schwartz said that, to set myself apart from your typical eighties musicians, I should wear expensive suits, and wear them casually, with no tie and a dress shirt buttoned to the top. I bit the bullet and bought three beautiful, classic suits, dark blue, beige, and a subtle gray plaid. Al had a feeling that the days of looking like a slob onstage were coming to an end. His instincts were right. Looking at those videos today, neither my suits nor my haircut looks the least bit dated. Before the decade was out, acts like Robert Palmer and Wynton Marsalis would also be dressing sharp.

My friend Paul Gayten was there all three nights, and he brought along his old boss, Phil Chess of Chess Records, who said he could have made a fortune with me back when he and his brother Leonard owned the label. Paul also brought the great bluesman Lowell Fulson, decked out in wine-colored, full-on bluesman finery: suit, tie, shoes, and bowler hat to match. Rickie Lee Jones came up onstage for our encore. I invited my Westchester homeboy Richard "Shaft" Rountree onstage and, not to be outdone, that wild man Robin Williams joined us. It was utter mayhem.

The exploitation of the album was well coordinated. In March, we spent two weeks in Japan, where we won the Gold Prize at the Tokyo

Music Festival. My personal prize came after the show, spending the night with a certain Italian movie star who latched onto me afterwards, along with her *Playboy* centerfold sister. During our trip, I came down with bronchitis but managed to struggle through our other performances by lowering the keys of the songs I sang (or croaked through).

When we arrived back home, the first single, "I Can Take Care of Myself," was all over the radio, eventually rising to #39 nationally. Alfa's top-notch promotion man, Bernie Grossman, and the label boss, Bob Fead, got into a disagreement, resulting in Bernie's departure, just when we needed him most, to promote the follow-up single, "At This Moment." Without his guiding hand, the record only reached #79 on the *Billboar*d chart. It was time to prepare for the next album.

Larry Brown came out to help write some new songs, and I grabbed Chip at his hotel one afternoon when he was in LA to attend the races. His gambling addiction had taken over and was his main means of earning a living now. We came up with a nice, Sam Cooke–styled tune called "I Don't Want Her" before he headed out to the Santa Anita racetrack to win some loot.

At a rehearsal studio, the band played the new material for Lorne and Fead, who loved what they heard and gave us the go-ahead to record. With Skunk again at the helm, the Beaters and I entered Cherokee Sound on Fairfax Avenue and made the album. But when Lorne heard the finished product, it pained him to tell us he was less than pleased and wasn't going to release it. Listening to it today, I hear three great sides out of the whole, one of which, "I'll Be There for You," especially illustrates my lifelong desire to ignore trends. Years later, I released these on a CD called *The Best of Billy Vera and the Beaters*, after acquiring ownership of my entire Alfa catalog.

Lorne and I tossed around ideas for a new producer, and I suggested my old mentor, Jerry Wexler, who by this time had been pushed aside at Atlantic, now owned by Warner Bros. Jerry flew out to hear the band and the songs, then sat everyone down afterwards and told us, "I can make a great record with Billy and these songs, but not with this band as it stands. You guys are a great live band, but are not yet studio caliber. I can use the horns, but I need a rhythm section I can count on. You can listen to what I come up with and learn, if you're smart, or you can pout and waste this opportunity."

Their fragile egos were understandably bruised, and all but Jim Ehinger, the pianist, whom Wex thought he could work with, immediately quit, leaving me to find replacements for our live gigs. I felt bad for them, they'd been friends, but I was faced with the difficult decision of whether to go along with the program or wind up back on the street again, with no record contract. Besides, as much as it bothered me to admit it, I knew in my heart that Jerry was right. The unreleased album had, for the most part, been too heavy-handed for the songs, which required more delicacy.

Wexler made plans to record at Muscle Shoals Sound and put together a rhythm section of Barry Beckett on keyboards, Jimmy Johnson and Pete Carr on guitars, Tommy Cogbill on bass, and Gene Chrisman on drums, all legends, with the Beater horns: Jerry Peterson, Lon Price, Ron Viola, and Bryan Cumming.

I had taken up with a slightly older soap actress from New York named Marie whose boyfriend was a very sick puppy, an actor on her show. I wound up living with her at a rented house in Laurel Canyon for a few months, but their twisted relationship pulled her back East to marry him, only to divorce once he got sober. After that, he was often seen at the Actor's Studio, cruising for young male actors.

This drama was going on in December when I headed to Alabama to record. The sessions went well. Jerry was still a master record producer and song man. The one gem from the date was "Hopeless Romantic," which, once strings were added in New York, became a masterpiece. To his dying day, Jerry insisted it was one of the five best records he ever made—this from the man who produced classics by Ray Charles, Aretha Franklin, Bob Dylan, and many more. As he had on "With Pen in Hand," years before, he carefully directed my vocal, telling me to sing the song with my lips practically touching the microphone and "let us worry about you overloading it." He managed to capture every subtlety, every bit of grit and emotion.

In their wisdom, Alfa declined to release "Hopeless Romantic" as a single, probably because a) ballads are difficult to get on the radio and

b) it sounded like nothing else on the album, so if it were to hit, they would have nothing to follow it with. So they went with a rocker that sank like a rock, "We Got It All." Listening today, the album, despite the legendary players and producer, sounds too polite.

The only other hit they had on the label was by the sixties British star Lulu, so the writing was on the wall. The Japanese soon pulled the plug on the American operation and I was without a record deal. At age thirty-eight, my prospects were dim. Rock 'n' roll is a young man's game, and I was now on the wrong side of young.

The popularity of the Beaters, in our current iteration, had shifted to LA's West Side, mainly Santa Monica, where yuppies packed the places where we worked, mainly our monthly appearances at Matt Kramer's At My Place. There were girls, lots of them, actresses, models, all kinds, all lovely. One comes to mind, a little girl half my age with a 189 IQ named Tracie, who, without regard for my needs or anyone else's, would pop in and out of my life for years, often ringing my phone at 2:00 a.m. She resembled a young Ava Gardner and embodied my lifelong addiction to narcissistic beauties. She had boldly come to my dressing room at the Roxy and invited me to write my phone number on her forearm. I was hooked, a willing victim, unable to say no anytime she felt like calling me in the middle of the night for years afterward.

One minor problem we had in the band was that some of the guys liked to put too many friends on the guest list, posting as many as ten some nights. Remembering that sign backstage at the Apollo, I realized that, with a ten-piece band, if everybody had ten guests, a two-hundred-seat club would, even if sold out, have only one hundred paying customers. Why would a club owner want us back under those circumstances? So I instituted a new rule: only one guest per band member. If a member had no guest, he could give his comp to another guy. In this way, there would never be more than ten guests. If friends asked to get in free, the band could blame mean old Billy "No Guest List" Vera, which let them off the hook. "If your friends won't pay to see you, who will?"

I was now living in a gorgeous old 1920s apartment on Sycamore Avenue, near La Brea and Beverly, with a high-ceilinged living room, wainscoting on the walls, and a Murphy bed for guests. I began to write again, grown-up songs now, and my acting was taking off. I had small parts on TV shows and my first movie, *The Adventures of Buckaroo Banzai*, which flopped in theaters but went to number one when it came out on video and turned into a perennial cult favorite. People still write to me about it, and a year ago there was a sold-out screening at the New Beverly Cinema, with Peter Weller and myself as guest speakers. The manager told me it was the biggest ticket seller in the theater's history.

That movie had a fantastic cast. Almost everyone went on to bigger and better things. The eponymous star was Weller, who had to learn a little guitar for his role. Ricky Hirsch from the Beaters and I helped him out. Like my sax player, Lon Price, Peter had gone to North Texas State, which had a strong music department, and he could play a tiny pocket trumpet quite well.

It gave me the giggles each morning to see that either Peter's trailer or that of his costar Ellen Barkin had been moved closer to the set, each one's ego demanding the better position.

Often in the mornings the producer, Sidney Beckerman, would come on the set. When he did, I'd be the first one he would speak to. Having seen Sidney come over and put his arm around me, Weller would later say, "Why does Sidney always talk to you first thing in the morning? I'm the fucking star of this movie." What no one knew was that the late Mr. Beckerman's longtime mistress lived in my building and I'd occasionally run into him bringing her home from a date. Discretion has its rewards.

In his final years, I'd sometimes see him lunching with his cronies at Caffé Roma in Beverly Hills, where all the old showbiz geezers hung out. He would always treat me like a star in front of them, perhaps in remembrance of my sealed lips.

Other *Buckaroo* cast members included Jeff Goldblum, Christopher Lloyd, John Lithgow, and jazz singer Bill Henderson, along with several very good, lesser-known actors like Clancy Brown, Carl Lumbly, and Pepe Serna. Jamie Lee Curtis played Buckaroo's mother, although her scenes were deleted when it became necessary to shorten the film. They even hired Beater Jerry Peterson, whose unforgettable look added to the film's weirdness. The studio had high hopes for this flick, signing us up for five sequels that never came to pass.

About this time, 1983, TV director Steve Binder, who was best known for directing *T.A.M.I. Show*, one of the all-time great rock 'n' roll films, and the 1968 Elvis comeback special, wanted to manage me. Al Schwartz was long gone. Al's problem, aside from being a degenerate gambler, was that he was great at starting someone out, but less great with the follow-up. He loved the battle, jumping up on some bigwig's desk, telling him he's a moron if he doesn't sign his act, but once success starts to come, Al loses interest, becoming bored with the day-to-day nuts and bolts of sustained career management.

Binder saw me, not as some silly teen idol, but, in his words, as "a rock 'n' roll Willie Nelson." He believed in me, and we got off to a good start. But the directing side of his career began taking off, and the management was handed over to a woman named Kathie Wasserman, who was not in Steve's league or anywhere near it. From what I could see, she bungled just about everything she touched and practically destroyed what was left of my career. With regret, I had to leave. Steve and I are still friends, and he still comes to see me perform and makes the occasional call on my behalf. Before his retirement, he used me whenever he could to sing on telethons or the ice skating specials he directed. One song I was especially fond of singing for him was "I Wanna Be Like You," which Louis Prima made famous in Disney's *The Jungle Book*.

Just prior to the end of my contract with Warner Bros. Music, Paul Gayten suggested that Lowell Fulson and I get together and write a song. In Lowell's kitchenette, while watching *General Hospital* with the sound turned off, he had the idea to write a song called "Room Full of Blues," in hopes that the excellent New England band of that name might record it. We knocked it out in twenty minutes.

As I was eating my dinner at home that night, I glanced out my kitchen window at the apartment across the courtyard and spotted a beautiful actress emerging from the shower with no towel covering her. As she pranced down the hall, through the kitchen, the living room, and finally her bedroom, I said, "Man, I got a room with a view of the blues."

A light went on in my head and I called Lowell to tell him we needed to change our title. He agreed, and "Room with a View" has gone on to become a modern blues standard, with recordings by Lou Rawls, Eric Burdon, and Johnny Adams, to name just a few. I've done it myself, both with the Beaters and with a big, eighteen-piece band. My only regret is that Lowell passed away before getting around to recording it himself.

The Beaters would occasionally play private parties for wealthy people. I hated doing them, because nobody paid much attention. We were just the help. But the money they paid was hard to turn down, and I felt an obligation to the band to do some good-paying gigs when possible.

Binder introduced us to Jerry Perenchio, former partner of Norman Lear and one of the quietly richest men in LA. He was also one of the most generous, throwing lavish parties, treating even us lowly musicians like guests.

One example was his wedding to his girlfriend Margie. In addition to the Beaters, the entertainment included Les Brown and his Band of Renown and Peter Allen. There were 120 strolling violin players and Jerry's former client Andy Williams, singing the old standard "Margie" from a balcony. All the entertainers ate the same delicious food as the guests in a tented space over the tennis courts. We were paid three times our normal fee, and at the end of the night, when the guests had gone, Perenchio came up to me and asked me to play a blues. So, for Jerry, Margie, and Angie Dickinson, I sang a blues and received a handshake containing a $1,000 tip. We played a number of such gigs for him, including the couple's fifth anniversary, where the entertainment included a ten-piece mariachi band and Tony Bennett, and the guests ranged from Herb Alpert, to Steve Lawrence and Eydie Gorme, to Ronald and Nancy Reagan.

We were playing another of these gigs on a huge property in the hills above Beverly Hills, owned by Marvin Davis, then-owner of MGM Studios. The pool house where we changed clothes was bigger than most upper-middle-class homes.

During our break, a good-looking, well-turned-out woman in her forties initiated a conversation with me. She was in her cups, and, as I usually do to divert the talk away from myself, I asked what she did for a living. "I'm a rich man's wife," she slurred.

"And what did you do before that?"

"I was a high-priced call girl."

This was getting interesting, bringing out the gossip in me, so I asked her, "I've heard that some of our biggest movie stars were in that profession before they made it big. Did you ever work with any of those?"

She said yes and rattled off a short list of A-list actresses, including a woman I had briefly dated.

Hollywood is many times as decadent and depraved as you've heard, although not everyone falls into that category. There are some who live normal, respectable family lives. Water seeks its own level, I've always maintained. You wind up with friends that are like yourself, those who share your values or lack thereof. My mother always warned me about "showbiz phonies," so I tend to stick to my "regular Joe" friends or interesting people not in show business.

Case in point: it is my habit to go sit at the bar and nurse a Pepsi on my breaks between sets. You meet the most fascinating people. It also gives fans a chance to meet you and tell you how much they like what you do. When they're drunk and stupid, it's not so much fun, but usually they're okay.

This one night, an attractive blonde sitting next to me gave me a compliment and I thanked her and asked what she did for a living. Without batting a false eyelash, she told me she was a professional dominatrix. Never having met anyone in that line of work, I was intrigued and asked, I suppose, more questions than necessary. She handed me her card and said that if I wanted to see what it was all about, I should come to one of her parties. My curiosity got the best of me and I took her up on her invitation.

The party was held at a large apartment in Hollywood. I arrived early and was introduced to the other girls as a friend who was "auditing the class," so to speak. In other words, I was not a customer or slave, as they're called, just there to observe.

Since I can remember, I've always been a good listener, thus women tend to reveal to me things they would never tell others. I spoke with one girl and learned that sex is not part of the equation in that world; it's all about exchange of power. That way, they stay on the right side of the law. The slave, usually but not always a male, pays by the hour to be humiliated or caused physical or emotional stress. There are any number of types of slaves, depending on the particular fetish, ranging from ones who are made to run endless errands, or financial slaves, expected to buy unending gifts for the mistress . . . and from there it can get pretty wild.

The guys, who to my surprise were mostly in their late twenties and early thirties, started to arrive. I said I'd expected to see older men and was informed that a lot of these younger guys mistreated or cheated on their wives or girlfriends and felt the need to be punished. As I sat on the couch, chatting with one scantily dressed girl, a young guy crawled up on his hands and knees. Without a word, she handed him a nail polish applicator, indicating that he should hold it between his teeth and apply her nail polish to her fingers and toes, without spilling a drop. Across the room was a large, wooden X to which another young guy with long hair was chained, naked, facing the wall. No one spoke to him, but while passing, the mistresses would crack a whip or riding crop across his backside.

A fat guy came in with a duffel bag and proceeded to a bedroom to change. The girl told me that the guy was a "sissy slave." When he emerged, almost a half hour later, he had morphed into the spitting image of Ethel Merman. Nobody spoke to him all night; he just paraded around like that, thankfully not breaking out into "There's No Business Like Show Business."

There were other things a little, or a lot, rougher. One guy was spread out and tied to a massage table while hot candle wax was dripped onto his naked body. I saw a homemade contraption, made from a child's chair, with a hole cut in the seat and a toilet seat placed over the hole. Its intended use was that the slave would lie on the floor, face up, under the seat and the mistress would sit on the chair and, well, you can guess the rest.

I suspect you don't see much of this stuff in Des Moines, or maybe you do, if you know where to look.

My new friend's professional name was Princess Seva or Mistress Aves, depending. I enjoyed knowing her. She had a 169 IQ and loved to talk on a variety of subjects and we have remained very close friends over the years.

She once invited me to the annual Fetish Ball, held at the Hollywood Athletic Club, a large facility that holds a few thousand people, and it was packed to the gills with men, women, couples, straight and gay, all into "the scene," as it's called.

I had a gig with the band earlier that night, but she said it was no problem; she picked me up in a white stretch limo at midnight, the hour when things started to get going. Walking in with her and her girlfriends was like walking in with rock stars and, as I found out, she was a true star in that world. Male groupies would come up and hand her fifty or a hundred bucks to give them a few whacks with a riding crop or flogger.

There were all kinds of rooms. Some had tables and booths where various fetish items and implements were sold, as well as books on the subject and photos of the more famous dommes. There were booths where, for a fee, you could have your picture taken with a real, live dominatrix.

In a room filled with unusual and strange contraptions, I saw a bearded man in leather leading a woman in her mid- to late forties by a leash. He led her to a wooden structure to which, limb by limb, he slowly attached her, suspended, face up. Men and women both were then invited to do anything they wanted to her. Then, all of a sudden, I recognized her. It was a woman I'd gone on one boring date with, set up by a director I knew. She was a rich divorcee who lived up in the hills, by the 405, in a modern, gaudy condo with too much expensive, shiny furniture. We hadn't hit it off, so there had been no second date. Yet there she was, naked and hanging there for all to see and use.

My friend eventually moved back home to Tucson, where she supports herself and her child by dominating submissives online and making bondage videos.

In 1984, during the run of a play I was in, I was approached by a woman named Ames Cushing, head of the theatrical department at the Agency for the Performing Arts, where my friend Danny Robinson worked. She and her colleague Donna Perricone said they'd like to have me at their agency. I said that if Danny would agree to represent me for music, I'd be happy to be an APA client. Danny said yes, and I'm with that agency to this day, although Ames eventually moved on and Donna left the business altogether. This was a shame, because while she was my agent I did quite well as an actor, actually earning a basic living, something fewer than five percent of Screen Actors Guild members can claim.

One night I was at some show at the Forum and had to go to the men's room. Doing my business in the stall because I'm shy, I heard a voice singing "Room with a View." Thinking it was a friend who'd seen me enter, goofing on me, I said in my best deep, dangerous Barry White voice, "Who's that singing my song?"

"It's me, David," came the reply.

I zipped up, came out, and looked up . . . and up. It was David Hasselhoff, then star of the show *Knight Rider*. "How do you know that song?" I asked as he reached to shake my hand, before I had the chance to wash. He took out his phone and dialed his home number and the song came on. He said, "I've seen you guys; I'm a huge fan. Hey, I'm getting married, would you play my wedding? I can get Universal to pay whatever you want." I agreed and this former Knight-Rider played the TV Knight Rider's wedding. His bride, actress Catherine Hickland, and I became fast friends, and she'd often call me with the latest soap opera gossip from her dressing room on the CBS daytime drama *Loving*, where she worked.

Budd Friedman, owner of the famed comedy club the Improv, was a good friend to the Beaters, hosting our very first TV appearance at his club. Danny Robinson and his parents spent practically every evening there. When Budd asked me to play for his wife's son's wedding reception, I readily agreed.

This was not the most enjoyable gig of all time, as many of the guests were comedians, not the politest audience on the planet. We were engaged to play two sets, and after the first I was more than ready to beat it out of there. Danny came over and said that Milton Berle's fiancé, a fortyish blonde, was a fan and wanted to meet me, so I went over to their table.

Milton got right to the point: "Sit down, kid, she likes you. Talk to her." As the lady and I were making small talk, the best man got onstage to deliver his best man speech. Not paying attention, Berle figured this was just a bad comic and made some crack about how the kid stank. Seeing this as an opportunity to get out of playing a second set, I egged the old ham on: "Yeah, Milton, it's a crime how these young comics don't know how to deliver a punch line. Why don't you go up there and show him how it's done?" Danny, standing behind Berle, was waving his hands, trying to stop me, knowing that once Milton was onstage he'd never get off, which was exactly what I wanted. So I kept instigating until Berle suddenly jumped up, hopped on the stage, pushed the poor kid off the mic, and took over, doing forty-five minutes of stale gags from the Paleolithic Age. Bottom line: we didn't have to play a second set.

When we were doing *Buckaroo Banzai*, Jeff Goldblum and I had adjoining honey wagons, those RVs that serve as dressing rooms for the principals. He'd recently been dumped by a girlfriend, and we commiserated about our pitiful love lives. I'd run into him periodically after that; he liked to play piano and was pretty good. A couple of years later, he was doing a movie called *Into the Night* with Michelle Pfeiffer, one of the great beauties in all of moviedom. He brought her to see us at our Santa Monica home base, At My Place, and came backstage during our break to say that Michelle wanted to meet me. Like any guy with a pulse, my heart was pounding during our brief conversation. I was too shy to even ask her out and was convinced I'd made a complete fool of myself.

The first time I'd ever seen her was in a rotten flick called *Grease II*, which was so bad that I was just standing up to walk out when into the frame came this young blonde goddess. With my mouth hanging open, hypnotized, I eventually remembered to sit back down and sat through the rest of that dreck just so I could look at her.

A couple of years after she came to the club with Jeff, we were appearing on New Year's Eve at the Palomino, the legendary country-and-western club in the Valley. Michelle was in the audience, with her soon-to-be-ex-husband and a table of friends. At the stroke of midnight, it is traditional for the wives and girlfriends of the band members to come up onstage and give the boys a kiss. As is my habit, I had no date; seeing this, Michelle ran up and gave me a kiss, a real, deep kiss I thought would never end . . . a kiss I shall never forget.

LA was a great place to meet many of my blues and R&B idols. I got to play with the likes of Joe Turner, Floyd Dixon, and Lee Allen, and to meet Percy Mayfield, the great poet of the blues, Johnny Otis, and so many more. Once, I was asked to play a Malibu movie star party thrown by Michelle Phillips and Alana Stewart but was already engaged, so I recommended Joe Liggins, who had had a huge hit in 1945 with his song "The Honeydripper." Joe went over very well, and it made me feel good, not only to provide one of my heroes with a good gig, but to enlighten these movie folks about this important American music form.

Looking back, I spent too much time and energy romancing actresses, although I did find time for my work, playing the clubs every week and acting on TV shows. It just wasn't leading anywhere . . . yet.

My mother had by now contracted lung cancer, and it was judged to be terminal. It would take four years for the disease to take her life, during which she suffered greatly. She was more than ready to let go when the end finally came.

11
Family Ties

O ne of our steady gigs was at the Central, a dive on the Sunset Strip, since renamed the Viper Room. One night, a guy came up to the stage and said he'd seen my name on the marquee and just had to come say hello. He'd worked as a bartender at Peter Weller's New York bar, and Peter had bought a couple hundred copies of my album and given them to friends, including this guy, whom I now recognized from this new TV show with Cybill Shepherd called *Moonlighting* that had just premiered.

I said, "Man, you're great on that show and I predict you're gonna be a big star." He asked if he could play harmonica with us, and since it was a pretty dead night, I said okay. Bruce Willis became a friend and started coming to all our gigs, until he got so famous that people refused to leave him alone. Little did we know that one day we'd end up working in a movie together.

One afternoon, while I was reading in my living room, it came: the golden phone call, the one that would change everything.

A man came on the line and said, "Is this the Billy Vera who has the band?" I said yes and he continued, "My name is Michael Weithorn, and I write and produce a show called *Family Ties*. My secretary couldn't find your agent and she looked through every phone book on both sides of the hills before finally finding you. I caught you at the club last weekend and you sang a song we think might be right for an episode we're planning."

I asked the title and he couldn't remember, so I figured it must be "At This Moment," because no one ever gets the name right. It was, and I told him to call Warner Bros. because they administer the publishing. He got ahold of our record, which he said they couldn't use because the audience on the live recording would distract from the dialogue. So could we record a studio version, which they'd pay for? I said of course and we did.

In the interim between recording it and the episode airing, I worked as a hit man on a show called *The Insiders* directed by Bobby Roth, a director I would work for many more times over the years, becoming part of his own personal stock company.

When the *Family Ties* episode aired, the one where Michael J. Fox's character, Alex P. Keaton, meets Tracy Pollan's Ellen, something unusual happened. A bag of mail arrived, asking about the song. I'd had songs on TV shows before and it had never meant more than a nice little windfall influx of cash. This was different. It meant that this song touched people in some way and maybe I should do something about it. I made a few calls to anyone in the record business I thought might still pick up the phone to me, in hopes that one of them might let me rerecord it, but no one was interested. So I let it go.

Things weren't going so well at my lovely apartment on Sycamore Avenue. There had been a number of rape attempts on the street, two of which I managed to foil by yelling out the window and running the guy off. The second time this happened, I heard a girl cry out, "Help, they're going to rape me!" I yelled out the living room window, which overlooked an alley, "Hey, Leo, get my gun," and heard the bad guys drive away. My bluff had worked.

I went downstairs and found the girl, who grabbed onto me tightly, shaking in her shoes. She said they'd held a gun to her head and planned to take her inside and do all kinds of awful things to her, but this clever New York kid had told them her nonexistent boyfriend was inside, so just as they were about to attack her in the car, they heard me yell and took off.

Just then, a car came speeding down the alley from the other end of the block. "That's my car," she cried. I pulled her back into the garage and these two little savages pulled up, pointed a pistol at us, shot, and missed, driving off again. The half-wits couldn't even shoot straight. The cops later told us that this was some new kind of gang initiation, to come into this area and rape a white girl.

I told all this to my mother a few days later and she said it was time to move. Since she wasn't expected to be living much longer, she offered to give me part of my inheritance right then, for a down payment on a house. Ron Viola, one of the Beater horns, was hip to real estate and calmed my fears, saying that after the down payment my mortgage would be no more than my rent was now and that, unlike rent, it would never increase, so I felt confident that I could handle being a homeowner.

So I found a cute little place in the neighborhood known as Larchmont, near the Paramount Studios, and hired my buddy Chuck Fiore to put the house in livable condition. He paid special attention to the bathroom because, as he said, "Chicks dig a beautiful bathroom." That Chuckie, always thinking!

A sexy soap actress named Kristen Meadows heard I was moving and called to ask if she could have my apartment. She wanted to move in right away, but my house wouldn't be ready for a month, so she suggested I stay where she was staying, at the home of longtime APA agent Hal Gefsky. I've never been able to say no to a pretty face, so we switched living accommodations and Miss Meadows rewarded me nicely.

Living at Hal's was great. He'd been a Hollywood agent since 1946 and had enough stories to fill ten books. I loved hanging out with the old guy and the wacky showbiz types who came by. He was an easy mark, generous to a fault, and many a freeloading actor or actress mooched off him, filling the rooms of his big house above the Sunset Strip, designed by Frank Lloyd Wright.

One story he told me was especially sad. He'd been friendly with Marilyn Monroe early in her career, and even after she became a star they would occasionally break bread together. One day at lunch, she looked at her watch and cried, "Oh my God, it's almost two o'clock! I have to run over to Columbia and give Harry Cohn a blowjob!"

Now, many an aspiring actress, from time immemorial, has performed fellatio on many a man who they thought could fast-forward their career, but it saddened me to think of Marilyn Monroe never realizing, no matter how successful she became, that she wasn't obliged to do sexual favors for anyone. Apparently, she allowed this kind of thing the rest of her life, when her "friends" would pimp her off to gangsters and politicians.

A day or so before I moved out of my apartment, I went downstairs and across the alley to the deli where I often bought a sandwich for my lunch, and ran into the elderly woman who lived in the building next door. I'd often seen her sitting on a chair in the sun, where people would stop to speak with her.

When we'd cross paths at the deli, I would flirt, as one does with old ladies to make them feel good. That day, I told her we wouldn't be "meeting like this" anymore, as I was moving away.

Oddly, she said, "I know. You're going to be very happy in your new home." I gave her a questioning look and she said, "You don't know me, but I'm a psychic. I don't do it for money," and, after a beat, "You're in show business, aren't you?" I nodded and she continued, "You write songs. A song you wrote, nine years ago, is going to be successful beyond your wildest dreams, and very soon. You didn't write it all at once; you put it away, then came back a year later and finished it."

Well, since my process is always to finish what I start the same day, and there was only one song that fit her description, I said, "The song you describe was on TV last season. But I have three other songs coming out in a movie."

"No," she said, "I see this song on television, not in a movie, and it is in the very near future. I can see it on the screen vividly, even now." I've never been one to take psychics seriously, even though my mother claimed to be psychic, but this woman was so specific that there had to be something to it.

When I told the deli guy what she'd told me, he laughed and said, "She does this all the time. She's amazing; even the police come to her for help. Just last week, a guy ordered a sandwich and reached for his wallet and it wasn't there. She was standing behind him and told him his wallet was at a parking structure in Beverly Hills, on the third floor, and that an attendant with red hair had it, which was freaky, because almost all Beverly Hills parking attendants are Mexican."

The wallet was exactly where she said it was.

I was now doing a weekly radio show on the Santa Monica College NPR station KCRW, similar to the one I'd done back in New York. Tim Hauser, of the jazz vocal group the Manhattan Transfer, did a show there and had asked if I would sub for him when he was out of town, which led to me getting a show of my own. It became very popular, especially among industry types, so much so that, when I went in on acting auditions, maybe one in five would say "Love your band," while virtually five out of five would tell me they never missed my radio show.

The basic format was, I'd pick a year, say 1953, then research what R&B records had been released that month. There were always enough to fill the time. I'd tell stories, and it made for a fun and informative two hours each week.

Occasionally, I'd bring on a guest. LA was still rich with old music makers from the past. There was a fine grand piano in the next studio, and I'd get a Charles Brown, Floyd Dixon, or Little Jimmy Scott to perform live on the radio to promote their upcoming appearances. The Charles Brown recordings we made wound up on a posthumous album called *Alone at the Piano*, one of his best.

One of my regular listeners was Bonnie Raitt, who, hearing Charles on my show, hired him to tour as her opening act, bringing this once-great star back to where he belonged.

Other legends who graced our microphones included LaVern Baker, Johnny Otis, Lowell Fulson, Jerry Leiber, the Spaniels, the Robins, and a behind-the-scenes guy named Berle Adams. Aside from being Louis Jordan's manager, Adams was a founder of Mercury Records and later a big shot at MCA, right under Lew Wasserman. Atlantic Records cofounder Herb Abramson was another trove of information.

Johnny Otis broadcast on another station, and we'd appear on each other's show from time to time. Johnny and I had both married black women and self-identified as part of that community—I for a decade or so and he for the remainder of his life—so I felt a certain affinity with him. He was also a good cartoonist, and once, while I was guesting on his show, he drew a toon for me that proudly resides on the wall of my office. Johnny's was another funeral I was asked to speak at.

I did that show for six years on KCRW, later moving over to CRN (Cable Radio Network), but eventually had to quit when I got too busy to continue.

Meanwhile, our drummer, Peter Bunetta, hooked us up with his brother Al to record a song for a Blake Edwards movie called *A Fine Mess*. The song, "Slow Down," was a remake of a Larry Williams fifties hit I'd recorded for Alfa on the Jerry Wexler album. It was no big deal, but it led to our appearing and performing three of my songs in Blake's next movie, *Blind Date*, starring Kim Basinger and our old friend, Bruce Willis.

The day before our scenes were to begin filming, I was brought to the set to meet Blake. As the crew was relighting the set to shoot the beautiful Kim Basinger from another angle, Blake said, "Julie [Andrews, his wife] and I used to go to hear music at all the little jazz clubs around town. We saw all the great musicians."

"Really? I had no idea you two had been together that long."

"Oh, yeah, I've been banging Mary Poppins for years," he said, looking me right in the eye.

I sensed this might be a test, so I said, "Wow, that must be wild. What does she do, hop up on the roof with that little umbrella, then jump off and land on your face?"

With a naughty grin, he said, "You . . . are a very sick man . . . I like that. We're going to have fun on this movie." And we did.

Working with one of the great directors is a huge difference, and the man who directed the *Pink Panther* series, *Peter Gunn*, *Breakfast at Tiffany's*, *Days of Wine and Roses*, and *Victor/Victoria* was indeed one of the true greats.

Edwards, who lived in Malibu, hated traffic, so shooting would end promptly at 4:00 p.m. so he could hit the road and beat rush hour. He worked with the same crew for decades, so he never had to raise his voice. A nod or a raised eyebrow was enough to convey what he wanted. This carried over to his dealing with the actors. I never saw one diva moment on a Blake Edwards set.

During the barroom brawl scene when Bruce finally catches up with Kim and they fall in love as they dance to my song "Oh, What a Nite," Blake had two stuntwomen attack me, not telling me ahead of time, so as to get an honest reaction. In the ensuing scuffle, my pants ripped and my leg got cut. The next day, Blake's longtime stunt coordinator, Joe Dunne, and all his stuntmen gave me a badge, a hat, and a T-shirt proclaiming me an honorary stuntman, an honor I will always treasure.

Blake, his producer, Tony Adams, and the rest made us feel like part of the family, often coming to see our shows. One night, bored silly in the middle of some big event, Julie said, in that one-of-a-kind English voice, "Let's go see Billy!" They all hopped into their limo and off they went to see us play.

Another night, on Halloween, Blake's number one assistant, Trish Caroselli, called to ask if Tony could borrow one of my suits to wear. Later, onstage at the Santa Monica Pier, overlooking the merry-go-round, I felt a tap on my shoulder, and there was Tony Adams, in my suit, with his hair and beard done by the makeup department to look like me!

Tony and Blake have since passed on, but Blake's daughter, actress Jennifer Edwards, is still a friend who comes to see us from time to time.

Because of this *Blind Date* connection, Peter Bunetta was beginning to get ideas about taking a larger role in the band. He was a nice guy with a big personality, but his idea was not what I had in mind. We had a band meeting. Musicians tend to be insecure and will go where the wind blows. I could feel them getting shaky on me, so I secretly vowed to double my efforts to try and make something of this *Family Ties* thing.

Richard Foos, my friend and owner of the reissue label Rhino Records, and I were having one of our periodic lunches, during which we argue over arcane things like whose version of "Mustang Sally" is better, Wilson Pickett's, the Rascals', or the original by Mack Rice.

In the midst of this silliness, I broached the subject of *Family Ties* and asked how many records Rhino needed to sell to break even. He said about two thousand pieces, since the company had a low overhead. I told him I'd guarantee two thousand, which I could sell in the clubs if need be, if he'd license my Alfa material and reissue a "best of" album. He said yes, mainly because he likes me, never thinking he'd make any money off it, so I got my attorney, Chuck Hurewitz, to facilitate the deal and set about compiling the perfect Billy Vera album, which Rhino named *By Request*.

By the time it came out, we'd missed the *Family Ties* rerun, but, as luck would have it, the following season, in September 1986, they used the song again, in the episode where Alex and Ellen break up. This time, the story of the song and episode matched—boy loses girl—and America went berserk. In an unheard-of organic explosion, fans of the show started calling radio stations and record stores, demanding this song. NBC told us they'd received more calls than at any time in the network's history. Now, unlike the first time the song had played on their show, they were prepared to tell them the song title and the name of the artist. Best of all, we had a record out and ready to sell.

The night the episode aired, it was a complete surprise to me. A nice lady friend had taken me to see the Everly Brothers in concert and we were lying in my bed at Hal Gefsky's house when the phone started to ring. Calls kept coming in, dozens of them, and I finally turned up the sound to hear the messages, fearing it might be bad news about my mother. It was friends calling to tell me they'd heard my song.

The next morning all hell broke loose. Poor little Rhino Records had no idea what to do with this record. Their forte was leisurely reissuing old rock 'n' roll records, something they did better than anyone else. They had never had, nor even wanted or expected to have, a hit on the radio. But here they were, stuck with a record that the public wanted to hear and purchase.

So they quickly hired a guy to do promotion. I would drive over to Rhino headquarters every morning and we'd call stations. I would do telephone interviews and record station IDs, like "Hi, this is Billy Vera and when I'm in town I listen to the Good Guys on KRAP, 93.6 on your dial," until I could barely remember my own name. This was one of those rarities, a true grassroots record. The folks called in demanding it, and stations were forced to play it, without any payola.

While all this was going on, Bobby Roth was editing a TV movie the Beaters and I had appeared in for him, ultimately titled *Tonight's the Night*. The action takes place in a nightclub, and we had performed six of my songs in it, including, fortuitously, "At This Moment." Bobby called me every day, saying, "Jesus, the network keeps wanting more of you. By the time I finish editing this thing, it's gonna look like a goddamn Billy Vera video!"

Every day now, my phone was ringing every five minutes. Starting at 6:00 a.m., it kept ringing until long after midnight. I was getting calls from people I hadn't been able to get on the phone a month earlier, old girlfriends who "missed" me and wanted to get together, girls who hadn't been interested in me when I was hot for them, "friends" I hadn't heard from in years, people I barely knew, all "so proud" of me. The only surprise was that I didn't hear from any "relatives" I'd never heard of before.

Bear in mind that I was a free agent, signed to no record company or management. My deal with APA was a handshake deal. Once the word got out, I was besieged by more industry types who wouldn't have given me the time of day before this. There were offers from several major record labels and top talent managers, all of whom "had always known how great" I was, blah, blah, blah.

My old pal Steve Binder phoned to say he'd just gotten off the line with Sandy Gallin, who represented Dolly Parton, Neil Diamond, and other top names. Sandy had told Steve that he'd heard I was one of the best actors in town as well as a great singer/songwriter and he just had to have me on his roster. Could Steve please talk me into signing with him? I asked Steve for his opinion and he replied that they don't come much more powerful than Sandy, so I went for a meeting. Sandy's partner, Jim Morey, impressed me when he said, "Listen, I'm a greedy son of a bitch. I love money and I think I can make a lot of money with you." His candor and confidence won me over and I became a Gallin/Morey client. Another top manager I'd been talking to threatened to sue me for not signing with him!

Mike Trost, who was assigned to be my submanager, had a solution for the never-ending ringing on my phone: let the machine take messages on my old number but never answer, returning calls in the order of their priority. Then get a private line and only give it to those who need to reach me quickly. There were few cell phones in 1986. This solution served me well for the next couple of years, until things slowed down and the phone calls dwindled to their previous infrequency.

All this action served another purpose. Since Peter Bunetta had nothing to do with "At This Moment" or *Family Ties*, it stripped him of any power he may have had to influence the band. This was a hit record he had neither produced nor even played on. He was along for the ride now. The success had come from my efforts alone, leaving no question in anyone's mind about who was in charge.

Everything started to pop, so fast that most people would've cracked under the pressure. The second of my childhood dreams (my first had been to play the Apollo) came true when I got to sing my song and be interviewed by Dick Clark on *American Bandstand*, the day after my first appearance with Johnny Carson on *The Tonight Show*, all before I'd even signed with a manager. Carson's people didn't want to pay for the band, so I sang "At This Moment" with Doc Severinson's big band. For my next eight appearances, however, the Beaters would join me. Johnny liked us so much that we were even hired to perform at the party for his thirtieth anniversary as *The Tonight Show*'s host.

I was doing more acting auditions than ever, in addition to the radio promotion each day and gigs with the band. As the perfect ending to 1986, we taped a second appearance on *The Tonight Show* and played at our home base, At My Place, on New Year's Eve, where Matt Kramer set up a large TV screen so we and the fans could watch our moment of triumph with the great Carson.

12

Top of the World, Ma

New Year's Day 1987 was spent at Paul Gayten's house in the upscale black community of Baldwin Hills. It was just where I needed to be. With all the madness surrounding my record zooming up the charts, it was comforting to be among the people I still felt most at home with. It was also where I got to meet one of my favorite singers, Arthur Prysock, and to talk on the phone to another hero, Fats Domino. They both congratulated me on my success, and Arthur later recorded "At This Moment." Odile Gayten's killer New Orleans Creole cuisine was an added delight, along with the chitlins traditionally served in so many black homes on New Year's Day.

Danny Robinson was fielding booking requests from every music TV show in existence. Everybody wanted us. I was interviewed by *Rolling Stone* and *People* and was on the cover of *Cashbox* and *LA Weekly*.

There was a James Brown tribute for the Cinemax cable channel that had to be shot in Detroit, because Aretha Franklin was afraid to fly. The other guests were Wilson Pickett, Robert Palmer, Joe Cocker, and me. Each of us had to sing a James Brown tune with the Godfather's band. I chose "Out of Sight." The coolest part was that, when I turned around to say, "Maceo, blow your horn," it really was Maceo Parker, the alto saxman who had graced so many JB classic 45s.

After rehearsal, Aretha's sister Erma came over to me and said, "Your record is on top of the black charts in Detroit. Come with me, Ree wants to say hello." There she was, the Queen of Soul herself, relaxing in a booth. She looked up, smiled, and said, "Well, if it isn't Mr. Storybook Children," letting me know that she hadn't forgotten my days with Judy Clay. I'd like to think it was Lady Soul's gentle way of saying, "Don't ever forget who you are and where you come from."

Her spot on the show got a little weird. She was scheduled to sing "It's a Man's, Man's World," and the band started playing the opening riff while James did a long, rambling introduction, the purpose of which was clearly to make Aretha uncomfortable and throw her off her stride. Seeing that she didn't know how to handle this, her brother Cecil came up to the stage and shouted, for all to hear, "Don't let him do you like that, Ree! Step down, baby, step down!" But she didn't, and when the two began to sing, it was obvious that her mic wasn't as loud as Brown's, and that it was his doing. It was an ugly, unnecessary moment that had to be edited out in postproduction. Show people can be very competitive, and sometimes that can get pretty nasty.

For the show's finale, we were all onstage together and the rivalry between Brown and Pickett threatened to get even uglier. These were the two greatest screamers in the business, and each was willing to shred his vocal cords bloody in order to outdo the other. Joe Cocker and I looked at each other and rolled our eyes. I told Joe, "Let's just stand back and let them work it out." With all those major egos on one stage, what else could you do?

Another of the Beaters' main clubs, the Blue Lagune, a second-floor venue in Marina del Rey, was going out of business, and the owner, Don, a sweet guy who'd once given me a large poster from *Rock, Rock, Rock*, one of the first Alan Freed rock 'n' roll exploitation flicks, asked us if we'd play the final weekend. He'd given us one weekend a month when we needed it. No way was I going to turn him down.

The record was roaring up the charts, leaping over established stars like Madonna, Janet Jackson, and Bon Jovi, so there were lines around the block and Don had to clear the house after our first show to let in a whole new crowd, which was also overflowing. The thing people always recall about that club is how the floor would shake up and down on certain numbers. Miraculously, it never collapsed.

Next door was another club called Hop Singh's that played mostly jazz acts. I would often sneak over on our breaks to catch a portion of jazz greats like Benny Golson or Hank Crawford. It hurt my heart to see these brilliant musicians playing to twenty-five people while we, a simple R&B band, were next door, packing 'em in. After the Blue

Lagune closed and the hoopla over our hit had passed, Hop Singh's became one of our homes and we drew large crowds for them, too.

Dick Clark really liked me and put us on every show he produced, even having me as a presenter on his *American Music Awards*. I also presented, alongside Diana Ross, on the *Soul Train Awards*. "At This Moment" was a hit on the pop, country, R&B, and adult contemporary charts, crossing every demographic boundary. It was a hit with kids who made it their junior high prom song as well as with senior citizens. Seldom in modern times has a song resonated with such a broad cross-section of America. Such is the power of television.

The one offer from a record label I liked came from Joe Smith, whom I knew socially through Steve Binder. Unlike other record execs, Joe didn't have his secretary call and say, "Mr. Smith would like to speak with you," or "Hold, please, for Mr. Smith." I picked up and heard, "Hey, Billy, Joe Smith. I just became president of Capitol Records and I'd like you to be my first signing." If that wasn't enough to charm me, the idea of being on the same label as Sinatra, Nat Cole, the Beach Boys, and the Beatles was good enough for me. I had Jim Morey and Chuck Hurewitz negotiate the deal.

On my mother's sixty-seventh birthday, January 24, 1987, "At This Moment" hit the top spot on the *Billboard* and *Cashbox* national charts. Her little Billy was number one. Shamelessly, she had called all the radio stations in South Florida, where she was now living, told them who she was, and asked them to play my record. They would put her on the air, for a joke. She didn't care that the disc jockeys were making fun of her, as long as they played her boy's song.

For Valentine's Day we played Disney World in Orlando, and my mother, my sister, and Ronnie Hinds and his wife, Bernie, came to see us, along with my high school sweetheart Pam with her sister Rosalie, who was godmother to my daughter Maria. Later, as my mom drew closer to the end, Rosalie went to the house regularly and looked after her. These were the good old friends, the ones who stick by you in good times and bad.

You've all heard the expression "fair-weather friends," those who are with you when times are good, but desert you when things are not going

151

so well. I coined a phrase during this period, "foul-weather friends," to describe people who are there to comfort you when you're down, but who when things pick up don't know how to fit into your new, happier circumstances. Too many of these drifted away once I found success. Not that they were bad people; they just couldn't figure out their place in the new scheme of things and I didn't know how to help them. It was one more painful discovery about human nature.

With the Capitol record deal came the need for songs and a producer. Capitol's A&R staff and I discussed the matter. I felt obligated to toss Peter Bunetta's hat in the ring because of the work he'd done on the things we'd recorded for the Blake Edwards movies, but Capitol's staff felt I was more of an album act and that what Peter did was more suited to singles. So I thought some more and came up with Tom Dowd, the legendary producer/engineer who had done so many classic Atlantic records. Not only was Tommy brilliant, but his name would add class to the project.

Capitol agreed and went about making him an offer while I called Chip and Larry to come out and write some new material with me. Both Capitol and Dowd would contact publishers and "name" writers for radio-friendly songs, but in truth we did not get one good song, much less any great ones.

Chip had not yet embarked on the performer part of his career. Today's he's become unbelievably prolific, knocking out an album's worth of songs every year. I think I deserve some of the credit for getting him back in the songwriting groove. He came and stayed at my house and we wrote a slew of terrific songs, including "La-La for What's Her Name," which ended up on the album, and one called "Papa Come Quick (Jody and Chico)," about which more later.

One of these tunes came about after I got a call from a TV producer I'd worked for, asking me to write and sing a theme song for a new show he was doing about a Marine, played by Burt Young, who goes back to college and rooms with a snotty kid played by Cory Haim. We concocted a cute little Ricky Nelson-esque thing called "Answers" in a half hour.

I waited another half hour, so they wouldn't think I'd just pulled something out of the trunk, and called to ask if we could come by and play what we'd written. When we arrived, I told them they had to come into the men's room to listen, for the echo. All those executives and secretaries huddled by the urinals, listening to our song, was a comical sight. Amazing what people will do when you're hot. They loved the song and I said that my only demand was to have Ricky's old guitarist, James Burton, play on the session for authenticity. It was such a thrill to work with this master of the Telecaster, but unfortunately the show, called *Roomies*, was canceled after only three episodes.

Larry Brown came out, too, and we wrote some nice things, a couple of which wound up on the album, including "If I Were a Magician," a song that Lou Rawls would later record.

I grew up in a house where politics were not discussed, especially at the dinner table. In my family it was considered vulgar to subject friends and family to opinions that might lead to contentiousness and bad blood. I never knew whom my parents voted for, although in later years I strongly suspected that, given his work with his union, my father might've been an old-fashioned Roosevelt Democrat. But my mom never gave any indication of where her sympathies lay. She was a believer in the great American tradition of the secret ballot and I take after her in that regard.

As a result of this upbringing, I've always thought it best to keep my politics to myself. Truth be told, I never had a political bone in my body, until well into middle age. I subscribed to the old radio comedian Fred Allen's famous line, "I never vote . . . it only encourages them."

In New York, the motto was, "If you want to get along with people, never discuss religion, baseball, or politics." The entertainers I admired never expressed political opinions in public. I mean, when have you ever heard any actor or musician say anything intelligent on the subject? Most of them just parrot what they've heard, the kind of "wisdom" you see on bumper stickers. On the other hand, you never knew what Johnny Carson or Dick Clark thought about world events.

My thinking was, and is, if you take one side, you stand to lose the opposite side, and who can afford to lose half their audience? I know I can't. My attitude is, before you take seriously the political opinions of an actor, remember these three words: John Wilkes Booth.

That said, at one point I was asked by Blake Edwards's producer, Tony Adams, a guy I loved and who died too soon, if we would play an event at the Hollywood Palace to present to the public this guy who was going to run for president. "He's great, just what the country needs!"

I told Tony that I didn't believe in using my name to promote politicians. I think it's wrong to influence people dumb enough to take the word of a musician, taking advantage of their gullibility. People should do their own research and think for themselves. If you need a musician or an actor to do your thinking for you, you have no business voting.

"We can pay you five grand," replied Tony Adams. To refuse felt like taking money out of my musicians' pockets, so I said, "We'll do it, only you can't use my name and I won't speak on the guy's behalf."

Tony agreed to my request and gave us our orders: we were to play for eight minutes, the guy would speak for exactly thirteen, then we'd play a forty-five-minute set, after which we could eat the free food and hit on the actresses who'd be there. Easy gig. I didn't know the candidate's name or even what party he belonged to and didn't care.

The night of the presentation, my old friend, the famed jazz producer Michael Cuscuna, was working across the street at Capitol and stopped backstage to hang with me. The band played our eight minutes, after which a large American flag was unfurled behind us and Springsteen's "Born in the U.S.A." came over the loudspeakers. The guy marched up, his adoring wife at his side, and spoke for precisely thirteen minutes, saying nothing. Nothing, but pablum, corny bromides and tired platitudes. "I'm against war! I'm against hunger!" Every dreary cliché in the book. Cuscuna and I were laughing our asses off in the wings at this schmuck, wondering, where'd they find him?

Two weeks later, the guy was caught on a yacht in Florida with a model named Donna Rice, bringing down the curtain on his "brilliant" career in politics.

When we came offstage after our set, I was accosted by a reporter. She stuck a microphone in my face, saying, "So here we have Billy Vera, who's here for Gary Hart."

I said, "I don't talk about politics."

"But you're playing at this event for Gary Hart."

"Read my lips. I don't discuss politics."

"Are you against Gary Hart?"

"Listen, I'm just a dumb musician and I don't believe dumb musicians or stupid actors have any business telling people who to vote for. People should think for themselves."

"You want me to print that?"

Cuscuna quipped, "It's probably the only honest thing anybody's said here all night."

As always happens when you have a hit, some of my old records found their way back into the marketplace, courtesy of those looking to capitalize on my newfound good fortune. The 1971 album I did at Doug Moody's came out, repackaged as *The Hollywood Sessions*. The Bob Reno stuff from 1976 was reissued on some nondescript label, and "She Ain't Johnnie," released as a single, actually made it to the lower reaches of the country charts. The people who put out records like this are scavengers, bottom-feeders, and whatever money is earned never finds its way to the artists or songwriters.

The Beaters and I did relatively little touring off our massive hit. One hit record usually gets you an opening slot with a big-name act, and these acts prefer a young and hungry, four-piece outfit who'll work for peanuts, doubling up in rooms and traveling jammed together in a van. With a nine-piece band of veteran sidemen who demanded a decent salary and one room apiece plus two crew guys, it was fiscally unfeasible to be anyone's opening act. So the few road gigs we did were ones where we could headline. This deprived us of the opportunity to show America how good we were and make permanent fans in other parts of the country.

In May, we took over Capitol Records' Studio B and, under Tommy Dowd's supervision, started on our album. When Peter Bunetta had found out he was not to be the producer, he had quietly departed the band, and so he was replaced on the record by veteran studio drummer Jim Keltner.

The late Richard Tee, the last of the great keyboard accompanists, was brought in to play on two of my ballads, "Between Like and Love" and "If I Were a Magician." As always, Richard played with so much soul, and "Between Like and Love" was released as the first single. Working and hanging out with my old Atlantic friend Tom Dowd was great fun, but the resulting album lacked a certain warmth, and although

"Between Like and Love" reached #9 on the adult contemporary charts, the album failed in the marketplace. Joe Smith soon left the company and Capitol declined to pick up my option.

13
Back to the Clubs

We were still a big draw on the Southern California club scene, and Danny was able to book the occasional big-money gig, but this was generally a time of letdown.

Bobby Roth hired us to portray a Western swing band for a movie called *Baja Oklahoma*, based on the Dan Jenkins novel. I played the part of bartender Lesley Ann Warren's drunken, coke-sniffing ex-boyfriend whom she pesters to help her do something with the songs she's written. As was his habit, Bobby loaded up his cast with a number of good-looking females, some of whom were seen with the band and me, half-naked, in a dressing room scene that had to be cut for network TV. Lesley Ann's daughter was played by a bright-eyed newcomer with a wide smile named Julia Roberts, with whom I had a lot of fun after shooting one night at Billy Bob's in Fort Worth, Texas.

The movie opens with a song Larry Brown and I wrote called "You've Got Me," a country weeper, done up in our typically soulful Beaters style. I got to play some Ivory Joe Hunter–style piano on it. Jerry Wexler later heard the song and planned to have Willie Nelson cut it, but the deal for him to produce fell through, so he had the great Etta James sing it on one of her albums. That may have been some unconscious reciprocation, since the first record of note I ever made, "My Heart Cries," was written by Etta with Harvey Fuqua.

The climax of the film takes place during a concert scene at Billy Bob's, when I surprise Lesley Ann by bringing Willie Nelson onstage to sing "her" song (actually written by Willie and Jenkins), then bringing her out to join us for the last verse.

The day of Lesley Ann's pre-record I got a frantic call from Bobby, saying he was unable to get her to sing; would I come over to the studio to help out? Right away, I could see that Lesley Ann, a good singer herself in the Broadway tradition, was intimidated by the idea of singing with a couple of guys who did it for a living. So I asked Bobby to shut off the mic in the booth and began to sweet-talk her, telling her how pretty she looked and what a nice color her blouse was on her, laying it on thick to make her feel beautiful and at ease. She soon was comfortable enough to sing and gave us a good performance. Bobby was grateful and all was well in movie land.

Back at Billy Bob's, there were a thousand extras, pretending to be an audience in that huge club that covered a whole city block. When we broke for dinner, Willie said, "These folks have been here all day. Why don't we give 'em a little show while they eat?" And Willie performed for over an hour for his loyal Texas fans, backed by the Beaters. Later, after we wrapped, Willie invited me out to his bus and took out his guitar so we could sing songs for each other. I made requests, one of which was "I Just Can't Let You Say Goodbye," perhaps the darkest song Willie ever wrote. At the end the narrator strangles the object of his obsession. I'd heard it years before on a live album Willie recorded back when he still had short hair and wore a black suit and skinny tie onstage. What a memory, my own personal Willie Nelson concert.

A casting director named Vickie Huff brought me in to audition for a show called *Wiseguy*, starring Ken Wahl and Ray Sharkey. It was produced by the great Steven J. Cannell, who'd risen to the top with the James Garner vehicle *The Rockford Files*. *Rockford* was one of my favorite shows. I admired Cannell's use of richly colored secondary characters, as opposed to TV's typical habit of having them there merely to feed lines to the star.

My character was well written and fully developed and the centerpiece for that week's episode, an aging club singer who lucks out with a big hit record. His boss, played by Ray Sharkey, refuses to give him time off to capitalize on his success by playing some big-money gigs, so he goes to the boss's Mafia godfather to complain and ends up in the hospital, his larynx crushed by a sadistic detective on the mob's payroll, played by my friend Dan Lauria. Vowing revenge, he gets a gun but is reluctantly gunned down by one of the good guys at the end.

I gave a good reading, and Vickie called Cannell in so I could read for him. Steve said, "You've got the job," very unusual for Hollywood people, who traditionally have a hard time making up their minds. "Glad you like him, Steven," said Vickie, "I didn't bring anybody else in. Billy's the only guy in town who can do this part." They needed someone who could really sing and really act, so off to Vancouver, Canada, I went.

Shooting went well. Finally, a real, well-rounded character to play, even if it was a singer. Ray Sharkey, a real-life recovering addict and in good shape, was a great help, more than willing to run lines with me as long as I needed. Ken Wahl and everybody in the cast were nice as could be. I got to perform two of my tunes from the Capitol album, "Poor Boys" and "Ronnie's Song."

In November, the National Academy of Songwriters honored a number of composers, including myself, at an event at the famed Wiltern Theater. The twelve-story building, built in 1930 as the Warner Bros. Western Theater, is one of the most beautiful examples of Art Deco architecture in the world, with its blue-green glazed terra-cotta tile and facing the corner of Wilshire Boulevard and Western Avenue.

It is a thrilling place to perform. Everyone was backed by a house band. When it came my time to sing "At This Moment," the conductor counted it off much too slow. I had to make a split-second decision whether to make him start over or to continue and take my chances. I chose the latter, resulting in one of my best performances and a standing ovation that I thought would never end.

Some twenty-odd years later, I met one of Frank Sinatra's former girlfriends, who told me she had produced the show and videotaped me that night. One night she'd played it for Sinatra, who said, "Who is this kid and why isn't he the biggest star in the country? This is one of the greatest performances I've ever seen." He made her play it over and over that night, as well as every time he came to her house.

I was blown away by this knowledge and wished I'd only had the chance to meet the great man and maybe hear him say that that to me in person. I knew his best friend, Jilly Rizzo, felt strongly about my singing. He'd been at the session in 1968 when I recorded "With Pen in Hand" and told people I was the only singer who came close to Frank when it came to phrasing. During the run of "At This Moment," we played a club in Palm Springs, where both Frank and Jilly were living. Before the show, there was a knock on the dressing room door. It was a big guy with a crooked nose holding a dozen roses in his arms. He said, "Dese are from Jilly. He says he's sick in bed or he'd be here to see you. He said to tell ya he loves ya and Frank is still the only one who can outsing ya."

On New Year's Eve weekend, we were booked to open for Chuck Berry in Las Vegas at Caesar's Palace. I'd worked with Chuck, one of the maddest rockers of them all, many times over the years, from when he was a $1300-a-night act in the 1960s to his $15,000-a-night days in the seventies, to whatever insane amount he was getting for this gig. I had even worked with Chuck at a Beverly Hills mansion, for the wedding of the scion of a Chicago department store fortune turned movie producer, and a call girl he'd met in Vegas. Ironically, the call girl had more class and charisma than ninety-five percent of the movie stars and Beverly Hills doyens there, making every man there, from the biggest mogul to us little musicians, feel like the most important man in the room.

Waiting for our baggage at the Las Vegas airport, I spied Chuck coming up an escalator, carrying his guitar. He was dressed in a 1970s paisley polyester shirt with a long collar and a pair of yellow, double-knit bell-bottoms, straight from that decade of hideous taste. Knowing he was notoriously frugal, I asked where he'd gotten his outfit. Proudly, he said, "At the Goodwill, man! Three dollars for the shirt and six for the pants." This from a man whose songwriting empire has grossed him millions. Coda: he wore the same clothes onstage that night! As cheap as they come, Chuck was known for sleeping in his Cadillac to avoid having to pay for a hotel. And, in his case, you can't blame it on growing up in poverty; his family was solid middle class. I have to admit, though, he did give me a copy of his autobiography, free of charge, signed by both himself and his longtime piano player, Johnnie Johnson.

Once, back when I was with the Shirelles, we were playing somewhere like Erie, Pennsylvania, at the local arena. Chuck was, as always, the headliner. I was strolling down the hall backstage with Gary Bonds and Bo Diddley when we passed Chuck's room. He called us in to see his newest toy, one of the first video setups. "Wanna see something?" We looked at each other and entered the room.

On the screen came a video of Chuck having sex with some girl. As the kids would say, "TMI," too much information! We laughed about that for days.

Chuck notoriously would not rehearse. His contractual requirements included two Fender Dual Showman amps, every knob turned to ten, a band that knew his songs, and full payment, in cash, before he went on. Once, during the seventies, my band and I backed him at a festival for three days straight. He not only refused to rehearse, but he never said what song was next or what key it was in. He'd just start playing. To make matters worse, to test us, he'd play the songs in different keys each day. Not once was I stumped, and after a while he smiled at me and gave up being a dick.

His contracts were for union scale, something like $298. He neglected to report the huge cash portion to the IRS. This little trick eventually got him some time in prison, his third round behind bars. Before he ever made records, he did time for armed robbery, and in the midst of his fifties fame he did another stint for Mann Act violation, transporting an underage prostitute across the state line for immoral purposes.

Another time during the seventies, when cable TV was new, the HBO network hired my band to back Chuck and Little Anthony and the Imperials for a special to be taped at the Beacon Theater on Broadway in New York. Rehearsal with the Imperials went well and I spotted Chuck's silhouette at the back of the theater. I asked Ray Renieri, the stage manager, if Chuck was ready to rehearse and got a "Shhh, he wrote five new songs on the plane and wants to do those."

"That's crazy," I said. "Didn't you put in the contract that he's to do his three biggest hits?"

"Yes, but you know Chuck; he's out of his mind."

In the end, Chuck refused to go on, forgoing a $10,000 fee, for which he would have had to sing only "Maybelline," "Roll Over Beethoven," and "Johnny B. Goode." His motivation known only to himself, he may have feared that HBO would be free to use his taped performance in perpetuity, without further payment. Or maybe he just wanted to be paid in cash. He was only comfortable in situations where he could withhold performance until he got paid in advance, often winding up with less than he would have made otherwise.

I've often thought that you have to be at least half-crazy to be a major star in rock 'n' roll. Consider the big triumvirate of Chuck Berry, Little Richard, and Jerry Lee Lewis: mad as hatters, all of them.

14
Blue Note

Capitol went all out to do a video for my first single, "Between Like and Love," a lovely ballad, backed by Richard Tee on piano, with strings arranged by Arif Mardin, who'd written the chart for my 1968 hit, "With Pen in Hand," twenty years before. Other than bassist David Miner, there were no Beaters on this track. The video was to be shot in Paris, France, the city of romance.

My romantic interest in the video was a beautiful blonde model/ actress named Rosalee Mayeux, who'd posed with me for the album cover, shot in an old railroad car in Perris, California, some seventy miles east of Los Angeles. We had been dating casually since then, and I was still seeing other girls. Rosalee, who was from Louisiana, spoke fluent Cajun French and was thus able to defend me from the wardrobe girl who'd brought only one outfit, including an embarrassingly lame pair of big clunky shoes that she insisted were the fashion statement of the season. My taste, being more classic than trendy, was offended by these gauche clods of leather. I've always resisted wearing trendy garments, like those you see at awards shows on musicians whose outfits look hopelessly dated twenty minutes after the closing credits. Rosalee let the girl know, in no uncertain terms, that these monstrosities would not do, and she and I took off to find a more suitable pair.

During our time in Paris, my son, Charlie, was conceived, which would result in marriage by the time Rosalee started to show.

Back home, Dick Clark had me back on *American Bandstand* and I did the next of what would eventually be nine appearances with Johnny Carson. I received two ASCAP awards, one for writing and one for publishing "At This Moment," that share wall space with my previous plaque for "I Really Got the Feeling," and a star on the Hollywood Walk of Fame now bore my name. It wasn't over for me just yet.

Despite the heavy sales of both "At This Moment" and the *By Request* album, I wasn't getting rich. For the past twenty years since my first marriage, I'd been a confirmed rock 'n' roll bachelor. I knew how to make ends meet on a small income and never suffered, mainly because my needs were never great. My mother had advised me years earlier that "Show business is a business of peaks and valleys. One year you'll make a bundle, the next year nothing. So always live below your means." You'd be surprised how few in our line of work are able to live by that simple, seemingly obvious rule.

But now, here I was, faced with having to support a new baby on the way, a young stepson, and a model/actress wife who could barely support herself. On top of it all, I'd never even had a roommate and wasn't used to living under the same roof with other people. It was a formula for trouble.

Work took me out of town for a couple of movies—*Finish Line*, with James and Josh Brolin and Mariska Hargitay, and *Desperate for Love*, with Christian Slater. They changed the title of the latter when I let them use Chip's and my song "Desperate Frame of Mind." The Beaters and I played Caesar's Palace again, this time for two weeks as the opening act for magician David Copperfield.

On November 7, 1988, I watched Charlie being born, in a blood-spattered C-section, at Cedars-Sinai Hospital. I was scared as hell for the future, but when the nurse brought Charlie to me, he grabbed ahold of my thumb and didn't let go for the next three hours. The nurse said, "This one's gonna be a daddy's boy."

Toward the end of the year, two things fell into my lap that would expand both my horizons and my pocketbook. First, a friend brought me to the offices of Specialty Records, the record label that in the 1950s was home to some of my favorite artists: Little Richard, Sam Cooke, Larry Williams, Percy Mayfield, and Lloyd Price. I met with Beverly Rupe, the daughter of the label's founder, Art Rupe, a producer and businessman whom I admired greatly. Art had left the music business in the late 1950s to concentrate on his more reliable holdings in oil and real estate. More recently, Beverly had come back into his life after many years and convinced him to let her oversee Specialty, a job for which she was woefully unqualified.

For some reason, she entrusted me to put together a Little Richard box set and, after her dad was pleased with my work, set me to work on six more single CDs by some of Specialty's best artists. All these were well received in the oldies and blues press, and I continued at the company, pretty much calling my own shots. I would remain in this freelance capacity, even after the label was sold to Fantasy Records, compiling and annotating over fifty reissues for Specialty.

In time, Art and I became friends. A private man, he opened up to me on a variety of subjects. Once, he confessed that he felt letting Sam Cooke go had been his biggest mistake, as Sam had gone on to become a major star at RCA Victor.

Sam, who'd made his name on Specialty as lead singer for the gospel group the Soul Stirrers, made his first secular recordings for Specialty, produced by the label's A&R man, Bumps Blackwell. Blackwell, who saw Cooke as "a modern Morton Downey," booked a session to record a new song of Sam's called "You Send Me." Art happened to stop by the studio and, seeing a background vocal group of two white females and two white males, was not pleased, as he had envisioned Sam being backed by an all-male black quartet, like the Soul Stirrers, whose richer sound would lend weight and provide contrast to Sam's light tenor. An argument ensued, resulting in Rupe selling the session and artist to Bumps, who took it to the fledgling Keen Records, where the song became Sam's career-making hit. Sam then claimed that his brother L. C. had written the song, in order to deprive Art of his share of the publishing.

I told Art that selling his publishing arm, Venice Music, had been a bigger mistake than losing Sam, since songs last forever and don't give you any grief, as human beings tend to do. Venice Music's copyrights included five songs recorded by Elvis Presley, three by the Beatles, and one by the Rolling Stones, not to mention songs recorded by every fifties rocker of note—Bill Haley, Buddy Holly, the Everly Brothers, Pat Boone, and many more. Art's reply was that Venice had been his wife's bailiwick. She'd grown tired of doing the paperwork and he'd found it difficult to find good, trustworthy administrative help to replace her.

During my time at Specialty, I was able to release a lot of great music that had fallen by the wayside, by artists who, in the constant push for the new and fashionable, had been forgotten by the public. Some of the songs I reissued were used in motion pictures, providing nice income for the company and for those songwriters and artists who were still among the living.

The second break came by way of a call from my friend Michael Cuscuna, saying that his boss at Blue Note Records, Bruce Lundvall, had signed Lou Rawls and would like us to produce his first album for the label.

The three of us went to Las Vegas to meet with Lou and his manager, David Brokaw, whose father, Norman, headed the William Morris Agency. The meeting went well. Lou's last few albums for Epic had been dreadful examples of what can only be described as Vegas disco, feeble attempts to recapture his grand success with Gamble and Huff, "You'll Never Find Another Love Like Mine."

Bruce's idea was to take Lou back to the jazz and blues that had first made fans fall in love with him, plus some of my songs, where appropriate. We would recruit respected name musicians and do a couple of duets with other stars. Lou and David loved our ideas, and plans were made to record in New York, as Brokaw thought it wise to keep Lou away from his friends in LA.

So in January, with a rhythm section that included Richard Tee and guitarist Cornell Dupree, we began recording the great Lou Rawls. I picked some cool old songs, two new ones written by Lyle Lovett and published by my friend Bo Goldsen, and four of mine, "If I Were a Magician," "Oh, What a Nite," "Room with a View," and "You Can't Go Home." The last of these featured a guitar solo by George Benson, who sang background with Lou and me; the three of us called ourselves the Lou-rettes. To my surprise, as had happened with my Capitol album, we put out the word for songs and got nothing but a pile of stiffs. You'd think songwriters and publishers would give anything to have a song recorded by a great singer like Lou or, for that matter, an artist coming off a number one hit like mine.

Michael chose "At Last" for a duet with Blue Note artist Dianne Reeves. This one boasted a splendid tenor solo by Stanley Turrentine and a string arrangement by Bobby Scott, who also did the honors on an achingly sad chart for "If I Were a Magician." Dianne and Lou also revived the Nellie Lutcher chestnut "Fine Brown Frame," and we cut a track and Lou's vocal for his childhood friend Sam Cooke's "That's Where It's At," destined to be a duet with Ray Charles.

Michael hired tenor saxophonist/arranger Benny Golson to write some of the horn charts. I told Benny that the first jazz album my dad had ever brought home from the NBC library for me had been his record *Meet the Jazztet*. He smiled and told me he'd been introduced to my music by his daughter, which blew me away. When you hero-worship someone, it never occurs to you that they might even know who you are, much less be a fan of yours, too.

In New York for three weeks, I enjoyed the comfort of seeing my old friends and living in the relative peace of Cuscuna's hundred-year-old house in Stamford, Connecticut's upscale Shippan peninsula on the Long Island Sound.

Back in LA, I was taking any job that came my way: band gigs, acting gigs, whatever. Word of my reissue work for Specialty was spreading, and I began getting hired by RCA Victor and Rhino, too. One I did for Rhino, *Songs That Got Us Through World War II*, sold well for them, taking the company beyond their narrow realm of fifties and sixties rock 'n' roll.

We brought the tape for "That's Where It's At" back to LA, and Michael and I went to Ray Charles's studio to add his vocal. A few days prior to the session, I'd called Jerry Wexler, who'd produced all of Ray's Atlantic hits in the 1950s, including the one that introduced him to the white teenage audience, "What'd I Say," and asked for advice. "You don't produce Ray Charles, man," said Wex. "You just get out of his way and let him do his thing."

At his RPM studio, Ray took the tape box from my hands, threaded the tape into the machine, and listened. He said, "That's Fathead, isn't it?" referring to his former saxophonist, David Newman. "You know, that solo would sound better eight bars earlier." And with that, he took a razor blade and cut our $10,000 tape and spliced that solo where he wanted it. A blind man, taking a razor to our session! But you know what? He was right, it did sound better.

He sang his harmony to Lou's vocal and that was that. We had "produced" the great genius Ray Charles. Unfortunately, Ray's studio was a piece of crap, filled with aging, poorly maintained equipment, so our engineer back in New York had a hell of a time matching Ray's vocal to Lou's.

I was still doing my weekly radio show on KCRW, which Ray listened to when in town. Sometimes I'd come home to a message on my machine, "This is the old man. Call me," meaning he wanted to talk about a song or artist I'd played. He loved talking about the old days and the performers he'd known back then.

One Saturday I came in to find a message from an ad agency: "He's got an interesting voice; you believe him when he talks. Would he be interested in doing voiceovers?" Would I? Work with the band was slowing down again, and with money flying out of my bank account, things were getting scary.

The first commercial I did was for Nissan, which I read very low-energy, in a deadpan style I stole from the 1960s comedian Jackie Vernon, a staple of the old *Ed Sullivan Show*. The week after it aired, my picture was on the cover of *Adweek*, an industry magazine. My phone started ringing off the hook, and I figured I'd better look for an agent. My attorney, Chuck Hurewitz, suggested Cindy Kazarian, whom I knew from when she'd been a secretary at the agency she now co-owned. So, with no further exploration, I signed with her company. Don Pitts, an old-line voice agent, headed that department and it was off to the races.

My dad got a kick out of me going into his old line of work. He was now retired and living in San Diego with his wife, Olga. I asked if he had any advice. He said, "Show up early, work quickly, have no opinions, and don't give anybody any crap." I knew from record producing that I had no interest in what the bass player or drummer thought, so why should a commercial producer care what I thought of a script? I would just read what was on the paper, and if they didn't like it, the worst that could happen was that they'd rewrite it, bring me back the next day, and pay me again.

Voiceovers is a solitary line of work. You're alone in a studio, with an engineer, a producer, a writer, and maybe other clients in the booth.

Occasionally you run into someone you know in the lobby, while you're waiting to be called in to read.

The receptionist at LA Studios was a pretty young girl who had previously worked as a mud wrestler at the old Tropicana nightclub in Hollywood. Very friendly and chatty, she always talked to me. One day she said, pointing to the elderly man on the sofa near me, "Hey, Billy, look who's here. It's Robert Mitchum!"

Sure enough, there he was, the coolest guy in the movies, Mitchum himself. I got up the nerve to say that I'd just been talking about him on my radio show a few days prior, mentioning all those black-and-white films noir he'd made in the 1940s. He replied that, in those days as a contract player with RKO Pictures, he'd often be making three films at once.

"How'd you manage to do that, man?"

"Ah, it was nothing. I'd be shooting exteriors for a cowboy picture on the back lot in the morning, then doing love scene interiors in the afternoon, then at night, exteriors for some detective piece of crap."

"Holy shit, that must've been hard."

"Nah, acting's no big deal. Anyone can do it."

"You're a wonderful actor, maybe my favorite. One of my favorite scenes of yours is in *Maria's Lovers*," the 1984 film he made with Nastassja Kinski, the most beautiful actress of that era. In that one, she's mopping the kitchen floor in a crummy house, backlit so we can see her body through a diaphanous summer dress. "You hardly move, and on your face we can read every woman you've ever been with, every girl you've ever loved. It's an extraordinary piece of minimalist acting."

"Oh, yeah, I remember that flick. Those assholes from *Entertainment Tonight* crossed in front of the camera in the middle of the scene and I had to do another take."

His humility aside, dear reader, that scene is a must-see for any movie buff or fan of great acting. The tone of Mitchum's voice when he asks Kinski for a kiss is heartbreaking.

In October, my mother finally let go and passed away. It was a blessing. The cancer, plus a stroke, had made her suffer for four long years. She was in a better place now. I flew to Boca Raton for the funeral, where there were only a handful of people: my sister, Kat; my daughter, Maria; Maria's godmother, Rosalie; my former sister-in-law, Carole; and my mom's boyfriend, Bill. My mother had no other real friends.

Although they had tried their best, Gallin-Morey had done little to move my career along. Everything positive had come from my own efforts or by sheer dumb luck. Disc jockey Rick Dees, another client, had always wanted to be a TV talk show host like Johnny Carson, so, against his better judgment, Jim Morey went about the task of talking ABC into giving Rick a shot.

One obstacle: Rick's TVQ wasn't high enough to warrant him having a show of his own. TVQ is a secret method by which networks measure public recognition and popularity. Jim came up with a solution: to have a known bandleader, one whose TVQ plus Rick's might add up to a sufficient number. As it turned out, while Rick was known locally in LA, my TVQ was higher nationally than his.

That was enough for ABC to do a pilot, which got picked up.

Before we started work on Rick's show, Lou's album, titled *At Last*, went to number one on the *Billboard* jazz chart, my third time at the top. Lundvall rushed us back into the studio for a follow-up. We used the same rhythm section and most of the same horns, adding Hank Crawford, another Ray Charles alumnus, this time.

I had loved Hank's playing ever since I stumbled across a 45 of his two-part version of "Misty" in the six-for-a-dollar bin at the magazine stand I used to frequent near the White Plains train station as a kid. So it was a thrill to meet and work with yet another of my heroes. Hank told me he was a fan of mine and that he had written the horn charts for both Arthur Prysock's version of "At This Moment" and Etta James's version of Larry's and my song, "You've Got Me."

Cuscuna and I chose some more good oldies plus three more songs of mine: "Moonglows," "One More Time," and "Good Morning Blues," thanks to a suggestion from my old Knight-Rider pal Ronnie Hinds, who reminded me that it would be perfect for Lou.

One morning Lou had a hangover and didn't show up to the studio on time, so I had to sing his part for the tracking session. Michael overheard Hank and Benny Golson say that they wished they were doing this record with me instead of Lou. Some time later, jazz producer Joel Dorn told me he'd run into Hank and Benny on Fifty-Seventh Street in Manhattan and they'd told him the same thing. Now Hank is gone and I never got to make a record with him.

I did get to sing with Benny one night when Michael and I went to see him perform in Los Angeles. He was playing the old Don Redman song "Cherry," and after his solo he turned it over to the piano player, then came offstage over to me and said, "You know this song, man, get up there and sing a chorus." I said I wasn't sure of the words, but for the chance to sing with Benny I went up and faked it, getting a huge hand. Benny told the crowd, "If he's going to get applause like that, I'm going to have to take him on the road with me."

Back in LA, I overdubbed sax players Eddie Harris and Plas Johnson soloing on two of the tunes. In conversation, Eddie, who seemed a little bit nutso, told me that he'd gotten his start "playing for nickels and dimes on the corners in Chicago with Bo Diddley." It sounds odd for a jazzman and a rocker like Bo Diddley to be playing together in the streets, but stranger things have happened.

The ever-loyal Bobby Roth hired the band and me for another of his movies, *Rainbow Drive*, starring my old Buckaroo Banzai pal Peter Weller and the exquisitely beautiful Sela Ward. We performed two of my songs, "Is That the American Dream, Johnny?" and "Papa Come Quick (Jody and Chico)" at the venerable Mayan Theater in downtown LA, where Duke Ellington's only musical in his lifetime, *Jump for Joy*, was performed from July through September in 1941.

One morning the phone rang and it was Bonnie Raitt. With the surprise success of her multi-Grammy-winning Capitol album *Nick of Time*, she needed to record a follow-up and was in desperate need of songs, since she wasn't a prolific writer. Would I please send or find her some? I said sure and, being a fan of her ballad singing, went through my ballads. I mentioned this on the phone to Michael Cuscuna, who'd produced her second record, her only Warner Bros. album to go gold. Bonnie had written the song "Nick of Time" about Michael's first wife.

His current wife, Lisa, overheard the conversation and got on the phone. "Why don't you send her that little Cajun number you wrote?" I resisted, saying it had been written from a male point of view, a redneck one at that, something I felt Bonnie had little empathy for. But Lisa was so certain that I added it at the end of the cassette and gave it to Bonnie.

As things turned out, they already had a killer ballad, "I Can't Make You Love Me," for my money one of the five best female vocal performances of all time, but there was still a slot open for something up-tempo. Chip and I had written the song with my guitar player, Ricky Hirsch, over a guitar lick he'd played us. When Bonnie expressed interest, not only in cutting the tune, but in playing that lick herself, I told Ricky to get over to her house and show her how to play it, "even if you have to move in with her!"

She had one concern. "That line, 'It must've been that wine-eyed, silver-tongued beaner.' I know it's the kind of thing the character in the song would say, but my liberal fans won't get it and will be offended by the word *beaner*. I hate to ruin the truth and authenticity of the song, but is there another way of saying it?" I fixed it with one word: *schemer*, and that did the trick, mollifying the PC police.

On the day of the session, I got a frantic call from Bonnie, saying that she couldn't get her band to play with the same feel as our demo. "That's because your musicians are too good," I told her. "It needs to be dumb, amateurish, like I play."

"Can you come over and teach them?"

I got Ricky on the phone, told him to meet me with his little five-dollar keyboard, and headed to the studio. First, I told the drummer to put his hands in his pockets and just play one and three on his bass drum. I had the bass man do the same. Bonnie played Ricky's lick and Ricky played a little Cajun accordion rhythm on that keyboard. I played my old Telecaster the only way I know how. The producer, Don Was, looked on quietly. Basically, I produced the track, uncredited. But I didn't care. I got our song, "Papa Come Quick (Jody and Chico)," on the follow-up to a three-million-selling album.

When I was back in New York, I mentioned to Bruce Lundvall who, in addition to heading Blue Note, was the East Coast chief of Capitol, the mother company, how thrilled I was to have had Bonnie cut our song. He said not to get too excited; *Nick of Time* was a fluke. She probably wouldn't sell more than four hundred thousand on the next one. That next one, *Luck of the Draw*, wound up selling over five million copies and remains the biggest seller of her career to date.

In May, I went back to New York to finish Lou's record. After having seen the Broadway show *Cats*, he insisted on doing one of the awful songs from the show. Cuscuna said, "Let's throw him a bone; he's been good about singing what we gave him so far," so we ultimately stuck it on at the end, where it wouldn't spoil the flow of the album.

Some moron label exec suggested that Narada Walden produce one track to appeal to radio for a single. It wound up not fitting at all with the rest of the record and may have even hurt sales, as it was the opening cut and the title song, "It's Supposed to Be Fun." Still, in between the lousy opening tune and the final piece of corny show-tune rubbish was a good album that reached the top five on the jazz chart in spite of those two mistakes.

I began work on Oliver Stone's biopic *The Doors* at the end of May. I played the promoter of the infamous concert where Jim Morrison, portrayed by Val Kilmer—who remained in character, on and off camera, throughout shooting—exposes himself. The concert scene was filmed in the old Olympic Auditorium. The couple thousand extras who played the audience were mostly real-life lowlifes from the gutters of Hollywood. After shooting, the cleanup crew found used condoms and hypodermic needles throughout the place. Every third "person" you see is actually a cardboard cut-out, to save money.

Stone, like most directors, was a man with a gigantic ego who thrived on ordering around a few thousand people at once. However, he let me continue ad-libbing at the end of one scene where I yell at the Doors' manager, turning the poor actor, the son of Steve McQueen and Ali McGraw, into a sniveling wreck, calling him fourteen different kinds of punk-ass motherfucker. Later, Stone came to my trailer and said, "I love what you did for me. I am definitely going to use you again." I am still awaiting his call. I love Hollywood bullshit, especially when it's unnecessary.

The release of the Little Richard box set happened to coincide with Richard receiving a star on the Hollywood Walk of Fame. I was sent to represent Specialty Records, the label for whom he recorded all the hits that made him a star. What's interesting is that Richard recorded all of those classic hits within an eighteen-month period.

I treasure the photo of us together taken that day. But with all the rockers he'd influenced, why, I wondered, was I the only one who'd showed up to honor the self-described King and Queen of rock 'n' roll?

The remainder of 1990 was basically taping the Rick Dees show five days a week, doing voiceovers or auditions in the morning, my radio show on Saturdays, and weekend club dates with the Beaters.

I had very little home life. I'd get home around seven and have dinner—mostly a lousy, tasteless meal prepared by a nanny who couldn't cook—with Charlie and my stepson, Lee, while my wife talked on the phone with her girlfriends. Living in a houseful of people, I had never been so lonely in my life.

The good part was that I was finally earning enough to support my family. I'd cowritten the show's theme with Rick, and I got to sing a couple of my songs each week, so there were ASCAP royalties there in addition to my salary. The Beaters were earning a steady paycheck for the first time since we'd started the band, so I was happy for them.

Many of the guests were lame Top 40 record acts that late-night viewers had no interest in, but at least once a week someone good came on: Frankie Valli, Merle Haggard, and Dion DiMucci come to mind. The guys were overwhelmed with pride to play "Peter Gunn" with its composer, Henry Mancini, conducting. I tried in vain to get the talent coordinators to book Judy Clay, but I did manage to get Lou Rawls on, and he did "If I Were a Magician."

As an interviewer, poor Rick left much to be desired. For the more substantial music artists, the director would often bring me over to help out. One day, the guest was Sherman Hemsley, who played George Jefferson on *The Jeffersons*. Having been told that Hemsley was a music lover, Rick asked who his favorite singer was, to which Sherman excitedly replied, "Little Jimmy Scott." Befuddled, Rick, looking like a deer caught in the headlights, tossed the question to me, and I started singing Jimmy's one obscure hit from 1950, "Everybody's Somebody's Fool." Sherman jumped up and ran over and hugged me.

That night, Jimmy's then-wife Erline was watching, and when he returned home, she told him what had transpired. At the time, Jimmy Scott was a forgotten man, one of the neglected greats, living in the slums of Newark, New Jersey. Before long, after several similar events, Jimmy was rediscovered and went on the have the career and admiration he deserved, living out the remainder of his life as the respected artist he was.

15
Back Stabbers

Between the income from the show, my voiceovers, and royalties from my songs and the Rawls albums, I was finally making good money. I called my accountant, Ron Lederman, and asked him if I had enough to pay off my mortgage in full, as the Italians back home do. I hate paying interest and have always resisted buying anything on time.

"Absolutely," he said, "Great idea."

Fifteen minutes later, he called back, his voice quivering. "You know, we ought to rethink this and maybe wait a while."

I smelled a rat and dialed my attorney. Chuck got on and agreed that something smelled. "Let's get our ducks in order first, so we can catch him red-handed. I'll alert the Beverly Hills Police."

I called my bank and asked how much was in my account. It was down to almost nothing. A second account, which Lederman had no access to, had a little over $30,000. I was fucked. I told them to cash no more checks unless I okayed them. They said one for $18,000 had just come in a few minutes earlier. "Do not honor it," I cried.

My road manager, Bobby Reid, a head breaker from Glasgow, Scotland, and I headed over to Lederman's office, but he'd taken to the hills. His bookkeeper had a box for me on her desk with my financial records and a stack of cashed checks made out to him in large amounts. Bobby was ready to toss him off the roof, as was I. Good thing Lederman wasn't there, because we don't play where I come from and there is no question in my mind that Bobby and I would have done him in that day, to our later regret.

After he was arrested, his wife called me, sobbing, "Oh, my children's father will be a convicted felon. Isn't there something we can do?" I knew her family was from what passes for old money in Beverly Hills. I think they once owned a pier or something. I knew that, once the police were involved, there was nothing I could do to stop prosecution from going forward, even if I'd wanted to. It was now a criminal, not a civil matter. But I played it cool and kept this to myself. I decided to con her.

"How much money do you have?"

"I have my inheritance, about $350,000." This was less than half what that worm had stolen from me.

"I tell you what, you get a cashier's check for that amount over here within the next two hours, and we'll see what we can do." I made sure to make no promises, allowing her to draw her own conclusions and hear what she wanted to hear. The check arrived and I was out of the poorhouse at least.

A day later, the thieving bastard had made bail and showed up with his lawyer at my attorney's office, unshaven and sitting in a fetal position. I knew the wife owned an art gallery, peddling what's known as "naïve art," the kind of crap your kid paints and the proud mother posts on the refrigerator. This stuff goes for big bucks to the *nouveau riche* suckers in Beverly Hills and Malibu. Lederman claimed the art was all gone and his house was mortgaged to the hilt. He was claiming to be broke. Obviously, like any clever thief, he'd taken care to hide his assets well.

Over the next few months, he went through three lawyers (translation: he probably stiffed all of them) and wound up with the noted criminal attorney Harlan Braun by the time it went to court in Santa Monica, a location that would be significant to the outcome of the case. Lederman was active in the local Democratic Party, and Santa Monica is a very liberal town, so chances were that the judge was in their pocket. As things turned out, it seems my suspicions were proven correct.

I'd had hopes of seeing Lederman sharing a cell with a horny perv named Bubba and becoming the dude's bitch, but in the end he would not do even one night in jail. He lost his CPA license but basically got a slap on the wrist.

The California courts allow the victim to speak after sentencing, so I stood up. I was pissed. "Your Honor," I said, "I fail to see how justice was served in this case. This man stole over $800,000 from me and has not done one night in jail."

ABOVE: The afternoon before we recorded "At This Moment" at the Roxy. (AUTHOR'S COLLECTION)

LEFT: My best LA friend, Paul Gayten. (AUTHOR'S COLLECTION)

With Jerry Wexler.
(AUTHOR'S COLLECTION)

ABOVE: *Buckaroo* plays in my 'hood.
(AUTHOR'S COLLECTION)

RIGHT: As Pinky Carruthers in *Buckaroo Banzai*.
(AUTHOR'S COLLECTION)

RIGHT: Lowell Fulson, my co-writer on "Room with a View." (AUTHOR'S COLLECTION)

BOTTOM: Alfa publicity shot, 1981. (PHOTO BY MARK HANAUER)

The Beaters with Dick Clark on *American Bandstand*. (AUTHOR'S COLLECTION)

Publicity shot. (PHOTO BY VERA ANDERSON)

ABOVE: With Johnny Carson holding my gold album.
(AUTHOR'S COLLECTION)

In my T-Bone Walker pose. (PHOTO BY ROB LEWINE)

Got the wall on Tower Records. (AUTHOR'S COLLECTION)

In Vegas, baby! (AUTHOR'S COLLECTION)

Singing with Willie Nelson in *Baja Oklahoma*.
(AUTHOR'S COLLECTION)

With Julia Roberts on the *Baja Oklahoma* set.
(AUTHOR'S COLLECTION)

I finally win my Grammy. (PHOTO BY BARRY DRUXMAN)

Forty-five years later, holding the *With Pen in Hand* album.
(PHOTO BY STEPHEN PALEY)

The judge replied that he'd been on the bench for twenty years and had never seen anyone recover as much money as I had. This condescending piece of shit was trying to jerk me off in front of the whole court.

"With all due respect, Your Honor, that was no thanks to this court. And furthermore, I suspect that, within the hour, one of those black or Hispanic prisoners in the dock over there will be going away for five years for stealing a couple hundred dollars or a necklace."

With that, the judge turned as red as a pot full of marinara sauce. From the look on his face, it appeared that he wanted to put *me* in jail. The crowd murmured. They knew I was right and were on my side. I hated that judge, the corrupt bastard.

The case was over, adjudicated wrongly. I'd been robbed by a man I was supposed to be able to trust and betrayed by a judicial system that was supposed to protect victims like me. But this was just the beginning of my betrayals.

Where I came from, betrayal was always met with revenge, cold and hard. But revenge was never my style; the old ways are not for me. I find it simpler to put the person out of my life forever.

Some years later, after another particularly bad and costly betrayal, I eventually found it in my heart to forgive the person. It wasn't easy. I had to follow the rule to "fake it 'til you make it." I pretended to like, even love, this person until one day I realized that I'd come to a place of forgiveness. I remembered the saying "Forgiveness is the doorway to Heaven." It felt as though a tremendous weight had been lifted from my shoulders and I was at peace.

The guys at Rhino Records were good guys. They loved the music of their youth and hired people who shared their taste. One such guy was James Austin, who ultimately became responsible for so much of what came out on the label. His tastes ran from country to R&B to rock 'n' roll to Christmas songs. I called him Mr. Christmas.

Over the next two decades, thanks to James, I got to compile and write notes for many Rhino CDs, leading to three Grammy nominations, one for producing *The R&B Box*, an anthology of rhythm and blues hits from the 1940s to the seventies, and two others, for producing and best album notes for *Genius and Soul: The Ray Charles 50th Anniversary Set*.

I did seven other Ray Charles sets, a Drifters box set, three doo-wop boxes, and many more, including one that almost didn't get made.

While having pizza one day, it occurred to me that just about every major ethnic group had had their music reissued, except the Italians. Back on the East Coast, there were a few million people of Italian descent who would jump at the chance to own a CD of the songs they'd grown up with. I pitched the idea to James and he forwarded it to his bosses, where there was some resistance. Understandable, as Rhino's owners were frat-house boys and had no feeling for what makes the Italian heart beat.

I urged Richard Foos to check with his East Coast distributors, and to his credit he did, probably because he has a soft spot for me thanks to that gold record hanging on his wall for "At This Moment." The distribs loved the idea and I was given the go-ahead.

I gathered songs by Dean Martin, Connie Francis, Louis Prima, Jerry Vale, Lou Monte, and others heard on jukeboxes back in the old Bronx Italian neighborhoods. We were unable to license any by Sinatra or Tony Bennett. For the cover and booklet, I asked a Sicilian friend, Thom Williams, to art direct. He came up with the idea to use the Ronzoni packaging and call the album *Eh! Paisano!* It went on to be Rhino's best-selling CD for the next six months.

Before Rhino came along, lots of older music sat in the vaults of record companies, gathering dust. Periodically, there would be surges of interest in "oldies," but it was becoming clear that a more general discontent with contemporary music reflected a public hungry with nostalgia for the sounds of their youth. And the new CD format got people interested in replacing their old 45s and LPs with cleaner-sounding CDs that took up less space.

To the owners of these old recordings, reissues represented found money, so they were supportive at first, charging reasonable fees to license songs. This enabled Rhino and others like them to make a profit on minimal sales.

A small group of us, taking a cue from our jazz brethren and our European and Japanese counterparts, began to treat the music with greater respect than others had. Rather than simply slam together a bunch of titles, we wanted to include more information: recording dates, personnel, vintage photos and extensive liner notes, and previously unissued recordings, making for a more historical as well as a listening experience. This was unheard of outside of jazz. We were sending the message that rock 'n' roll and rhythm and blues should be taken seriously.

I was doing this as early as 1988, when RCA Victor gave me the opportunity to compile two CDs called *Billy Vera's Rock 'n' Roll Party* in two volumes. The booklets were thick with photos and information. I'm sure RCA didn't expect great sales, and in that respect I didn't disappoint them, but my approach set an example for other American vault men.

One of my favorite projects during my time with Specialty was a five-disc box-set history of Specialty Records that chronicled the label's years from 1945 to 1958, when owner Art Rupe ceased operations. I felt it was one of the most important record companies in the history of rock 'n' roll, right up there with Atlantic, Chess, and Sun, and wanted to honor both the label and its founder.

During this period, I was doing lots of reissue work, ending up working on over two hundred albums and box sets. In addition to compiling more than fifty CDs for Specialty (which had been sold to Fantasy), I was in charge of the Vee-Jay catalogue, rereleasing their soul, jazz, doo-wop, blues, and gospel gems. Pete Welding at Capitol put me in charge of their blues series, the *Capitol Blues Collection*, and Alan Warner gave me a series of my own, *From the Capitol Vaults*, so I could acknowledge the pop artists of the 1940s and fifties who made Capitol the greatest label in the business. I also compiled and annotated CDs for the great Ace reissue label in the UK and Bear Family in Germany, as well as the seminal jazz and R&B label Savoy Records, where I got to play in the vaults with legends like Charlie Parker, Jimmy Scott, Johnny Otis, and Big Maybelle.

In addition to these, I've been privileged to work on artists like Sam Cooke, Duke Ellington, Count Basie, Louis Jordan, Louis Prima, Etta James, T-Bone Walker, Allen Toussaint, and so many more. My historical work has been some of the most gratifying of my lifetime, although it's the kind of work that one does for little pay and a small but devoted audience.

An example of just how devoted came about one night at Sandy Gallin's annual Christmas party. It's an A-list event, lots of big stars, and not just Gallin-Morey clients. My wife was down with the flu but insisted that I go. A little shy offstage, I'm not very good at parties. I tend to plop myself down in a spot where people have to pass me and hope they'll speak first.

After a few minutes with Dolly, who was acting as Sandy's hostess, and a couple of others I kind of knew, I was sitting alone at the bar, nursing a Pepsi, when a woman I knew peripherally came up and said that "Bob" would like to have a word with me. I looked over her shoulder and saw that the "Bob" in question happened to be none other than Mr. Dylan.

Actress Lainie Kazan had told me that her friend Dylan was a fan of my acting (she said nothing about my music), so this wasn't that much of a shock. The first thing Dylan said to me was how much he loved the three Percy Mayfield CDs I had produced and how he agreed with my assessment that Percy was indeed the poet of the blues.

As the Madonnas and Shirley MacLaines and Ryans and Farrahs all approached to kiss the ring, Dylan blew them off, and none too politely. All he wanted was to talk about Percy and his wonderful blues lyrics.

Two and a half hours later, the great Dylan suddenly stood up and said in that voice of his, "Startin' to fade, man. Gotta split." And with that, he left and went home, presumably to listen to some Percy Mayfield.

The ratings for the Rick Dees show, while never good, were abysmal now. I'm always surprised now whenever someone mentions having seen it. ABC went through three different producers, the last of whom was a guy best known in the industry for "failing upward," as the word among the stage crew had it. I always make friends with the crew, who can make or break you. The crew and the hair, makeup, and wardrobe people always know more about what's happening than anybody else. Plus, I'm comfortable around them because they're real, down-to-earth, normal people.

This producer asked me to lunch at the ABC commissary (always a bad sign) and pontificated on his ideas for attracting a larger audience to the show. Then, treading lightly, he suggested I consider getting rid of two of my front-line sax players whose main sin was, in his words, the fact that they were "overweight white guys in their forties." How would I feel about replacing them with, say, some younger black guys or even a girl or two?

"Nothing doing," I said. "These guys have been with me for thirteen years and are doing a fine job playing the music. They're my friends and I have to look myself in the mirror in the morning." For emphasis, I added, "Plus, you don't want to find yourself on the wrong end of an age-discrimination suit, do you?"

That shut him up for the time being, but I knew it was just a matter of time before the proverbial shit hit the fan. His type doesn't take kindly to someone getting the best of them.

A week went by and I got the word that they wanted to keep me (for my TVQ) but could "no longer afford" a nine-piece band, and would I consider cutting back? "No," I replied, "It wouldn't be the Beaters." So that was it; we were let go.

The union rules for network shows state that musicians are hired in thirteen-week increments. If you fire them before that period ends, you have to pay them for the full thirteen weeks. Well, they screwed my guys out of their last nine weeks' pay. We called in the union, and in typical union fashion, after some big words ("We're your union brothers and we're gonna stick by you"), they crumbled, as Jim Morey had predicted they would.

Unlike the other guys, I'd had the foresight to pay my attorney to negotiate my contract, rather than trust the union to take care of me, and I walked out that day with a check for $45,000.

Later, I found out that a couple of the band members had gone behind my back and, thinking we were being let go because of the songs I chose to play coming in and out of commercial breaks, told the producer they'd be happy to play any songs they were told. In other words, after I'd stood up for them, these guys had betrayed me.

I never said anything. What would have been the point? Fear and desperation can make the strongest among us do things we wouldn't normally do.

16
Pick Up the Pieces

On March 26, 1991, I lost the best friend I ever had in LA. Paul Gayten's wife, Odile, called that morning to tell me he had suddenly passed away the night before. He had told none of us, except his aunt in New Orleans, that he'd had bloody stools for some time, probably the result of taking his daily aspirin in too-large doses or without eating. By the time it got to the point where he got weak from loss of blood, it was too late. At the hospital, he was given a transfusion and the resulting pressure caused a fatal heart attack.

Odile asked me to sing his big hit duet with Annie Laurie, "I'll Never Be Free," at the funeral. Our mutual friend Teddy Edwards, the great pioneer bebop tenor saxophonist, wrote me a chart but was too heartbroken to attend. I asked Lou Rawls to come and sing a hymn. The pallbearers included Phil Chess, master drummer Earl Palmer, saxophonist Lee Allen, and other New Orleans greats.

Paul's career included hit records, productions, and songs such as "But I Do," the Clarence "Frogman" Henry hit, and "For You My Love," originally sung by Larry Darnel and covered by many artists, including Dinah Washington and, as a duet, by Nat Cole and Nellie Lutcher. His passing was a tremendous personal loss. His friendship and loyalty were the kind you seldom find in this treacherous town. I'd managed to reissue two CDs of his work, the second of which came out posthumously.

Aside from band gigs, my radio show, and small parts in movies and TV shows, my main income was now from voiceovers. I was recovering financially from the episode with Lederman. I was asked to sing the theme for a new sitcom called *Empty Nest*, starring Richard Mulligan and Kristy McNichol. Singing a TV theme can be lucrative, especially when the show lasts a few years. You sing it once, and for that one day's work you get residuals at Screen Actors Guild scale every time the show airs, the same as the on-camera actors. *Empty Nest* lasted four years, plus endless reruns.

A special treat that summer was playing for the fortieth anniversary of the songwriting partnership of Jerry Leiber and Mike Stoller, arguably the best composer/lyricist team in the history of rock 'n' roll, with such songs to their credit as "Kansas City," "Stand by Me," "Yakety Yak," "Charlie Brown," "Ruby Baby," "On Broadway," "Hound Dog," "Jailhouse Rock" (a total of twenty-six tunes for Elvis alone), plus "Is That All There Is" for Peggy Lee.

The performers at the Hollywood Palladium that night included Miss Lee, the Coasters, Dion, and others. Before she went on, Peggy asked me to open the curtain slightly so she could see. "It's been fifty years since I've played this motherfucker" were words I never expected to hear uttered by this classy lady!

My old fan David Hasselhoff called one day to say that he was starting a new show and was asking friends to do him a favor and come on as guest stars. Would I be willing? I told him I'd be happy to, and that's how I wound up doing a guest shot on the first season of *Baywatch*.

Though I didn't get to meet Pamela Anderson, years later she would dance to my song "At This Moment" on *Dancing with the Stars*. She looked beautiful in a lavender gown, with her blonde tresses in an upsweep, and waltzed very nicely.

In April 1992 Michael Cuscuna and I started work in New York on our third Lou Rawls album for Blue Note. It was to be an all-blues set of genre classics. We had the same musicians, plus guest artists including Joe Williams, Phoebe Snow, Lionel Hampton, Buddy Guy, Joe Lovano, and Junior Wells. Benny Golson and Hank Crawford were back on hand to write horn charts.

Lionel Hampton was one of the greatest musicians in the history of jazz, but by this time he was getting up there in years. When I watched him being helped into the studio by two women, I got nervous. But once the music started, Hamp dropped thirty years and played like, well, Hamp. On the old Lucky Millinder wartime hit "Sweet Slumber," he kept getting one chord wrong, making it a minor instead of a major.

He knew he was flubbing it and said, "Don't worry, Gate, I'll stay here as long as you want; I just love to play."

Hamp could afford to be generous. Thanks to his late wife, Gladys, a tight-fisted woman if there ever was one, he was one of the richest men in Harlem, owning real estate galore, including the Hampton Houses, between St. Nicholas and Eighth Avenue, near 130th Street.

Thanks to guitarist Steve Kahn, son of the great lyricist Sammy Cahn, we got a spectacular track on the old Clyde McPhatter hit "A Lover's Question" for Lou and Phoebe to sing over.

Joe Williams told me a less-than-discreet story about the time Ava Gardner came to Birdland to catch him and Count Basie's band. Joe wound up back at Ava's place, and it was only during a postcoital cigarette in her bed that he remembered he'd promised to bring his wife a fried egg sandwich after work. Ava told him to phone the wife so she could speak to her and make up some excuse.

"Next time we played Birdland, Ava showed up and, as my wife was there, invited the whole band for a little after-the-gig party. My wife was a very hip British lady and, without saying a word, made sure Ava knew that she knew what had transpired."

On our album, Joe and Lou had a ball reviving Louis Jordan's 1940s hit "Saturday Night Fish Fry," with a tasty solo by Hamp.

Later in the month, I got to travel to the Netherlands to do some local television shows to promote the Dutch release of "At This Moment" and an album of my music. For some reason, Holland had always, even back in the sixties, been a good market for me. Of course, with a population and square mileage only twice the size of New Jersey, how many record sales could that translate into?

Amsterdam is beautiful. The people from the local record company showed me around this historic city. Dutch women are some of the most breathtaking in the world. It was the first time I'd ever been to any of the countries of my origins and I loved it there.

Back home in LA, I was doing voiceover spots for Mervyn's, Applebee's, Toyota, Sparklets, just about any product you could name. And then I got a big steady gig: I started doing promos for a CBS show called *Northern Exposure*. That ended a couple of years later with the show's demise. I was walking down the hall, feeling sorry for myself, when a guy stopped me and said, "I'm glad I saw you, Billy. It gives me an idea. The network is thinking about changing their comedy voice, and I think you'd be perfect."

This chance meeting resulted in a five-year gig as the voice of CBS comedies, bringing in more money than I'd ever dreamed of, making it easy to overlook what my thieving former accountant had done to me. CBS was five minutes from my house, so the travel time was nothing. The announcers had our own parking spaces. I'd walk in, wave to the guard, go down to the basement, work for half an hour once or twice a day, reading inane things like "Watch *The Nanny*, tonight, 8:00 p.m., seven Central," and earn as much as my former girlfriends upstairs on *The Young and the Restless* and *The Bold and the Beautiful* did for spending sixteen hours a day in hair, makeup, and wardrobe, in addition to having to memorize forty pages of dialogue per day. It was the perfect lazy man's gig. I would eventually announce promos for all the other networks as well.

With all this going on, I managed to squeeze in teaching a class on the history of rhythm and blues at UCLA and doing a recurring role as Duke on the hit show *Beverly Hills, 90210*. Duke was the bookie for Jason Priestley's character during the period when he had a gambling problem.

A Westchester musician named Joe Ferry asked me to do an album for a label called Shanachie for which he'd been doing some producing. My recording career was nowhere at the time. He said I could duet with anyone I liked, and I thought it would be nice to finally record "Storybook Children" with Nona Hendryx, so we did it. The album came out and disappeared quickly. Ferry then had another idea, to do a multi-artist live album at the Lone Star, a popular club in Manhattan. It was a nice event, with Chuck Jackson, Cissy Houston, myself, and a couple of others. Richard Tee and Cornell Dupree backed me on "Room with a View," and I did "If I Were a Magician" alone with Richard, one of the last recordings he ever made, as he was dying of cancer at the time.

It was a good thing I got a little taste up front, because Shanachie not only never paid artist or publishing royalties, they never even bothered to apply for licenses for the songs.

Rosalee and I were going to therapy and Al-Anon meetings in an attempt to fix our marriage, but things weren't getting any better. I was terribly unhappy, and I'm sure she was, too. It was just a matter of time, but I was determined to stay as long as I could stand it, if only for the sake of my son. I didn't want him to be without a daddy. I was so lonely in that house and longed for female companionship and understanding. I wanted to cheat, but, despite a few temptations, I somehow managed to control the urge, mainly because I didn't want Charlie to have that kind of a father. My only happy moments were when I'd come home and hear his little feet running to meet me at the door. I felt no one in the world loved me but him.

Before long, I began to see signs around the house that caused me to look over my shoulder. One of these was an advice book, left lying around, with a title something along the lines of "How to Get the Most out of Your Divorce." The writing was really on the wall, in all caps. Rosalee wanted me to get my record collection out of the house and was after me to rent an office for that purpose. She wanted to use that room so her son could have his own bedroom, rather than share with our son.

I'd been noticing a lovely old Spanish-style house on my way to the park where I walked each day. One morning, there was a For Sale sign, and I decided to buy it. I had enough to pay cash, so there was no mortgage, and I moved my collection and the furniture my mother had left me into it. I would use the house for an office and have a place to live, a safe haven for my records, when the inevitable came. I desperately feared that, in one of Rosalee's rages, she might lose it and smash my irreplaceable treasures, a common nightmare among collectors.

That inevitable arrived in April 1994, after an ugly argument that let me know that, if I didn't get out of there, I was bound to crack. I hated leaving the boys, but what good would I be to them if I were to have a nervous breakdown? And there was no doubt by now that I was on the verge of one. I had to get out, to save myself and my sanity.

I spent my fiftieth birthday on May 28, 1994, alone and unwanted in my new house, for the first time in my life knowing what it feels like to be hated and despised.

Unlike the ending of my first marriage, which was fair and friendly, this divorce process was horribly vitriolic, and it will do no one any good to go into it here. So we'll just say it took three long years to work out a settlement, thanks to a weasel of a lawyer who was not man enough to stand up to his client and convince her to do the right thing.

Bonnie Raitt asked me to join the board of directors of the Rhythm and Blues Foundation, a nonprofit organization set up to help needy former R&B stars from the 1940s, fifties, and sixties. You'd be surprised to know how many of our musical heroes fall on hard times, either from being cheated by managers and record companies, or simply by not knowing how to handle the money they earned in their heyday.

Bonnie said they needed me because, whenever you're giving money away, there are always hustlers and frauds ready to steal some of it. In this case, there'd be people claiming to be former members of famous groups. Since I'd worked with and known many of the players involved, I could tell who was a fake and who wasn't.

The Foundation also threw an event each year at Grammy time, during the same week, in the same city. They'd honor around a dozen veteran performers and, instead of just presenting them with a plaque or statuette and a slap on the back, give them a $15,000 check, which was impressive, considering that many of these people had never seen a check for that amount in their lives. The shows were done first class and I was proud to be a part of both choosing the artists to be honored and working on the shows.

Often, egos being what they are, problems would arise from old scores wanting to be settled and I'd be called upon to put out the fires, as the performers tended to trust and listen to me.

One show comes to mind. Since the Coasters were more of a rock 'n' roll act than R&B, I'd suggested a solution whereby we'd honor them in conjunction with the Robins, the group out of which the Coasters had evolved. All was good, until the day of the concert in New York.

Carl Gardner, my old friend from the Coasters, egged on by his wife, hadn't wanted to appear onstage with his former colleagues in the Robins, due to some past grievances, probably long forgotten by everyone but Carl. He wanted to give them a piece of his mind during his acceptance speech.

In a panic, one of the Foundation assistants came running to me, begging me to do something. I sat Carl down at a table and calmly said,

"Carl, we go back a long time and had a lot of fun together. You taught me so much of what I know about show business."

"Yeah, baby, we had some times, didn't we?"

"I'll never forget one thing you told me," I lied. "You said, 'Sometimes a simple thank you will suffice.' Well, this is one of those times, Carl. This is a night to be the bigger man. Show them your class. Let them see the gentleman I know you are."

He nodded, taking in what I'd said, and we shook hands. Later, during the ceremony, my old friend got up there and said, as he accepted his plaque and his check, "As a dear friend of mine once said, 'A simple thank you will suffice.' Thank you all very much."

Whew! One fire put out. My old friends Ruby and the Romantics were also being honored that night. Sadly, all were dead now, except for Ruby Nash and Ronnie Mosely, who was in no shape to walk up the stairs, so a lift had been installed to accommodate his infirmity. Then, during the show, as the band was about to play Ruby on, she became too frightened to sing, as it had been years since she'd sung in public.

I caught her in the wings and said, "Ruby, there's a hall full of people out there who love you and would give anything in the world to hear your beautiful voice again. Please, for me, go out there and give 'em what they want." She went out and sang a gorgeous version of the group's biggest song, "Our Day Will Come," to a standing ovation.

My greatest failure during this period came when it was brought to my attention that acts who had recorded for the Cameo/Parkway labels in the late 1950s and early sixties weren't working the oldies circuit as much as other acts. I realized this had to do with the fact that their records weren't on the market, thanks to a bizarre business decision by the company's owner, Allen Klein, who believed this tactic would increase the value of his holdings.

In fact, with their records unavailable, these musicians weren't heard on radio, so demand for their services went down along with their fees. In addition, no records for sale meant no royalties, not only for the artists, but for the songwriters, too.

It occurred to me that this might be a basis for a restraint of trade lawsuit, a class action suit on behalf of all Cameo/Parkway artists and songwriters. I spoke with several attorneys, seeking to get some noble soul to work pro bono for these people, many of whom had no other way of earning a living. In an age when oldies were being reissued, right and left, this one small group of performers was being royally screwed by Klein. As hard as I tried, I was unable to interest anyone in helping.

I stayed with the Foundation for ten years, until most of the living artists from the era had passed on and they were moving on to seventies acts. I felt that by the 1970s most acts were lawyered up and had no excuse for being in desperate straits. Plus, someone had the bright idea to include more artists on the board of directors, which meant our meetings became huge, annoying ego fests that I had no stomach for, so I regretfully left the organization.

My acting career was winding down. An agent named John Gaines had taken over the theatrical department at APA after Ames and Donna left, and he and the guys he'd brought with him had no idea I was a trained actor. They just thought I was another singer who wanted to do a little acting on the side, and the roles they sent me out for reflected this view. I did two sitcoms in a row, *Double Rush* and *Boy Meets World*, which were essentially the same role in the same storyline, an old rock singer, played for cheap laughs. I needed a new agent.

Bobby Roth brought me on board to play the Judds' bandleader and straw boss in a biopic he was directing about that popular mother/daughter country act. I got him to include my bass player, Chuck Fiore, who had returned to the Beaters and needed some money. One night, at the end of a big, emotional scene, Bobby was shooting close-ups, and, as the low man on the totem pole, I was the last to be filmed. It looked like there might not be time for my shot without taking the crew into costly overtime.

Bobby asked if I could cry in one take and I said, "I can if you play that sad song of theirs." So he had them play the tune, and, with the crew quietly breaking down the scenery, my tears came down, on cue. Bobby was always good to me like that. On that ABC movie *Tonight's the Night*, he even wrote an unnecessary bathroom scene for me so I could have a few lines and show my stuff. Later, when ABC was advertising the Rick Dees show, they used my scenes in the promo for the rerun, to make it look like I was the star of the film. Boy, did we laugh about that one!

In San Diego, for a show called *Vanishing Sun*, I played a blind blues singer married to a black woman who in real life turned out to be the daughter of a real blues singer named TV Slim. I got to spend some needed time that week with my dad and his wife, Olga, who lived down there.

In the spring of 1995, Blue Note was planning a Christmas CD featuring Blue Note acts to benefit the Special Olympics, and Bruce Lundvall asked me to produce a song for Lou Rawls and Dianne Reeves. The song chosen was "Baby It's Cold Outside." It had to be done low budget so there'd be money left for the charity.

I booked an inexpensive studio in the Valley and hired jazz pianist Gerald Wiggins's trio, adding Teddy Edwards to play a solo on his tenor sax. All four of these exceptional musicians were willing to work for scale for me.

We arrived at the studio, but Teddy wasn't there. I called him at home and he answered. "Teddy, we got a date. You coming, man?"

"Yeah, baby, I'll be there. My ticker was giving me trouble and I have to wait for the nitro to kick in."

Teddy eventually showed up and played beautifully. I went over to Capitol afterwards and sweet-talked the girl up in the payroll department into putting my contracts on the top of her pile, so these old fellas could get paid while they were still among us. Record companies often find it cheaper to pay late fees to the union, rather than go to the expense of hiring enough staff so that musicians' payments can go out on time.

Lou Rawls had a recurring role on Hasselhoff's spin-off show, *Baywatch Nights*, as a club owner. I told him that "Room with a View" was David's favorite song and he should sing it on the show, so he did.

Not long after, I got a call to appear on an episode of the show, where I was to play a Brian Wilson character, the leader of a Beach Boys–type group. In a flashback, wearing a wig, I lie on a sofa, drunk, while, unbeknownst to me, the band rapes a groupie.

Cut to present day. The girl's daughter is murdering each band member, one by one, until she gets to me. Thinking that I participated in her mother's rape, she has me next on her kill list. She becomes my girlfriend, takes me out on her yacht, hits me over the head, ties me up, tosses me into a rubber life raft, sends me out to sea, and shoots a hole in the raft. All this while I'm in cut-offs and a shirt, freezing in the dirty, cold, shark-infested Pacific Ocean. All day long.

In the nick of time, Hasselhoff comes to save me and the girl is arrested.

After we wrapped for the day, I drove over to CBS and made more money in half an hour, doing comedy promos, than I'd made all week on *Baywatch Nights*. That was the moment of truth, when I knew I'd had enough of acting on camera.

The year ended with a tribute to Jerry Wexler at the LA House of Blues. The acts he requested to play for him were Etta James, Solomon Burke, Doug Sahm, and me. I felt honored to be included in that group and, more so, to play for my mentor and friend.

Wex was more than just a musical and showbiz mentor. He was my literary mentor, too. The first book he ever touted me on was by Harry Crews, *The Gospel Singer*, a novel about an impossibly good-looking young gospel singer who travels the South with his flunky in a big Cadillac convertible, preaching and singing in a big tent. Women find him irresistible, just as he can't resist the ones who throw themselves at him, having sex with them underneath the bleachers or anywhere he can.

I thought this would have been a great vehicle for Elvis to show he could really act; years later, I discovered that the King had optioned the book. Most likely the Colonel put the kibosh on that idea, preferring to have his boy make quick and stupid travelogue movies, filled with lousy songs they could publish.

One time, I thought I'd return the favor and tout Jerry on a book I was certain he'd never read, *Ask the Dust*, an obscure 1939 novel by John Fante that had been recently reprinted due to its being on Charles Bukowski's list of favorites. I sent Jerry a copy, and a week later, the mailman brought a package containing a first edition with a note from Jerry saying that he'd stolen this book from a neighborhood candy store at Bennett Avenue and 181st Street when he was twenty-two. He was convinced that Mr. Orenstein could not come after us at this late juncture due to a statute of limitations. I called him in Florida to thank him, and he said, "You know better than to think there's a book I haven't read."

Wexler was a superb writer himself, and when I had the chance, I hired him to write notes for a Guitar Slim set and a New Orleans compilation I produced for Specialty called *Creole Kings of New Orleans*. He didn't need the money, but he gladly accepted it and enjoyed himself immensely.

17
What Music Career?

While the dogfight known as divorce was at its height, my whole professional life, it seemed, consisted of doing three or more voiceovers a day, five days a week, with maybe two Beater gigs a month. I used to joke that I did the voiceovers for free and got paid for the endless driving from one studio to another. By the end of each day, I was so tired that I had no time or energy for a social life.

The clubs, as a rule, weren't paying that well. But the guys loved to play as much as I do and stuck with me, for money I was ashamed to be paying such talented musicians pushing fifty years of age.

One day I was at music publisher Mickey Goldsen's office, listening to his colorful tales of the old days of the music business in Hollywood. Mickey owned Criterion Music, which he'd formed from the ashes of Capitol Songs, the onetime publishing arm of Capitol Records. As they periodically do, our government had forced Capitol to divest itself of its publishing interests, citing monopolistic practices. Mickey had been in charge, so Capitol sold it to him for the proverbial song, giving him ownership of some great copyrights, like "Moonlight in Vermont," "It's a Good Day," and "Mañana." He built the company, later with his son, Bo, into one of the most successful latter-day independent music publishing houses.

Mickey's early experiences included a stint with Mills Music, owned by Irving Mills, Duke Ellington's manager. At night, Mickey, who had an accounting background, would scour the books in order to learn the business. He noticed that Duke lost money on most of his personal appearances. One day, he questioned Mills about this, and Irving said that, in order to have his "expensive gentlemen" on hand to learn the new songs as he wrote them, Ellington was willing to dip into his considerable ASCAP royalties to keep the band afloat.

I thought, if Duke could do that, so could I, and decided to give all the money on our low-paying gigs to the band and sell CDs after the show for my pay. On the high-priced engagements, I'd take the lion's share, as bandleaders traditionally do, but those were becoming fewer and farther between. The difference to each guy would be minor, but the gesture might be good for morale.

One great club we worked at a few times a year was the Crazy Horse, basically a country-and-western venue in Santa Ana in Orange County. The owner was a great guy who always gave us the star treatment. He told me that the only non-country acts he ever booked were Ray Charles and Billy Vera and the Beaters.

A rich couple who were fans of ours put up a little money so we could record a live album at the club. Our soundman, Brad Spurr, engineered it, and my friend Thom Williams did me a favor and designed a cover, gratis, that was in the style of a vintage Pepsi-Cola bottle cap, after my favorite beverage. That album, plus an additional six tracks, was rereleased a few years later as *At This Moment: A Retrospective* on the Varèse Sarabande label, one of the few companies from whom I still receive royalties.

The early days of 1997 brought the final judgment in my divorce. My attorney said that in over twenty years of practice, he'd never seen anyone get screwed as badly as I'd been. I was paying as much alimony as people like Burt Reynolds and O. J. Simpson, although I was nowhere near their league financially.

To make matters worse, CBS had a new president, Les Moonves. Upon his arrival, I suddenly, with no explanation, stopped getting calls from the network to do the promos I'd been doing for the past five years. I later ran into some of the recording engineers having lunch at the Farmer's Market next door, and they said they missed me and that one of Moonves's first acts as president had been to call downstairs and say, "Who's that guy doing the comedy promos? I hear him too much; he's all over the place. Get rid of him."

And with that my income declined by a quarter of a million bucks a year . . . just because the new boss wanted to mark his territory on what amounted to a random whim. Since the alimony was based on my previous year's income, I was now paying my ex more than I was earning. Luckily for me, I'd had a mother who told me to always live below my means, so I had enough savings to fall back on until I got something else.

Before my departure from CBS, one of my producers there named Jody Gottlieb had been telling me that, now that Don Pitts had retired, I needed to find new representation, because the person who'd replaced Don was not doing her job. Not knowing any other v/o agents, I asked her who was good. She named only two companies, ICM and Sutton, Barth and Vennari, the only difference between them being that the head guy at ICM was aggressive but mean to his clients and the agents at SBV, all women, were friendly and nurturing. Guess who I chose?

Rita Vennari came to see the band, which stroked me pretty good, showing me she really wanted me with the agency. I told her my predicament and she quickly got me a gig with the new UPN network, doing promos for all their comedies. Most of the network's shows were black sitcoms, like *Moesha*. I hadn't worked for a couple of months, but now I was back on the job. UPN kept me busy three or more times a day, along with the odd gig here and there for other clients.

Applebee's restaurants lasted for nine years, a steady gig if there ever was one. The Bill Cosby people liked me enough to let me promo every one of his shows in syndication. David Brokaw was Cosby's manager, but I don't think that had anything to do with me getting the gig. My agent got a call from a guy who knew me from CBS and somehow got the idea to take me in a totally different direction and have me do a creepy voice for NBC's *Saturday Night Thrillogy*, the network's trio of scary shows. I spoke over background music provided by porn star Traci Lords, something I'm sure the viewers never knew.

One day I got a frantic call to rush over to Toolbox, the studio in West Los Angeles where I did the UPN promos. It seems these people had auditioned every black announcer in town for a new Magic Johnson talk show and settled on a guy who, when he got there to do the actual job, had trouble pronouncing some of the guests' names. The Toolbox folks recommended me, as they needed someone quick because the spots had to go up on the satellite in twenty minutes.

I did what was needed and got the gig, which paid a thousand a day, five days a week. Unfortunately, Magic's magic didn't catch on with viewers and the show lasted only a few months.

Being a v/o guy is like being a whore; you read what you're told and get paid. Only once did I ever refuse, aside from doing political spots, that is. It was for those little cars Mattel makes called Hot Wheels. The director had me reading in an extremely harsh voice that hurt my throat. Worse, he couldn't make up his mind how he wanted it and had me do more than fifty takes, all of which were perfectly fine. This happened every time I worked for this jerk. Finally, I told my agent, "I have to sing with this voice. Tell them I ain't working for him anymore."

In early 1999, I was hired to do my first spot for the AM-PM convenience stores, kind of like a 7-11, only in Arco gas stations. They were very well-written and hip. The client wanted my cool, hip Billy voice. It has turned out to be my longest-running v/o job, over seventeen years as of 2016. They've been very good to me, keeping me on even after changing ad agencies, something that rarely happens.

I get a lot of people who approach me asking how to get into voiceover work. Their mother or their girlfriend tells them they have a good voice, or they're actresses who are forty plus, and on-camera work is slowing down for them. I never know what to say, because I got into it on a fluke. I recommend they take classes, because it's not as easy as it looks. You have to have good timing, be able to shave a half second off your read if called for, and, above all, be believable. A few times, a very few times, I gave a friend's demo to my agents, but, other than Lou Rawls, they've never accepted any of my submissions, and they were unable to get Lou any work. The answer is usually "We have too many like him already" or "She sounds fortyish. There's no work for a woman that age."

My friend Bob Hunka took me to lunch one day and said there was a new sitcom coming on about a New York UPS driver and his hot wife who live in Queens. They had a theme song, and would I listen to it and give my opinion? So I did and said it sounded like Paul Simon's idea of a country song, and not right for that show. Bob agreed but said the producers were tied to the song. Could I think of anything to make it work?

I said, "It needs to sound dumb, real blue collar, like the guy."

"Think you can do it?"

"Sure, I'd simplify the chords, play it real simple. Let me use the Beaters and I can give you what you're looking for."

That's how we got the gig to do the *King of Queens* theme. We recorded it in one take plus another for safety. The show lasted for nine years on network and is still running in syndication. It's probably airing somewhere as I type. Financially, it was like having a hit record. Singers are in SAG, the actors' union, and get paid scale each time the show airs. Musicians, on the other hand, have only the ineffectual musicians' union, so they get one scale payment each year the show is on the air. Quite a difference.

The show was a monster hit in Germany and Austria for some reason, and I used to constantly get messages on my website asking me to put the song out as a single. Everyone was sure it would be a huge hit over there. I had to explain that the whole song lasts only thirty-two seconds, much too short for a record.

18
Like It's 1999

The new millennium brought a Screen Actors Guild strike that lasted six months. This meant no TV commercials. I could still do radio voiceovers, as radio falls under a different union, AFTRA, but my v/o work was essentially cut to less than half.

Fortunately, my frugal ways allowed me to keep paying my high alimony and thus stay out of jail. For any of you contemplating a career in show business, I can't emphasize enough what my mother said about living below your means. A friend who owns a tiny indie record label has another bit of good advice I'll pass along. He met and married a European singer/actress who took him for a bundle. I asked if he'd learned anything, and he said, "Yeah, never marry anyone who has headshots."

Looking at the big picture, it was clear that the strike helped no one. Actors I knew lost their homes when they couldn't keep up payments. Any gains we made in increased fees were more than offset by the amount of work we'd lost. But I guess you have to show management, every once in a while, that you're willing to walk.

There was less and less work for the Beaters; club work was drying up. Clubs were hiring cheap bands or even bands that would work for free. Famous places like the Roxy or the Whisky let any kid band play that was willing to guarantee fifty customers at ten bucks apiece. They call it "pay to play." Any high school band can do that once. But will those friends show up a second time?

Another scam the clubs were running was to record your set for $250 or video it for another $250. Most of these bands were Beverly Hills kids whose parents could pay for them to indulge their fantasies of becoming big-time rock stars, at least until they went off to college to become lawyers or dentists.

AFTRA sent me down to New Orleans to sing at their convention. A local band led by Deacon John Moore backed me. The wife of a local Mafia chief's nephew was a fan of mine, and he asked if they could attend the private show. I said yes and he showed me around town, treating me at the best Italian restaurants in New Orleans. He told me, "Boy, whenever you come back to New Orleans, you own this town." Paul Gayten had worked for his uncle at a number of clubs he owned in the old days.

Most people think of New Orleans as a strictly black town, thanks to all the incredible jazz and R&B music that's been made there. But NOLA was also the first American city the Sicilians settled in, largely because of the climate, which was similar to that of Sicily. Louis Prima and Sam Butera were born and bred in New Orleans. It was also where the Black Hand first took hold in America, eventually morphing into La Cosa Nostra.

I had been in the Crescent City in the 1970s with the Shirelles, when the band that backed us was that of Dave Bartholomew, the producer and cowriter of Fats Domino's many hits. The band was great; Fats's drummer, Cornelius Coleman, a.k.a. Tenoo, and I made friends opening night, and he offered to take me the next day to meet all my heroes, Professor Longhair, Earl King, Frogman Henry, and the rest. But at the end of the night a strange thing happened. He leaned over, banged his head on the table, and peed his pants.

The next night, Bartholomew showed up with another drummer named Junie Boy and said he'd dropped Tenoo off at home, and fifteen minutes later his wife had called and said that he'd dropped dead.

While in New Orleans I heard more JFK stories from reliable sources, about how the father, Joe Kennedy, had promised New Orleans boss Carlos Marcello, Sam Giancana of Chicago, and Santo Traficante of Tampa that if they helped fix the 1960 election in their states, they'd be allowed to run their business without government interference. But when brother Bobby became attorney general he double-crossed them and illegally sent the Feds in to kidnap old Carlos and drop him in the jungle of Guatemala.

Carlos managed to escape and snuck back into the country via Grand Isle. His boys asked if he planned to kill Bobby, to which the old man replied, "No, you wanna kill the snake, you gotta cut off the head."

Lee Harvey Oswald's father worked as a bookie for Marcello, and Oswald's loser son Lee Harvey, with his Soviet and Cuban connections, made the perfect patsy, a culprit who'd confuse the public with rumors of communist or CIA involvement. Jack Ruby was another loser who'd been exiled from Chicago to run a strip club in Dallas, another city controlled by Marcello.

Traficante's son told a friend of mine that his old man had told him before he died that he, Giancana, and old Carlos "did" Kennedy or, better said, were behind the assassination.

I told all this to a friend, a former FBI agent who specialized in Mafia cases, and asked if he could confirm my story. He said I had it exactly right. So why, if law enforcement knew this, had they kept it secret all these years, I asked. Was it for fear the public might freak out? He said, "Something like that."

Believe what you want. This is how I believe it went down.

For reasons unknown to me, I was invited to a couple of Phil Spector's birthday parties, which were held each year at Montrose Bowl, a tiny, five-lane bowling alley done up in the same 1950s style it has always retained. Many of the local music freaks came to eat mediocre burgers and hot dogs and breathe the same air as the troubled genius record producer.

I stepped outside for some air at one point, just as Phil's limo was pulling up. He hugged me, saying what a big fan he was and how he loved my work. I mentioned this to my friend Art Fein, who said, "Don't take him too seriously; a half hour from now he's just as likely to pull a gun on you." I wondered if he knew I'd dated his ex-wife Ronnie. She believed he was having us followed the whole time we were seeing each other, although I didn't buy it.

While working on some reissues at Capitol Records during the SAG strike, I got to do seven Nat "King" Cole CDs and listen to that wonderful voice and piano playing of his. One thing that struck me about Nat was how he had a habit of clearing his throat before each take. Over the course of the two decades he recorded for Capitol, that cough got worse and worse, due to his cigarette habit, which he thought gave his voice the husky sound he wanted. It occurred to me that this would make an effective anti-smoking public service spot. Smokers might hear the deterioration and be inspired to quit. On the other hand, I've been told that the addiction to nicotine is harder to kick than heroin. So good luck to those who are struggling with this nasty habit. I hope you win. I am so grateful that I've never had a cigarette in my mouth.

Another thing that caused a girlfriend of mine to quit cigarettes was something Kim Basinger once told me. I'd asked her what it was like shooting the erotic movie *9½ Weeks* with Mickey Rourke, and she said, "We hated each other, wouldn't even ride up in the same elevator together."

"That must've made the love scenes difficult," I replied.

"You have no idea. He smoked like a chimney. Kissing him was like licking an ashtray."

I found some previously unissued songs of Nat's in the Capitol vault and released them for his many hardcore fans. I wrote extensively about him, becoming an even bigger fan than I already was.

This gave me the idea for Ray Charles to do a Nat "King" Cole tribute album, since Nat was one of Ray's main early influences. I spoke to Bruce Lundvall about it and he said that if I could convince Ray to do it for either Capitol or Blue Note, he would fund the project. I approached Ray with this proposal a number of times, but he refused each time. His only excuse was, "Once Nat sings a song, it belongs to him."

I countered with, "That's nonsense. What did people tell you when you wanted to do your country albums, the ones that made your career?" The stubborn cuss wouldn't listen to reason. I can't imagine the great Ray Charles being afraid of the comparisons people might make, but who knows? I am still convinced it would've been a Grammy winner and the first big seller he'd had in ages.

Finally, in September, the strike was over and the Cosby people put me back to work. Good old Bobby Roth hired me and the band in December for his movie *Dancing at the Harvest Moon* with Jacqueline Bisset, Valerie Harper, and a supporting cast culled from Bobby's little stock company. We did three songs, including an instrumental I wrote and taught the band on the spot in the studio.

Voiceover-wise, besides AM-PM and Cosby, I got the Toyota and Jiffy Lube accounts, so work was picking up, but although I was loving the historical and reissue work, I was missing performing my music.

Toward the end of June 2001 I took my son, Charlie, then twelve, on his first trip to New York. We stayed at the home of my friend Ralph Newman, a former executive at BMI, and did all the usual tourist stuff, the Statue of Liberty, Ellis Island, Rockefeller Center, Central Park, and the Guggenheim Museum. We even went to the top of the World Trade Center, a little over two months before that horrible event of September 11. There is a photo of Charlie and me, taken from the Statue of Liberty, showing the Twin Towers over our shoulders. Charlie kept a little shrine with that picture in his room for a long time.

He got to see his first Broadway show, a fantastic revival of *42nd Street*, with those fabulous songs by Harry Warren and Al Dubin, including "I Only Have Eyes for You" and the title tune. We also took a ride up to Stamford, Connecticut, where my former mother-in-law Betty lay dying of cancer. Charlie met my first wife, Maria's mother, Barbara, and Betty's husband, Fred, who made him feel like part of the family.

A wealthy guy who wanted to give his wife a special treat for her fortieth birthday hired her favorite band, the Beaters, to surprise her. She apparently used to come see us in LA when she was younger.

He flew us to Lake Okoboji, Iowa, where his family owned the local phone company and used to own the amusement park on the lake. I had forgotten how genuinely nice Midwesterners are. These people treated us, not like royalty, but like family. We got to eat Midwestern beef, which actually tasted like meat, as opposed to the cardboard facsimile we get in Los Angeles. It was a happy, sweet experience for nine jaded LA musicians.

On the flight back, a woman with a two-year-old and an infant sat next to me. Still in a mellow Midwestern mood, instead of letting crying children get to me, I offered to take the baby and laid it, face down, on my chest. It responded to my body's warmth—my body temperature has always been one degree higher than the normal 98.6—and was quiet the whole flight. I got up to walk it around the cabin. The guys saw this, and one cracked, "I know you work fast, BV, but damn!"

The mother was grateful and brought her husband to one of our gigs.

But generally, my life was in a rut. Between my alimony and expensive private school for Charlie, my need to earn was unrelenting. Doing voiceovers was the easiest way to make money, but I also took anything that came my way, even a small on-camera role.

When my friend Alan Swyer offered me a day's work playing a priest in his suspense movie, *A Time of Fear*, I jumped at it, as much to get myself out of that rut as for anything else. My scenes were shot down in Long Beach, so it got me out of town for a day, too.

I felt like a prisoner on a work-release program. By day, I was out driving to studios all over LA, selling computers and Mercury automobiles, telling people which TV programs to watch or which cheap restaurant to eat at, then going home, cooking myself a dinner, and collapsing into my easy chair and vegging out in front of the TV. I had no social life at all.

Then, in June of 2003, David Brokaw called. He said he was having a hard time getting a record deal for Lou Rawls and asked whether I had any ideas. I thought for a second and said, "I don't know about you, but I'm not too proud to use a gimmick. How about Old Brown Eyes Sings Old Blue Eyes, a tribute to Sinatra?" David loved it and made some calls, but came up dry.

At the time, I was doing some reissue work for the old jazz and R&B label Savoy Records. I approached them about Lou and they went for it. So we now had a home for the project.

And then it occurred to me that songs like "Come Fly with Me" could be used in TV commercials, and that if Lou owned the masters, he could make the licensing money if a client like American Airlines didn't want to pay for Sinatra's version. If Lou paid for the album and leased it to Savoy, instead of Savoy paying and owning it, he could own the record and be master of his own fate.

Lou and David loved the idea, and I went about the task of putting the album together. My first call was to Benny Golson, to have him write the arrangements for a ten-piece band. I wanted to record at Capitol and phoned the pretty studio manager, Paula Salvatore, who generously gave us a good price to record the album there.

Benny had horn players he wanted to use, and I respected his wishes. I hired the fine session pianist Mike Melvoin to rehearse Lou, get his keys, and play on the session. Mike was a hustler, though, and behind my back he begged Lou to let him write some of the charts. Lou, a typical people pleaser, didn't like to say no to anyone, so now, instead of Benny doing the whole album, I was stuck with Melvoin writing one-third of the charts. Benny, always the gentleman, was gracious about it.

Mike quoted me a price that was absurdly high, so I said, "I ain't paying you more than Benny Golson, man. Benny's a fucking legend, so either come down or don't take the job." He backed down, but it left a bad taste in my mouth. He also insisted on using his own trio. The day of the first session, his bass player showed up forty-five minutes late, while a roomful of musicians sat there, twiddling their thumbs. I was pissed, but the guys were all pros and we got everything done in the three hours allotted by union rules.

Benny's arrangements were gorgeous, as always. He is a master arranger. After years of not playing saxophone, he'd been back on the European jazz festival circuit and was playing beautifully, as can be heard on "In the Wee Small Hours of the Morning" and "All the Way" on Lou's album.

Lou's voice was in rough shape and he was badly in need of an operation. Normally, he was strong as a bull, but this time I could tell he had no more than three takes of each song in him, so I paced him like a racehorse with a bad leg and later combined takes to get good vocals. For the most part, only a few could tell the difference.

On "The Lady Is a Tramp," I asked Lou if he'd ever done any scat singing; to my surprise, he said no, so I suggested he try it. He did so, in one take, and got a big round of applause from the guys in the band.

One potential problem was Lou's girlfriend, later to be his third wife. She was bad news, very controlling and always wanting to put her two cents in. I had to cut her down to size at the beginning of the sessions, giving her little tasks, like downloading the lyrics off a computer, to distract her and keep her from butting in. Privately, Lou appreciated me standing up to her and later told me so. He asked me to come to the photo shoot for the cover, something he'd never done in the past. She was a nuisance there, too, trying to tell the photographer how to shoot pictures. Photographers are artists and don't like being bossed around by amateurs. Somehow, I managed to keep the photographer from walking off the job.

The album came out on Savoy and remained on the *Billboard* jazz chart for over six months. Sadly, it would be Lou's final record before he passed away from cancer.

My father died in January of 2004, after a long deterioration. It had been sad, seeing dementia take its toll. Little by little, conversation with this once-bright man had become more difficult, as he'd forget what we were talking about halfway through a sentence. I was happy that both he and my mother had lived long enough to see their son have some success in the music business, as well as in Daddy's field, announcing. I was now an orphan. At his funeral, the whole family, including my daughter, Maria, went down to San Diego, and I got choked up when I spoke on his behalf.

He was a good and decent man who could always be counted on to do the right thing, the honorable thing. He was not without flaws. He had a temper and little patience for children. They made him nervous and he was likely to snap at them when they were being boisterous or just being kids. Late in life, he recognized this tendency and told me it made him happy to see that I was a better father than he'd been.

Voiceover clients inevitably come and go; this year, a new stable client, Burger King, came in and picked up the slack. Billy Vera and the Beaters celebrated our twenty-fifth anniversary with a performance on the Santa Monica Pier in August that drew several thousand people. How many bands stay together that long, even ones with more sustained commercial success than we had?

Part of our secret may be the pride I was able to instill in the players, the sure knowledge that they were part of something that mattered: a band that could stand up to any other, the best band in town. While other horn bands who followed in our wake were content to play in the Stax/Volt style, the songs we played gave us a style unique to us. Not just another dance band, the Beaters played, in the words of saxophonist Lon Price, "nuanced music," music on a level of quality with jazz, music that required care and intelligence in the playing.

One thing I'd always tried to do was to encourage each guy to find his own voice on his instrument. This was not the norm in an age when every saxophonist, it seemed, wanted to sound like either Tom Scott or David Sanborn. I told them what the old-timers had told me, "If you ain't different, you ain't shit." It's been gratifying to see how, over the years, each long-term Beater has found a voice of his own. When you see me smiling during their solos, it's because I enjoy listening to their playing so much.

Later that year, my friend, screenwriter and producer Sally Robinson, was doing a pilot for TV and asked me to be in it, playing a Sunset Strip denizen, a hipster (in the old sense of the word) who knows everybody and everything on the street. The show was about a kid who inherits the Roxy and his struggles to keep the club a going concern. I think I was the only one in the cast who was over thirty.

The thing I dug about this show was that it was unscripted. In each scene, we were given a road map of what had to happen, and then we made up our own dialogue. Some of the ad-libbing got to be pretty wild. I loved it and was surprised at how well I took to this process. Sally was very happy with my work and had plans to expand my role if the show got sold, but, unfortunately, none of the networks picked it up.

This reminds me of another pilot, this one produced by Dick Clark. As I've said, Dick was very loyal to those who had made him, and he wanted to do something for Frankie Avalon. So he had his writers come up with a sitcom where Frankie would play a has-been teen idol who was now living in a small apartment in the Valley, surviving on oldies shows and rock 'n' roll cruises. He's the kind of guy who keeps a stack of eight-by-ten glossies at the door, to tip delivery boys, in lieu of cash.

Frankie's son, played by Michael Damian, comes home, giving up med school to become a rock star. Hilarity ensues. I played one of Frankie's old teen idol cronies who comes over each week for spaghetti and poker. I'll always remember hearing Dick's laugh. What a great, enthusiastic audience he was.

CBS was on the verge of picking up the show when there was a sudden regime change at the network. What always happens in those cases is that the new regime dumps anything pending from the old and brings in their own people. Frankie's show never got made.

For several years I announced the Annual Choreography Awards, which I enjoyed immensely. I loved seeing the gorgeous young dancers strutting their stuff and the great terpsichorean legends who appeared onstage. They also screened rare film clips of the great dancers from the past.

Honi Coles, whom I knew as the Apollo's stage manager, had been half of the great class tap act Coles and Atkins. His partner, Cholly Atkins, went on to Motown Records and taught the acts there how to dance. He said the most difficult had been the Four Tops, who "couldn't dance a lick," so he gave them the simple step you see them do on their hit "I Can't Help Myself." The Temptations were another story; all five were great on their feet and their routines were spectacular to see.

One of my few regrets in show business is that I never learned to tap dance. I've always loved the great tap masters, like Sammy Davis, Jr.; Stump and Stumpy; the Nicholas Brothers; and, of course, Fred Astaire. Unfortunately, tap wasn't considered cool when I was coming up.

Given my sedentary life, I suppose it was only natural that I'd start putting on weight. At my annual checkup, my doctor said I needed to lose forty pounds. I told him I didn't eat much and he asked what I did eat. He told me to cut out the Pepsi, the pasta and cookies. I could eat all the meat, chicken, and fish I wanted, all the fruits and vegetables, and drink water, and should come in once a month so he could check me out. I was also allowed to "eat bad" once a week as a reward.

Miraculously, I somehow managed to find the will power to do as I was told and, over the course of nine months, lost fifty-five pounds. I was down to my fighting weight when Danny Robinson called with an offer to appear on a summer replacement show called *Hit Me Baby One More Time*, a faux-contest show featuring people who'd had hits during the 1980s. Each artist would sing a truncated version of his or her own hit plus a current song.

I was able to fit into my best suit and looked good on camera. The day after the show aired, my Varèse Sarabande CD, only a year old, moved up on Amazon several thousand slots, surprising Cary Mansfield, who ran the company. What great timing. Talk about a reward for losing the weight!

I had attended way too many funerals in the new millennium so far—Charles Brown, Curtis Mayfield, Mable Scott, Floyd Dixon, and my songwriting partner Lowell Fulson, to name just five. But the first months of 2006 brought two passings that were even more painful. First came Lou Rawls. His road manager, John, called to say that he was at Cedars-Sinai Hospital, near my house, and wanted to see me.

I went over there and he was down to about eighty pounds. It was clear that it wouldn't be long. In full denial mode, he talked about making an album of his old friend Sam Cooke's songs, which he forgot he'd done some years before. I could see it was the powerful painkillers talking, so I went along with him and we sang some of Sam's tunes in the hospital room together. It was the last time I would see him.

A month later, my daughter, Maria, called to tell me that her boyfriend Steve, with whom she'd been living in Chicago, had died suddenly. They'd been at their respective AA meetings in the same building and Steve had fallen and begun to bleed from his throat. Within three hours he was dead. I asked my stepmother, Olga, a former nurse, and she said this often happens to alcoholics. A deteriorated liver can cause the thin membrane of the esophagus to weaken and rupture.

Rosalee and I got on a plane to take care of my daughter, who was inconsolable. I'd never seen such grief. She was so out of control that it scared the shit out of me. At almost forty years old, she had finally found a man she wanted to marry. Fortunately, she had a support system that gave her all the love and affection she needed to get through it. She had lost her mother and all her grandparents in such a short period of time, it was a miracle of her program that she never slipped and went back to the booze.

Another passing that came out of nowhere around that time was that of Joel Dorn. Dorn was one of the hippest cats in the room. A product of Philadelphia, he parlayed a gig as a jazz disc jockey in his hometown into taking over as head of the jazz department at Atlantic Records when Nesuhi Ertegun decided to step back from his duties. Joel took Atlantic into the future, producing acts like Roberta Flack and Les McCann. He later ran labels of his own.

When you reach a certain level of hipness, there are very few cats you can talk with about the more eclectic nuances of music and those who make the music we love. Joel was one of those guys. Whenever I'd pick up the phone and hear his voice, I knew I was in for an hour or more of deep musical conversation.

He gave me a few gigs writing notes for his projects and talked about wanting to do a jazz album with me. Apparently, he'd gotten the idea after running into into both Hank Crawford and Benny Golson one day

213

on Fifty-Seventh Street. Both of them had talked about working with me on the Lou Rawls albums and wanting to make a record with me. Alas, it was never to be. Joel died suddenly, a few days after completing one of his life's dreams, a five-CD box set of Atlantic jazz, a tribute to Nesuhi.

The year 2007 marked the sixtieth anniversary of the greatest independent label of them all, Atlantic Records. Due in part to my early connection to the company, my friend James Austin offered me the job of producing a box set of the label's vocal groups. I accepted on the condition that I be allowed to do a blues box and a soul box of second- and third-tier hits, rather than rehash the same tired old chestnuts the fans already have on twenty other compilations. James indulged me, and off I went to produce three of my all-time favorite projects.

Atlantic's former owners, Ahmet Ertegun and Jerry Wexler, were not vocal group fans. Jerry hated that they tend to sing out of tune, and Ahmet didn't care for the idea of having to deal with four or five egos instead of one. The company was blessed with three of the best vocal groups ever in the Clovers, the Coasters, and the greatest of them all, the Drifters. They also had a number of groups that had one or two hits, or none at all.

The original founders, Ahmet and Herb Abramson, were Harlem-crazed blues and jazz fans and record collectors, and those tastes influenced the label's earliest releases. Their first hit, "Drinkin' Wine Spo-De-O-De," by Stick McGhee, was a jailhouse blues, and over the years some of the greatest bluesmen and women made records for the label: Joe Turner, Jimmy Witherspoon, Professor Longhair, Champion Jack Dupree, and Esther Phillips, for starters.

Some of the greatest soul music stars have recorded for Atlantic; Ray Charles, Aretha Franklin, Wilson Pickett, and Solomon Burke are just the tip of the iceberg. The list is endless. I got to include some killer lesser-known tracks and obscure items galore that had never been reissued on CD.

19

All That Jazz

J erry Wexler called me "one of the best vault men in the business," meaning he liked my way of doing reissues of old recordings. He also said, "The only problem with being a vault man is, eventually you get to the bottom of the vault."

And so, as much of the great rhythm-and-blues music of the 1940s and fifties—my special area of expertise—found its way onto CD, I expanded my scope and began to become more involved in jazz. Michael Cuscuna, with his longtime involvement with Blue Note and his own Mosaic Records, was and remains the master of jazz reissues. For me, by comparison, it was just dabbling.

But I did get to release some important music. For Vee-Jay, I put out catalog items by Eddie Harris, Wayne Shorter, Lee Morgan, Wynton Kelly, little-known alto saxophonist Frank Strozier, and vocalist Bill Henderson. On Specialty, I released CDs by Elmo Hope, Frank Rosolino, Gerald Wiggins, and Buddy Collette. On Savoy, I did a set of early Billy Eckstine singing love ballads and the complete Jimmy Scott recordings, in addition to compilations of rare early items on that seminal bebop label. Then there were those seven Nat "King" Cole packages for Capitol that I mentioned earlier.

However, my proudest moments reissuing jazz were celebrations of the one-hundredth birthdays of two of my idols, Duke Ellington and Count Basie. For Duke, I was hired by EMI London to compile a centennial tribute culled from EMI-owned labels: Capitol, United Artists, and a few tracks from a Roulette album that Ellington made with Louis Armstrong, the only meeting on record of these two titans of jazz. Playing in Satchmo's band at the time was New Orleans clarinetist Barney Bigard, who'd played with Duke in the early years and cowrote

"Mood Indigo." I thought it only fitting to include the lovely version from these sessions.

Duke signed with Capitol in 1953, during a down period of his career, recording some great, if generally commercially unsuccessful, music. It was at the label that he recorded his last jukebox hit, "Satin Doll." On United Artists, he made a trio album with younger giants Charles Mingus and Max Roach. All in all, I put together a very satisfying album by arguably the most important musical figure of the first half of the twentieth century.

For the Count, I did two double CD sets. One was a reissue of a rare Roulette box set of late-fifties and early sixties remakes of his old hits from the 1930s and forties. The other, *Count Basie and Friends: 100th Birthday Bash*, included vocals by major stars like Nat "King" Cole; Tony Bennett; Sarah Vaughan; Billy Eckstine; Lambert, Hendricks and Ross; and the man Basie called his "number one son," Joe Williams, along with some of the best instrumentals the band recorded for Roulette during the Count's "New Testament" period. I still listen to this one often.

I produced a pair of Nina Simone CDs, one for Blue Note of her Colpix material, and the other for Verve of her major recordings for Phillips. Somehow, Nina heard an obscure song of mine called "Behind the Wall," written after reading a book entitled *The Walls Came Tumbling Down*, about the desanctification of a church during which the bones of dead babies were found buried in the foundation and walls. The song is told from the point of view of a convent gardener whose spouse, a midwife, commits this crime, goes mad with guilt, and runs off into a stormy night, never to be seen again, just the kind of story only Nina Simone could carry off. Her postcard said she loved the song and regretted not having a record deal so she could record it.

Rhino was now the catalog arm of Warner Bros. Records, which included Atlantic. Along with the other Ray Charles sets I'd worked on, I thought it might be nice to do one called *Blues + Jazz*, with one CD featuring Ray's jazz side. It was very well received. Also, for Rhino's *Masters of Jazz* series, I produced several multi-artist volumes dedicated to male and female vocalists, big bands, and jazz chart hits.

Saxophonist Lon Price, an original member of the Beaters, and I had been performing as a duo every couple of years, just for the fun of playing different songs and getting out of my rut. I'm not much of a piano player—I tell people I play like a songwriter—but I get by well enough to accompany my singing, and the audience seems to like the stories I tell about each song.

In 2008, we started doing a once-a-month gig at an old Italian restaurant in the San Fernando Valley called Vitello's, which has a performance room upstairs that features lesser-known jazz acts. Vitello's is best known as the place where actor Robert Blake did or did not shoot his wife. We did pretty good business and had a lot of fun making new fans and giving the old ones something new.

Some of my old soap opera friends came to see us, including that grand old dame of *The Young and the Restless*, Jeanne Cooper, who portrayed Mrs. Katherine Chancellor for some forty years. She was quite a character who had been through it all. Like her *Y&R* character, she was a recovering alcoholic and made no bones about it. Old enough not to care what people thought about her, she was quick with an opinion, too. I remember sitting next to her one night when she and other cast members had been roped into going to see the significant other of a certain cast member perform locally. Every song sounded the same. We were both getting itchy when she elbowed me and, in a stage whisper, said, "He really sucks, doesn't he?" After that, we couldn't look at each other for fear of breaking out in the giggles. She was a great old broad.

Lon and I were asked to perform for her eightieth birthday at the home of Lee Phillips Bell, who, along with her late husband Bill, created both *Y&R* and *The Bold and the Beautiful*. All of Jeanne's favorite cast members were there and beauty was on duty, so many gorgeous, well-turned-out soap stars, my eyes were popping all night.

It was a sad day when Jeanne passed away in 2013. *Y&R* did a beautiful two-day tribute to the show's most beloved star.

Since we're talking about soap stars, I guess it's as good a time as any to explain something about the women in my life whose names haven't turned up in these pages, especially given that *Soap Opera Digest* once named me the "Soap Opera Groupie of the Year" because of my habit of dating soap actresses.

You have to bear in mind that a lot of the women I dated back then were awfully young and, in some cases, wild when I knew them, and most are leading relatively respectable lives today, many with children who don't need to see in print what Mommy was doing with a rock 'n' roll singer during the 1980s.

I have always believed that it is the woman's prerogative to kiss and tell. A gentleman keeps his yap shut. So, to all the women I've known who are not mentioned in this book, it's out of my respect for your privacy, not because you didn't matter to me.

My late shrink, a brilliant old lady named Dena Whitebook, born in Harlem back when Central Harlem was a Jewish enclave, and raised on the Grand Concourse in the Bronx, treated me for a very long time and was a great help in solving a number of my issues. She was largely responsible for me figuring out how to become successful in this business I love.

Therapy certainly worked for me in business. The thing that makes entertainers want, or need, to get on that stage and sing, dance, and tell jokes comes from a need to be liked, to be loved. The love we get from all those folks out there behind the lights is a drug, and it's highly addictive. We get into trouble when that need spills over into real life. I recall one actress who would change her opinions every time someone expressed an opposing one. She was like the wind, desperately afraid that this or that person might not like her. Even her friends would sadistically make fun of her, pretending to take a stand on something or other just to see her change her mind. She was an extreme example, but an all-too-common one.

And then there was the young soap star, soon to be a movie star, who, the morning after she came home with me after a gig, went out to buy me breakfast and woke me with the sound of the vacuum cleaner going over the floors of my apartment. Her desperate need for love and approval was transparent in those eyes that have captivated movie audiences ever since.

I wasn't that bad, but I did need to change my ways and become more assertive. Assertive, not aggressive. One example: there was a guy in the band who played well, but there were problems. As the night went on he would play louder and busier, playing over other people's solos. When introduced, he'd take flamboyant bows. The other guys were complaining about him, insisting I do something. When I wondered why he acted this way, someone said, "Look under his piano at the end of the night." One night I did and there were at least fifteen beer bottles. Ah, so it was the beer. The band was on the verge of mutiny if I didn't fire this guy. The problem was, I was terrified of firing people, for fear this person, who likely didn't like me all that much in the first place, wouldn't like me. I was like the Duke and the Count, who always let people fire themselves.

It took several sessions with Dena before I got up the courage to speak to him. I ended up taking him to lunch and quickly ascertained that there was no reasoning with the guy. Nothing was his fault. Like most hard-core drunks, he was a master of self-justification. Luckily, Dena had given me the words to use, so I told him I was changing the sound of the band and needed someone to take it in a different direction. A little white lie, but this guy was unable to accept the truth.

Another thing I learned from my therapy was to observe others in my business and in life, both those who are successful and those who are not. There is much to be learned from both success and failure. Time management and priorities, for instance.

I was dating a popular television actress and marveled at how she managed to fit so many things into her day. For example, when she wanted to see a friend, she would find the time, even if it was only half an hour. Being English, she'd meet them for tea, then run off to her next appointment.

Her opposite was a guy who was in the band briefly. I'd tell him I wanted a rehearsal, say next Tuesday. He'd hesitate, mulling it over in his mind a moment, then reply without irony, "Uh, I planned to go to the post office next Tuesday. I don't think I can make it." The attempt to explain to him that a trip to his post office would have taken no more than twenty minutes didn't penetrate. Another extreme example, but you get the point: observe how winners conduct their lives, and losers, too. There is much to learn, about what to do and what not to do.

Many of Dena's patients were in show business, most of them actresses, in her words, "from the biggest stars to the biggest nobodies, and everything in between." A few of these were women I brought to her.

Dena saw me through more affairs of the heart than I care to remember. "You know what your problem is?" she quipped. "You are only attracted to exceptionally beautiful women. The trouble is, exceptionally beautiful women tend to be exceptionally fucked up."

I believe my proclivity stems from the time I spent as a little boy in those dressing rooms being pampered and petted by all those beautiful, half-naked dancers and singers. I admit it's not something that has served me particularly well. I've noticed that, in show business, relationships with people whose careers aren't riding on their looks seem to last longer. At 72, I'm still alone, envying those lasting partnerships. It is an issue of mine that I wish I could get past.

When my second marriage broke up, I asked couples I knew in long-term marriages what their secret was. The one constant answer that kept coming up was "acceptance." Accept the flaws, whether it be that crooked tooth she has or that he always leaves the toilet seat up.

Looking back over my romantic life, I can recall a high percentage of narcissistic women. As Dena said, "Of all the actresses I've treated, not one, let me repeat, *not one* was not narcissistic. In fact, you are the only entertainer I've ever met who is not a narcissist. You are the victim of narcissists. The good news is that, after all we've been through together in this room, you probably know more about the narcissistic personality than most shrinks."

The seductive thing about a narcissist is that, when you first meet one, you are the greatest, best-looking, smartest, kindest, funniest, best lover—any superlative you can name—she or he has ever met. You are perfection, that is, until she captures you and feels confident she has won your heart. At that point, she gets bored and looks around for a new challenge, at which point you can lay odds that you are on the way out.

I've lived out this scenario more times than I'd like to admit. It's embarrassing. Guys in this town who seem not to be affected by this kind of woman are the ones who have become jaded and lost the vulnerability that makes love so sweet. They don't take narcissists seriously, because they don't take anyone seriously. Or, as another shrink told me about one narcissist I wanted to break up with, "Tell her you're madly in love with her, can't live without her, and she'll run so fast your head will spin. The reason you can't get rid of her now is that you refuse to say 'I love you.' You're still a challenge."

One must never make the mistake of confronting narcissists about the bad things they do. Even though they love talking about themselves, they don't take criticism well. They interpret criticism as a "narcissistic wound," which must be met with a "narcissistic rage." These rages can get pretty ugly. The narcissist will have her revenge. Trust me on that one. I have paid the price, in spades.

Yet this hopeless romantic hasn't given up. Although romance hasn't worked out for me so far and, at my age, might never, I am thankful that I can still lose my heart to a pretty girl, even if it doesn't turn out the way I hope.

Some fifteen years since I'd last performed back home, the city of Stamford, Connecticut, contacted Danny Robinson about me appearing at a Billy Vera Homecoming Day at a small park in the center of town on July 31, 2008.

I contacted a local bandleader I knew named Billy Frenz and asked him to put together a group with the same instrumentation as the Beaters to back me for the show.

In order to have time to see as many old friends as possible, I took a week off and made plans to stay at Michael Cuscuna's house in Stamford. It was great to hang out with Michael and other dear friends and eat the great Italian food that's so hard to find in LA.

Billy Frenz arranged for a friend's company to video the show with a three-camera shoot and sound taken off the board. It made for a nice memento and can be seen on YouTube if you type in "East Coast Beaters," the name I gave the band. I had so much fun that I've managed to find a way to get a booking that allows me to get back home each year since.

To celebrate the seventieth anniversary of the great jazz label Blue Note Records, the company threw a party at the Club Nokia in downtown LA. Cuscuna was unable to attend, so he and Bruce asked me to speak in his place. There were some terrific performances by artists like Natalie Cole and saxophonist Joe Lovano. When it came my turn to speak, I stood at the podium and spotted Red Holloway, a wonderful sax player who had played on many of my favorite Chicago R&B records of the 1950s. It occurred to me that Red had never received the recognition he deserved, so I opened my remarks by telling the crowd that I was "an old doo-wopper from the streets, and the first doo-wop record I ever bought as a kid was 'Oh What a Nite,' by the Dells. And the lovely sax solo on that record was by the man sitting right here in front of me now, Red Holloway." The smile on Red's face as the audience gave him his props made it all worthwhile.

I went on to tell of how, when Michael and I were producing Lou Rawls, he was having a hard time singing my song "If I Were a Magician." It was a song requiring him to be vulnerable and take the loss, something he wasn't used to. Lou's forte was songs where he came out on top, as in "Your Good Thing (Is About to End)" and "You'll Never Find Another Love Like Mine."

So we took him out to dinner and got him drunk, so drunk that he walked right up into the back of a delivery truck without realizing what he was doing. The driver said, "Holy shit! It's Lou Rawls," to which Lou replied with his trademark "Yeah, buddy." The next morning, he came in suffering with a bad hangover. I told him to "use it in your performance," and boy, did he ever get vulnerable, for one of the most tender performances of his life.

The Internet was changing the world as we knew it. Websites, Google, at first MySpace, and later Facebook and Twitter became the new ways of promoting one's self and career. It was a way for old friends to find each other and to meet new friends and fans. To give you an example, a guy contacted me on Facebook and, as they say, "friended" me. He said he'd been Johnny Carson's bodyguard at NBC and had always wanted to let me know that I was Johnny's second-favorite singer, after Tony Bennett. As with Sinatra, and as thrilled as I was to know that Carson felt that way about me, I was sad that I'd never get to hear it from the great man himself.

Thanks also to the Internet, MySpace in this case, I became friends with a beautiful woman who worked under her first two names, Julia Ann, as one of the most famous stars in the adult industry.

Julia Ann Tavella said she was a big fan of mine, and I knew her work, too. She came to see me at Vitello's with her mother, and I went downtown to hang out with her at her booth at a huge adult industry event at the Convention Center. Her fans, male and female, couples too, were lined up for autographs and to have their picture taken with the gorgeous star. She was as kind and generous to those fans as any mainstream celebrity I've ever seen. In fact, many celebs could take lessons from Julia Ann on how to treat their fans.

As we got to know each other, she invited me to a Labor Day barbecue at the home of her aunt Marianna, where I met her whole family and her friends from both inside and outside the industry. It was as wholesome as any family gathering you can imagine, and her family clearly loved her dearly.

For her fortieth birthday, Julia and a group celebrated by coming to see the band. I bought her a nice, inscribed cake and got the whole club to sing "Happy Birthday."

One day she called saying that the eighth anniversary of Porn Star Karaoke was coming up at a Valley restaurant called Sardo's, where they hold that event each Tuesday night. She said, "All these jerkballs get up there and mutilate your song. Wouldn't it be cool if you came up and sang it for everyone?" I told her I'd do it, but only if she would introduce me. She said okay.

The night of the party, I entered the parking lot and spotted Julia in front of the place, being interviewed by the gossip show *TMZ*. Seeing me, she shouted, "There's Billy Vera. You should interview him, too," and we did a duo interview, letting them speculate whether or not we were a couple.

Later in the evening, I went up and sang "At This Moment" to the squeals and screams of a roomful of porn stars and fans. I got a lot of hugs and kisses and went home a happy man.

Contrary to what one might expect, the few adult stars I've known are very sweet girls who just happen to be more open about the things that they, and most people, do in private.

On November 10, 2010, I was invited to be one of the honorees at an event celebrating the fiftieth anniversary of the Hollywood Walk of Fame. Among the many celebrities there, big and small, who had stars on that fabled walk were Mickey Rooney, Barbara Eden, Jane Russell, Stan Freberg, Mamie Van Doren, Nancy Sinatra, Tippi Hedren, Pat Boone, Della Reese, Connie Stevens, Patti Page, David Hasselhoff, and Arsenio Hall.

I mentioned to Tippi that I'd acted in a play with her daughter, Melanie Griffith, playing a scuzzy drug dealer who seduces her. I also told her that, when I was eight years old, I'd stuffed the ballot box when she ran for Miss Rheingold Beer, a New York beverage that's no longer in business.

Celebrity photographer Harry Langdon took a picture of all of us in the Grand Ballroom of the Hollywood and Highland complex. Being there as part of this esteemed group made me feel like a member of the club.

Michael Bublé was becoming one of the biggest stars in the land, filling a vacuum for a modern Sinatra or Bobby Darin. His main appeal was to females, from sixteen to sixty-five.

Every so often, I go on YouTube and check for songs I've written, to see if anyone new has recorded them. This one day, I came across a live version of "At This Moment" by Bublé. Excited, I went to Amazon to see if it was on any of his albums and was happy to find that it was included on his latest upcoming release.

When the CD came out a couple of weeks later, it entered the charts at number one. It ultimately would sell over nine million copies, providing me with a huge windfall.

Meanwhile, on Facebook, I met a young singer named Tamela D'Amico. She told me she was a fan, so I checked YouTube for any videos of her. I liked what I heard and saw, and before long we became friends. She invited me to her big-band show at Catalina's Jazz Club in Hollywood. The girl was terrific. Not only did she sing well, in the pop/jazz vein, but she related to the audience in the same way that the great old-school show people did.

As our friendship bloomed, she told me I should go off in that direction and make a big-band album myself. Tamela was a real go-getter who I knew could make things happen. She offered me her arranger, Chris Walden, who I learned was one of the most in-demand arrangers around today.

All I needed was to figure out how to make my album different enough to stand out amidst the plethora of big-band albums everybody and his brother seemed to be making lately. Someone said, "What do you know better than anyone else?" And then it hit me. "I know black music and black showbiz really well. I'll do a tribute to the great black songwriters of the twenties, thirties, and forties, like Duke Ellington, Count Basie, Buddy Johnson, and James P. Johnson."

So that's what we did. We booked Capitol's famed Studio A, where Sinatra, Dino, Nat Cole, Peggy Lee, and Nancy Wilson had made all their classics, and booked eighteen of the best jazz musicians in LA. I picked some great songs, like "Since I Fell for You" and Louis Armstrong's theme song, "When It's Sleepytime Down South," plus a duet of Tamela and me singing "I'll Never Be Free," the song I sang at Paul Gayten's funeral. We made a killer album, courtesy of one of the checks from the Bublé CD.

But before all that, I had some medical issues to deal with. My PSA was getting higher, indicating a possible problem with my prostate. The doctor said we needed to keep an eye on it; meanwhile, I prepared to head to New York for the *TVLand Awards*, where they were honoring *Family Ties*. The entire cast would be there, and as they ran clips from the show, I would sing "At This Moment."

The show was one of the best-organized events I've ever been to. Each of the "talent," as the performers are called, had our own "wrangler" to take us where we had to be next. We were put up at the Loew's Regency, the finest hotel on Park Avenue, and had a limo at our disposal to take us where we needed to go. Big time star treatment, all the way.

The day I got back, Dr. Steven Sacks, reputedly the best urologist in LA, did a biopsy, which revealed a tiny bit of early cancer. Tests were done to determine whether it had spread beyond the gland itself. It hadn't, so I was given four options: ignore it, since prostate cancer is slow-moving and it's likely you'll die from any number of other maladies before it gets you; external beam radiation; radioactive seeds planted in the gland; or surgical removal. I spoke with a number of men who'd had the surgery, and all were glad they'd done it. Plus, I wanted that damn cancer out of me, so I decided to have it removed.

Dr. Sacks explained the process. The surgery was done robotically, by computer. Six arms enter through holes in your abdomen, a camera goes through a slit just below the belly button to allow the surgeon to direct the procedure, and the prostate is removed through another slit above the penis. It wasn't going to be anybody's idea of fun, but I had decided to man up and get it done.

In May, prior to my surgery, my boy, Charlie, became the first person in my family to graduate college, with a music degree from Loyola

Marymount University. It was a proud day for all of us. In June of 2014, my daughter, Maria, would become the second.

The few people who knew about my operation were informed on a need-to-know basis. I'm not a big believer in burdening people with my troubles. That's what shrinks are for. No "poor me" pity party on Facebook for this boy. The band didn't even know.

On July 5, 2011, Rosalee drove me to Cedars-Sinai to undergo prostate surgery. This woman who once hated the ground I walked on stayed in the hospital with me and at my house for five days, feeding me and getting up in the middle of the night to empty my piss bag. Whatever problems we had over the years, she's always been someone who can be counted on to come through in an emergency.

I recovered quickly, and one month to the day later I was onstage again, singing my little heart out, two nights in a row.

We made the album, my first in some years, in November. I loved the experience of recording live in studio with all those amazing musicians. In Capitol Studio A, you can feel the history. The ghosts of Frank, Nat, and Dino were in the room, making sure we lived up to the standard they'd set.

My friend Tim Hauser of the Manhattan Transfer came by to encourage me and let me know that I was on the right track. He said my singing was better than ever, the phrasing more mature, and he made a point of remarking on how I held certain notes so that I could extend a word or phrase into the next one without taking a breath. He was such a supportive friend.

Tamela insisted that I include a big-band version of "At This Moment." I thought it only right that we bring in Jerry Peterson, who played that emotional alto sax solo on the original version, to repeat his feat. Beater Lon Price played exceptional solos on "If I Could Be with You (One Hour Tonight)" and "Room with a View," which arranger Chris Walden turned into a Basie-like extravaganza worthy of Joe Williams. And former Beater Darrell Leonard played some beautiful trumpet solos on "Since I Fell for You" and "When It's Sleepytime Down South," evoking the spirit of Louis Armstrong on the latter.

To promote the album and let the world know I was stretching my wings into new territory, I embarked on a series of big-band personal appearances. The first was at the Syracuse Jazzfest, where Lon and I fronted an eighteen-piece band before a crowd of some thirty thousand jazz fans. The promoter, Frank Malfitano, raved and said we were one of the most exciting acts he'd ever presented in the many years he'd put on the festival.

Rob Christie, a fellow both Tamela and I knew from Capitol, started a little label of his own called Robo Records, mainly dedicated to what are euphemistically called "veteran" acts. His roster included Monkee Mickey Dolenz, Sheila E., and the Bangles. We played him the album and he wanted to release it.

I had my doubts that a photograph of my sixty-something-year-old mug would sell many records, so, remembering the great jazz album covers of the 1950s, I decided on artwork for the cover. To that end, I hired artist Roy Ruiz Clayton to paint me in a modernistic mode. His rendering made for a gorgeous, striking cover.

Rob put the album up on iTunes and Amazon, for downloading only, with plans to manufacture CDs later. We did some publicity and set up a date to debut the album at Catalina's, Hollywood's top jazz club. Beater saxman Terry Landry, who also played in the late Gerald Wilson's band, put together a hip eighteen-piece group for the occasion, and ticket sales ensured a full house.

Christie pressed up some four-song promo CDs to give away at the gig, where he introduced me from the stage as one of his "favorite all-time artists." The show was a smash, but when Catalina's had us back in February, there were still no CDs to sell. Something was up. As it turned out, Christie was not able to deliver the album as we had hoped. We needed physical product and distribution, so I got control of the album again. Luckily, my old friends at Varèse Sarabande picked it up and it was released in 2015 under Universal Music Group distribution.

20
Grammy Time!

Later that week, after four nominations, I finally won my first Grammy, for best album notes for the Ray Charles box set, *Singular Genius: The Complete ABC Singles*. I'd been recommended for the job by my old friends David Brokaw and Fantasy's Bill Belmont, and I thanked them from the stage.

For the first time since I'd started getting nominations, I shamelessly lobbied on Facebook, asking voting members to please consider me. Concord Records made five videos, very well done, that featured me talking about Ray and his career at ABC-Paramount. I'd post one of these on my FB page a couple times a week. They made me look like I knew what I was talking about, so I guess they worked.

I, who am scrupulous about promptness, almost didn't make it on time the day of the award ceremony. The hairdresser hired for my date, the young actress Augie Duke, showed up to my house late. The limo driver, a fan named Paul Leider, had gone out of his way to surprise me with a Rolls Royce and was waiting outside. Finally Augie's hair was done and we took off, speeding downtown.

We reached our seats and were about to sit down when my name was called. I ran down the aisle, Augie trailing behind, shooting pictures with her cell phone, screaming all the way, "You fucking won, you fucking won!"

I arrived at the podium, breathless, took a beat, and said, "Holy shit!" The audience cracked up. My acceptance speech was short and sweet and we went backstage for interviews with the press.

The award was, for me, vindication. I knew I was a well-respected writer and authority on this music, but I'd never gotten the physical proof. It had hurt to not have awards for my work, despite the fact that my peers, like Michael Cuscuna, Bob Porter, James Austin, and the late Pete Welding, treated me as an equal. I was always the guy called in at the last minute, when another writer missed his deadline, because I write quickly and accurately. Rhino's editorial staff voted me the writer who needed less fact-checking than any other.

So, unlike some of my pals who are jaded about awards, I am very proud and very grateful for that shiny item that sits on that shelf in my living room.

In the spring of 2013, I took the big band north to play the Bakersfield Jazz Festival, where they burned, as usual. Then it was off to New York City, to play my first Manhattan date in many years. Jimmy Scott's pianist, Alex Minasian, and I had become friends, and he put together a big band of young local jazz players, including the wonderful bassist Brandi Disterheft, formerly with Oscar Peterson, who also makes albums of her own.

We played the Cutting Room, a hip club on East Thirty-Second Street. Many old friends and fans showed up, including some of my old Harlem doo-wop buddies from the Harptones and the Willows. Michael Cuscuna introduced me, and we had a great time.

While in town, Michael and I had lunch with Bruce Lundvall and taped two episodes of his radio show, *The Blue Note Hour*. It was sad to see Bruce, the last of the great record men, suffering from Parkinson's disease. His sense of humor was intact, and he appreciated it when we made fun of the way he was talking, instead of treating him like a victim. I hope my friends are as irreverent with me when my time comes.

Speaking of the aging process, I must be reaching the age Benny Golson was referring to when he said, "When I turned forty-five, I couldn't get arrested. Then I turned sixty-five, and I became a legend." Benny's been working the jazz festival circuit ever since.

It's been happening that way for me recently. Hardly a week goes by when I don't get a request for an interview on radio or TV or in print. It looks like I've finally reached a place where I'm being taken seriously.

Appearances with the Beaters and the big band, in LA and New York, continue. We've made an animated video (by DreamWorks artist Ron Yavnieli) for "Room with a View," and there is a BV documentary in the works, so there's much to look forward to these days.

Writing this book has brought back so many memories of dear friends and family, here and gone; mentors who taught me so much about this business I love; the women, both faithless and true, who filled my heart with feelings I've been able to express in my songs; and the wonderful musicians who've helped make my music come alive. I don't believe in envy, so I can honestly say there is no one on earth I'd want to trade places with. As I've often said, I'm the most grateful son of a bitch in Hollywood.

Maybe I've never made it to the heights of the big stars, but I've never had to take a straight job and I still get to do what I love doing. My hero Duke Ellington said it best: "I Guess I'm Just a Lucky So-and-So."

POSTSCRIPT

Before we went to press, my sister Kat passed away on October 28, 2015, after a long bout with hepatitis C and lung cancer. She was sixty-three years old.

To save her embarrassment, I wasn't going to tell her story while she was still alive, but now I feel perhaps some good may come of it. Maybe it will help someone else.

As I said earlier, alcoholism is a disease common to the women in my family, and Kat was no exception. She was also addicted to cigarettes, and, as with so many of her generation, drugs played a big part in her life. She was a child of the sixties in every way.

As with many of us, contradictions abounded in her. She was all about "peace and love," and yet there was a deep rage inside. Unlike most addicts, she was honorable and trustworthy. She was the only person I ever loaned money to who actually paid me back, and when she said she would.

We didn't agree on a whole lot, but I learned to avoid certain topics and so we were able to love each other. We lived a continent apart but stayed in touch by phone every couple of weeks. Her final circumstances were not good. She was living in poverty, eking out a bare living caring for other people's animals and plants. I got a British record company to reissue a two-CD set of her old recordings. She had a cult following and this brought her the only royalties she ever earned in her life.

Kat had the goods. She was a pretty girl. She sang great and she wrote good songs. People wanted to help her, but it was not to be. What did she lack? Who knows? Life is not fair.

For her, life's unfairness struck at age five, when she was molested, repeatedly, by our next-door neighbor. His wife babysat for us, and he would take her down in the basement and perform oral sex on her. She told no one. There was no one to protect her. No one to save her. She kept her secret until she told me . . . at age twenty-two.

For the longest time, I was the only one who knew. Once the truth was out, I let her know that she was free to talk about it. And she did, not often, but at least it was no longer locked inside. Some years later, she confessed that she didn't feel abused because "it felt good." I asked my shrink about it, and she said that this is often the case where there is no pain involved. The victim knows what happened to her was wrong but feels conflicted because of the pleasure she experienced.

What happened to Kat explains so much about her—not just her awful choices when it came to the males in her life, or the numbing of her feelings with drugs and alcohol, not to mention the rage that could burst out at a moment's notice, but little things during childhood. For instance, when our parents would argue at the dinner table, Kat would spill her milk, instinctually, to divert the attention. Or the time she swallowed a bunch of pills and was locked up at the Grasslands facility for a few weeks. Neither of us was very big on formal education; she dropped out of high school and I managed to make it through one year of college.

She had a love/hate relationship with our mother, who saw her as "the weak one" and never required of her the same adult behavior or responsibilities that were expected of me. Kat was allowed to live rent free at home, where she would sleep until almost noon, then either sit at the kitchen table by the phone or hide in her room, getting high and doing her art.

From time to time, she'd move in with a guy, usually an unworthy one. But she'd always eventually come home to a life of suspended adolescence. She wasn't allowed to grow up. Hence, until her final days she approached her life as a teenager. Mom wasn't completely to blame; Kat was unequipped for adult life. When Mom died, Kat received a nice inheritance, enough to buy a small house. But the money ran out. I tried to get her to join Alcoholics Anonymous, but to no avail. Like our mother, she didn't see any problem with her drinking and using. To her credit, as the end neared, she told me, "Don't feel sorry for me, I lived the life I chose, and now I'm paying the price."

She had friends who loved her. Not just fellow drunks or druggies, but normal people, too, people who really cared about her. She didn't open up to many people, but she could be fun to be around, and that was the Kat people loved.

She always had a dog or two. She preferred them to most people, a trait not uncommon among victims of sex abuse, I'm told.

In the end, my little sister was a good person with a good heart. She never hurt anybody and was honest to a fault. She loved her big brother and was proud of my success. I wish she'd gotten the success she deserved, but hers was a life of potential unfulfilled. On her final day, her friend put the phone to her ear in hopes that she might hear me. I told her that I loved her and it was time to let go, that it was okay. Later that night, the call came saying she had done just that.

THE SONGS

Like so many who came of age during the rock 'n' roll era, I've been called an autodidact. This description holds true for me outside of music as well, as I left college some two months into my sophomore year at Fordham University in the Bronx.

My musical training consisted of a short span of lessons over two years on drums, piano, and guitar, and even more minimal training in voice and sight-reading. However, I was always an enthusiastic listener with a hunger for unique sounds. This search for the unique would inform my writing from the beginning, although I've always had a taste for the simple, too, as opposed to the simplistic.

I think my lack of extensive study may have helped my writing. Often, schooled musicians tend to write what is "correct," ending up with clichéd, formulaic work, something I've done my best to avoid at all costs.

Fans often write and ask how I work as a songwriter and why I make the choices I do. In this section, I talk about the little tricks I've used, like unusual chord changes or lyrical surprises, to give my songs a personal touch so they don't sound formulaic or like other writers' material. I hope to impress upon the reader the importance of developing a style of one's own. A number of my songs may be difficult to find—indeed, some fairly experimental compositions have never been commercially released—but the interested reader will discover many on collector sites, if not on YouTube. Here, in roughly chronological order, I will focus on those that have found their way to the marketplace.

"All My Love" was my first released song in 1962 on Rust Records as by Billy Vera and the Contrasts, a pseudonym for the Knight-Riders, who had to change their name because they were under contract to another label before I joined them. The tune was intended as the B-side, but in Louisiana and Texas it was a Top 10 record in those days of regional hits. I'd been listening to Allen Toussaint songs like "Mother-in-Law," and this was my teenager's interpretation of his New Orleans rhythm, as reinterpreted by four young New York boys. It's a verse/chorus tune with a typical rock 'n' roll bridge, made atypical by an odd surprise chord (A-flat in the key of F) at the end. The day I met the great songwriter Chip Taylor, he told me it was one of his favorite songs, a position he maintains to this day and will defend in detail.

"Mean Old World" was the first song I ever showed to a publisher. That story is in a previous chapter. Fascinated by Burt Bacharach's songs for that new girl singer, Dionne Warwick, I banged out the chords to the songs on the piano, playing them over and over until I came up with this song in that style in the key of E minor. At the end of the short chorus, I toss in a startling out-of-the-key A-flat to make the listener wake up. When I played the song for the publisher, it had no bridge, and he, correctly, felt it needed one. So I went into the next room and knocked one out in a few minutes. Lyrically, the bridge comes from a phrase James Brown ad-libs on his *Live at the Apollo* album. The song was recorded by Ricky Nelson, who performed it five weeks in a row on TV, helping it to become my first chart record.

After I was hired by April-Blackwood Music, David Rosner got me my first record there, by a girl named Cindy Malone, on "It's Up to You" on Capitol. The chords are like nothing else I'd heard, using suspended fourths, resolving to the tonic, and that's just the beginning. The bridge changes keys, then returns to the original key for the last verse. Professional songwriters need to know how to write in character, in this case a female voice. She is unsure of her guy and goes through various thoughts and feelings, ultimately admitting she'll sleep with him if he stays, albeit in the subtle language of the time. This was a big deal in 1965. "Nice" girls didn't do such things, at least publicly in song. American expat Madeline Bell later recorded it in England.

As mentioned earlier, "Make Me Belong to You" was the first song I wrote with Chip Taylor. It's easy to sing, written on changes from an earlier time. In parts, melodically, I was thinking of Lloyd Price. The point of view is neither male nor female, but it is submissive as per the title. The singer will be whatever his or her love object wants. Barbara Lewis had a hit with it, and many others did versions, including Fats Domino, British star Helen Shapiro, and singers in a number of foreign languages.

"Headin' Down Home," also with Chip, would have made a nice Ray Charles record in that country mode he had such success with. As it was, H. B. Barnum cut it for Capitol and I also did it on my Atlantic solo album. On songs like this, Chip would come up with a line and I'd usually follow with a rhyming answer. The six-bar bridge starts on the III chord and ends abruptly, a nice Chip Taylor touch that bothered H. B.'s arranger's mind, so he added a line to give it the "normal" number of measures.

Chip's memory differs from mine on the creation of "Storybook Children." He seems to think he wrote the whole thing in the car, but I recall talking about a housewife I'd see pushing a stroller in White Plains and how I had a crush on her. Chip asked me to play the chords of the Joe Cuba song "To Be with You" that I used to sing in the clubs, and we wrote the chorus on that. The lyrics were written the same way we wrote "Headin' Down Home"; he'd write a line and I'd answer it.

The band and I cut three demos in one day that all wound up being recorded. "Sorry Mama" was ruined by the producer of the Apollas, who took it much too fast, jiving up a song that was intended as a relaxed-paced Harlem Latin tune. Sometimes you write a song consciously, and other times you find out what you were thinking later, when someone tells you. Here, I open with the bridge, then go into a verse whose vocal is sung, incongruously, like Bob Dylan might with his unique, personal phrasing. This back-and-forth makes for an interesting contrast. Lamont Dozier of Holland-Dozier-Holland told me they too channeled Dylan's phrasing on the verses of their song "Reach Out (I'll Be There)."

I tell the story of "Don't Look Back" in an earlier chapter. Like "Mean Old World," it's in a minor key with a three-word chorus that repeats. The bridge is utter mayhem. It begins with an out-of-tempo stop chorus, an idea borrowed from Junior Parker's "Driving Wheel," like a black Baptist minister in church, then goes to a Bo Diddley beat over Motown chords. The Remains version takes it out into rock territory. It became a cult favorite, inspiring acts like Robert Plant and Cyndi Lauper to record it.

"People That's Why" was musically inspired by an obscure record by the Geminis, "Get It On Home," cowritten by Larry Banks, who wrote "Go Now." I was trying for Bill Medley, but my lyrics got a tad preachy, which was not uncommon in that era. The great producer Calvin Carter cut it with P. J. Proby, an American singer who made it big in England.

It was also recorded by another British act, the Idle Few, who sped it up, turning it into a Northern soul classic. The verse is in a minor key, colored by sustained fourths and ninths, taking the chorus into a major key. The bridge begins on the tonic and ends on a series of chords from "In the Midnight Hour," which the song's composer, Steve Cropper, told me he'd come up with by following the dots on his guitar neck.

One of my favorites from this period is "Good Morning Blues." Ray Charles told David Rosner it was the best blues song he'd ever heard, although he never got around to recording it, possibly because the publishing was not available. I wound up doing it myself for Atlantic. Jazz producer Creed Taylor cut a disappointing version with George Benson, who sang it beautifully over an unfortunate arrangement by Horace Ott. Years later, Michael Cuscuna and I produced the definitive version by Lou Rawls. Blue Note boss Bruce Lundvall listened to it over and over in his office the night after we recorded it and said, "This is no mere song; it is a composition, worthy of Monk." A very astute observation, as the piano line under the verse was inspired by Monk's "Misterioso."

"Are You Coming to My Party" was an extremely slow song Chip and I wrote that wound up on my solo Atlantic album. It was done at the "Good Morning Blues" session and, like that one, was more soulful than most of the rest of that album. I played guitar on it. One of the bits of songwriting advice Chip gave me was to "know the madness," and I think we achieved that madness in this one.

Ted Daryll was another writer who liked to take chances. His biggest hit was "She Cried," which he composed on a unique set of three chords a whole tone apart. We didn't write together often, but we wrote some interesting things, two of which he produced for Peggy March, "I've Been Here Before" and "Thinking Through My Tears," the latter covered in England by Madeline Bell.

The title for "Don't Try to Explain" was inspired by Billie Holiday's "Don't Explain." I'd been moved by her story of how she came to write her song as she told it in her autobiography, *Lady Sings the Blues*. This is me banging away on the piano in my office until I came up with a chord sequence I'd never heard before that sounds vaguely Old English. The bridge is an especially powerful combination of words and music that leads to an orgasmic climax. Zombies lead singer Colin Blunstone recorded a wonderful version as Neil MacArthur.

Sometimes you just want to write hits, so I wrote "Say You'll Never (Never Leave Me)" in the style of Curtis Mayfield and "You've Got a Deal" in Aretha Franklin's. In Alice Clark, I found the perfect voice to sing both. Alice never had a hit, but "You've Got a Deal" eventually became a popular Northern soul record in the English dance clubs.

Chip and I wrote "The Bible Salesman" for the Maysles brothers' documentary *Salesman*. As recorded in Memphis at Chips Moman's American Sound, it became a single for me on Atlantic, although the Maysles boys preferred our demo for their movie trailer. The song contains one of our cleverest lyrics.

I was in a jazzy mode when I wrote "Much Too Long," another of those tunes with unusual changes. It was recorded for RCA Victor by Margie Day, who'd been a popular R&B singer in the early fifties and was switching to jazz by the late sixties, rediscovered by my manager, Al Schwartz.

One of the last things I wrote at April-Blackwood was "I've Never Been Loved (Like This Before)," which I recorded in Muscle Shoals. Female singers seem to have liked this one. Two unknown girls recorded it at the time, and, years later, when I played it for the jazz singer Dianne Reeves, she loved it, although her producer decided against it. For the girls, I simply had to change the line "I've never had love like this before from a mother or a wife" to ". . . *as* a mother or a wife."

"Behind the Wall," discussed in an earlier chapter, was one of the first things I wrote upon leaving April-Blackwood. The subject matter left little chance that it would ever be recorded commercially, but then again, it was 1970. A band called Gotham, led by the great guitarist Linc Chamberland, did record it on his band's album on a Motown-affiliated label, after Linc wrote a new lyric to satisfy their singer, who feared lightning might strike him if he sang my lyric about the bones of dead babies. The great saxophonist Pee Wee Ellis and several top New York session men were in that group. I recorded it, as written, on an album that only came out years later, after I had a hit elsewhere. As I related earlier in the book, Nina Simone wrote to say she loved the song and would've cut it if she'd had a record deal at the time.

The early-seventies oldies revival led to renewed interest in fifties music, thanks to movies like *American Graffiti* and groups like Creedence and the Band. Even Chuck Berry had the biggest hit of his career with "My Ding-a-Ling." "Big-Legged Mama" was a Berryesque tune loosely based on my experiences in my mother's hometown in northern Ohio.

Steve Cropper and I wrote only one song together, "Hold On," which he produced me singing on at his studio in Memphis in 1973. Unlike anything he wrote for Stax, it's more like those songs like "Hit the Road, Jack" that Percy Mayfield used to write for Ray Charles. It's about a hard-luck guy who keeps messing up and going back to jail. Steve's TMI label, which he formed after leaving Stax, was going under, so he pressed up a single on a one-shot label he called Orange. It's probably my rarest single.

I was trying to write a Chip Taylor-ish song one day and came up with "Back Door Man," a story of a guy being used by a married woman he's desperately in love with. Chip often uses the I-IV-V chord structure of "La Bamba" to write his songs, so I twisted the order around, starting on the IV, going IV-V-I. The song captures the tenderness the guy feels for the woman while hinting at the coldhearted way she uses him sexually to cheat on her husband. During this period, adultery songs were popular in both country and R&B. I'm not proud to say that "Storybook Children" was one of the first of this genre.

Writing with L. Russell (Larry) Brown was a lesson in melody. With songs like "C'mon Marianne" and "Tie a Yellow Ribbon," he did quite well. For a Canadian sibling act called the Good Brothers, we wrote a bunch of songs, including "No Place Like Home" and "Don't Let It Die," which both had very singable melodies. Larry and I worked well together, since neither of us had any allegiance to formal structure.

As mentioned, I took what I learned from Larry about melody and came up with my first number one song, "I Really Got the Feeling." Shirley Reeves from the Shirelles was first to record it in its full length. Dolly Parton later apologized for leaving out one verse, one she loved. But she knew the song would be a hit and wanted to make it short enough for radio play. I'm glad she truncated it. Here's that verse, for those who have never heard it:

You're a funny man
You make me smile like a line from that old song "Funny Valentine"
And I smile with my heart
When I see your laughing face in a corner of my mind

Again ignoring formal structure, I opened with the chorus, one of those you can't get out of your mind, followed by a verse, then a chorus. Next is the bridge and another chorus. To thoroughly confuse the listener, I wrote a third section, a sort of tag that takes the song out.

Shirley also recorded "Private Clown." It was written on a common set of chord changes that have graced some great songs, like "Lover Come Back to Me" and "Lipstick Traces," although my bridge goes off into unfamiliar territory, chord- and melody-wise. For Shirley's record, Tommy Wolk and I arranged it in a style similar to that of "Love Will Keep Us Together," adding a calliope we found sitting around at RCA's New York studio to emphasize the circus metaphors in the lyric. Larry produced my first version, taking it in an overproduced Elton John orbit. In 1981, Jerry Wexler produced me, doing the song in a New Orleans jazz manner, along the same rhythmic lines as Dr. John's "Such a Night." A good song lends itself to different interpretations, and this one fits that description. I'd like to hear it in a swinging big-band version one day.

I like to surprise the listener with an oddly placed chord. On this one, I used a G-flat in the key of B-flat (a sharpened fifth) to open the bridge, taking it to a series of key changes that sound perfectly natural before returning to the original key. I always try for the element of surprise in my songs, little odd touches that pop up, seemingly out of nowhere, but that have a certain logic to them, too.

"She Ain't Johnnie," from my 1976 Midsong album, is a slice of country funk, a story song that anticipates Kenny Rogers's "The Gambler" by a couple of years. In Kenny's hands, or Waylon Jennings's, I'm convinced it would've been a number one smash. My reissued version scraped the bottom of the country charts in 1987. German star Mary Roos recorded it in her native tongue.

I was never in the habit of writing autobiographical songs, as so many self-absorbed artists do. My attitude is "professionals create fiction;

amateurs exploit their own lives." That said, my breakup with the infamous Nina resulted in a couple of semi-autobiographical songs and at least one that was completely autobiographical.

"Here Comes the Dawn Again" is dead-on autobiography. It reveals exactly how I was feeling at the time. Someone said that what raises this song to art is how it accurately details that window of time in which one has yet to accept that the affair is over but realizes on another, unconscious level that it's finished.

"At This Moment," the most famous song from that breakup, started out from Nina's previous boyfriend's point of view and ended from mine. The verse chords are borrowed from Motown. I merely slowed them down to ballad form, unrecognizable to all but the most astute listener. The transition bass riff into the bridge is out of James Brown's "Lost Someone." I had my doubts about the song's commercial potential, as it contains no obvious title. To this day, people don't know what to call it and often get the title wrong. This weakness apparently didn't matter to the great masses, who have turned it into a modern standard.

The granddaughter of one of the writers of the great standard "Moonlight in Vermont" brought to my attention the fact that neither song contains even one rhyme. Hard to believe, but I'd never noticed that before. It wasn't intentional. Now, I'm as capable as the next guy of a clever rhyme, but I guess rhymes weren't necessary here, and might even have distracted from the emotional content of the song. Perhaps the lack of rhymes made the lyric seem more conversational. Many people have recorded "At This Moment" or sung it in their act, including Tom Jones, Marilyn McCoo, Rita Coolidge, the O'Jays, the Manhattans, even Peggy Lee, but the biggest seller was Michael Bublé, who recorded both a studio and a live version, selling over eight and a half million copies.

"Between Like and Love" was inspired by my fling with a girl named Michelle, who came into my life on Nina's coattails. The affair was so sweet that we couldn't decide how we felt about each other. In both the chorus and the bridge, I use some adventurous chord patterns you're unlikely to hear in other songs.

One of the first songs I came up with after arriving in Los Angeles to write for Warner Bros. Music was "Someone Will School You, Someone Will Cool You." It combines several of my favorite styles. I was playing around with the rhythm of "Louie Louie" and altered it a bit for the verses. For the chorus, I played some Atlantic-era Ray Charles stuff. The piano riff between choruses is my clumsy reimagining of Professor Longhair's lick on his song "Big Chief." Story-wise, it came after my manager decided to find me a girlfriend, mainly because he was tired of me hanging around his apartment in the evenings, watching his TV. He took me, his girlfriend, and another girl he knew to dinner, where my date turned out to be a low-class type, what my mom would call a real floozy. When I walked her to her car, she asked me to call her. The song is how I imagined things might have turned out had I done so.

"I Can Take Care of Myself" is another example of what Larry Brown calls "song combining." This method requires skill in disguising your original sources, so that only a hint of them remains. The instrumental intro is based on the chords of "Satin Doll," although the melody bears no resemblance to the famous Duke Ellington tune. Larry says that people respond to melodies that start out high and end up low, so that occurs in the verses here. My use of the III chord (E7 in the key of C) at the end of each verse was inspired by a similar trick in Marvin Gaye's "Stubborn Kind of Fella." It's one Berry Gordy used often in the early Motown years. Then, on the last turnaround, when the phrase repeats, I take it down to the VI chord (A7 in the key of C) for variety's sake. The song became Billy and the Beaters' first hit. Too often, people mistake "I Can Take Care of Myself" for an "uplifting" song, when the opposite is true. The character is a fool for believing he can take care of himself, while the girl in question has him bamboozled. His friends tell him she's bad, but he thinks he can overcome her character flaws. We, the audience, can see he's being played. The happy music only emphasizes his blindness and stupidity.

Larry Brown and I wrote "Millie, Make Some Chili" just after Elvis's death, and it shows. The guitar riff is right out of Scotty Moore. I had taken Larry to a joint called Texas Lunch in Port Chester, New York, where a woman named Millie Kaplan served up the best chili dogs on the planet, and Larry, who can take his inspiration from anywhere, got the idea to write a song in tribute. We never again had to pay for chili at Texas Lunch. In fact, whenever she heard someone was heading to LA, Millie would give that person a quart to bring to me.

"Corner of the Night" sounds like the title of a soap opera. I wrote it for Esther Phillips after she sang with us one night. She loved it but had no recording contract at the time. The verses are in a minor key (E-flat minor, as I like to write on the black keys) to denote the darker feelings, while the chorus is in a major key to express the change to a lighter mood. The verse riff, at first played by piano, bass, and guitar, is later doubled by the horns. The horn line in the chorus sections also adds to the happier feel in those lyrics. The arrangements on most of the songs I've done with the Beaters are based on what I play on piano. The piano part I composed is the foundation around which the other instruments build.

"Hopeless Romantic" is the only song I ever wrote without the use of an instrument. I was living with a friend who was asleep across the hall, but the song needed to come out. Rather than "hopeless," the singer is actually hopeful that, despite the unhappy state of affairs, life will get better if he believes and finds a way to rediscover his innocence.

One day, with no other ideas, to keep in practice I decided to write a Shirelles-type song, despite the fact that their recording career had long been over. "Once in a Lifetime (Will Do)" is the kind of melody and storyline at which this major girl group excelled. Working for the Shirelles for several years as their guitarist/conductor had taught me exactly what Shirley's sound required.

In between my two issued Alfa albums was one the company chose not to release. While their decision was sound, there are three songs of merit that finally came out on the compilation *The Best of Billy Vera and the Beaters.* "I'll Be There for You," "I'm Gonna Marry You," and "I'm All for You" are all songs of devotion, but musically they're vastly different from each other. "I'm All for You" has a repetitive five-note melody played by the saxophone section that drives itself into the brain while I ad-lib for more than a minute. In the body of the song, the singer, noticing that his woman is losing her mind, struggles to come to terms with her madness and clumsily offers his help, pledging his love. Musically, "I'll Be There for You" is far more surprising. I know of no antecedent to it. I wrote the music first and had trouble coming up with a lyric, so I asked Warner Bros. staffer Jeff Monday for help. Later, when Jeff couldn't come up with what I wanted, a model named Cassandra

Gaviola gave it a shot. Not completely satisfied with either lyric, I kept small pieces of each one's attempt and, in a flash of inspiration one night, crafted a new lyric. How many songs do you know that rhyme "I'll jump right off a plane" with "I'll swim Lake Pontchartrain?"

Right before my contract with Warner Bros. expired in 1983, I wrote a blues with the great bluesman Lowell Fulson, "Room with a View." The story of writing it can be found in an earlier chapter. Suffice it to say that the song diverges slightly from the traditional twelve-bar blues structure, which keeps it interesting. It's gone on to become a modern blues standard, with recordings by Lou Rawls, Eric Burdon, Johnny Adams, and many others.

After a bout with writer's block and inspired by my freedom from a publishing contract, I hit a spurt of creativity with a series of more reflective, more grown-up songs. The first of these was "Moonglows," named after the fifties vocal group most famous for their hit "Sincerely." The verse melody probably comes from some 1930s movie that takes place in China, while the bridge makes me think of something Smokey Robinson might have sung. Lou Rawls did a nice job with it on the second album Michael Cuscuna and I produced for him.

Speaking of Smokey, "Heart Be Still" was my attempt at writing the kind of rhyming sequences Mr. Robinson excelled at. This one is overflowing with tasty little rhymes, interior and otherwise, as many as four the same in a row. Sometimes the mind is just working overtime.

"I've Got My Eye on You" was my take on my friend Paul Gayten's personality. Paul was the first New Orleans R&B artist to have a hit record, back in 1947. No less a talent than Mike Stoller praised this song as the kind of comedic tune he would have recorded with the Coasters. He then went into a dissertation on it, comparing it musically to the writing of Kurt Weill. As I'd done in "Private Clown," I took the bridge to a chord that was a half step above the dominant, a trick I haven't heard other writers use. When I was in the studio recording this for my Capitol album, David Lee Roth, who was recording next door, begged my producer, Tom Dowd, to ask me if he could record it. We foolishly declined. It would have made a perfect follow-up to his "Just a Gigolo."

I was now on a roll and went further into fresh-sounding territory with "You Can't Go Home," composing a chord sequence I couldn't even properly name. On the Lou Rawls recording Michael Cuscuna and I produced, George Benson immediately heard what I was doing and played a killer solo in one take.

My old boss at Warner Bros., Eddie Silvers, now retired, asked me to write something for his friend Dave Mason. Not being familiar with Dave's work, I just wrote something I liked. A line in the first verse,

Night-blooming jasmine gives off its perfume
Sycamore trees play hide-and-seek with the moon

was inspired by the fact that I was living on Sycamore Avenue at the time. My guitarist, Ricky Hirsch, said it was his favorite opening line of all time. The line "Way down the street I hear our favorite old song, 'Oh What a Nite,'" the Dells' hit, gave the song its title, "Oh, What a Nite." It wound up in the movie *Blind Date*, in which I appeared with the band. A lyrical twist is as good as a musical one. Here, after describing "such a lovely night," I wait a beat before I say "to be without you," to jar the listener and change the mood. Lou Rawls later recorded it on the first Blue Note album we did with him.

Also in *Blind Date* was "Let You Get Away," inspired by something I remembered Joseph Cotten saying in an Orson Welles movie about a woman he was recalling, "It's been all these years and not a day goes by that I don't think about her." The song is half sung and half spoken in a quasi-melodic way. I believed in it so much, I recorded it three times.

The brawl scene in *Blind Date* was shot over "Someone Will School You," but the director, Blake Edwards, wanted something else in the same tempo, so Larry Brown and I came up with something totally different that would be great for Frankie Valli called "Anybody Seen Her." Songs rarely end up sounding like your inspiration. How many would guess that I started this one by playing the guitar lick to "Monkey Time?"

After "At This Moment" hit, both Chip and Larry came out to LA to help me write songs for my follow-up album, one of which was "Papa Come Quick (Jody and Chico)." Chip and I were making demos at Ricky Hirsch's house. Ricky played us a guitar lick, and that inspired me to play a little Cajun riff on his keyboard and sing the opening line, "Papa come quick, Jody's gone to the city. What we gonna do now that

Jody's gone?" Ricky's girlfriend had a teenaged daughter named Jody. I'm a soap opera fan, so that inspired the line "Mama's been cryin' in the kitchen since morning, she cried right through *As the World Turns*," the name of the soap a former girlfriend acted on. The tune didn't make it to my album, but when Bonnie Raitt needed songs for her follow-up album to *Nick of Time*, I gave it to her and it sold over five million copies.

Another one from those sessions with Chip was "Is That the American Dream, Johnny," which came from a poem I'd written some years before. Jerry Wexler said it might make an interesting song, so Chip and I went at it. In the bridge, I do a little white-boy rapping. The song, as well as "Papa Come Quick," wound up in the movie *Rainbow Drive*.

I hope these little bits give inspiration and are helpful to any aspiring songwriters among you. As you can see, a song can come from anywhere. The only advice I can give is this: avoid cliché and don't give up until you find something that makes each song sound fresh and different.

DISCOGRAPHY

SINGLES

"January 1, 1962" [no B-side] (1961)
The Resolutions
Valentine 1001

"My Heart Cries" / "All My Love" (1962)
Billy Vera and the Contrasts
Rust 5051

"You Can't Have Everything" / "If I Could Have Your Love" (1964)
Billy Vera
Flavor 105

"No Strings Attached" / "You Can't Have Everything" (1964)
Billy Vera
Flavor 107

"Shadow of Your Love" / "Look Gently at the Rain" (1966)
Blue-Eyed Soul featuring Billy Vera
Cameo 401

"Something New" / "Tonight I Am a King" (1966)
Blue-Eyed Soul featuring Billy Vera
Cameo 423

"Storybook Children" / "Really Together" (1967)
Billy Vera and Judy Clay
Atlantic 2445

"Country Girl-City Man" / "So Good (To Be Together)" (1968)
Billy Vera and Judy Clay
Atlantic 2480

"When Do We Go" / "Ever Since" (1968)
Billy Vera and Judy Clay
Atlantic 2515

"With Pen in Hand" / "Good Morning Blues" (1968)
Billy Vera
Atlantic 2526

"I've Been Loving You Too Long" / "Are You Coming to My Party" (1968)
Billy Vera
Atlantic 2555

"Julie" / "Time Doesn't Matter Anymore" (1968)
Billy Vera
Atlantic 2586

"The Bible Salesman" / "Are You Coming to My Party" (1969)
Billy Vera
Atlantic 2628

"Reaching for the Moon" / "Tell It Like It Is" (1969)
Billy Vera and Judy Clay
Atlantic 2654

"J.W.'S Dream" / "I've Never Been Loved (Like This Before)" (1969)
Billy Vera
Atlantic 2700

"Little Darlin'" / "Imperial Gents Stomp" (1971)
The Imperial Gents
Laurie 3540

"Number Wonderful" [no B-side] (1972)
Silver Lining
Vanguard 35131

"Climb Your Tree" / "Big-Legged Mama" (1972)
Billy Vera and the Mighty Boogie All-Stars
Jive 100

"Big Chief" / "Hold On" (1966)
Billy Vera
Orange 5002

"Back Door Man" / "Run and Tell the People" (1975)
Billy Vera
Midland 10639

"Private Clown" / "Billy, Meet Your Son" (1977)
Billy Vera
Midsong 10639

"Something Like Nothing Before" / "Billy, Meet Your Son" (1977)
Billy Vera
Midsong 11042

"She Ain't Loni" / "I've Had Enough" (1979)
Billy Vera
Midsong 72014

"I Can Take Care of Myself" / "Corner of the Night" (1981)
Billy and the Beaters
Alfa 7002

"At This Moment" / "Someone Will School You,
    Someone Will Cool You" (1981)
Billy and the Beaters
Alfa 7005

"Millie, Make Some Chili" / "Corner of the Night" (1981)
Billy and the Beaters
Alfa 7012

"We Got It All" / "You Own It" (1982)
Billy Vera
Alfa 7020

"At This Moment" / "I Can Take Care of Myself" (1986)
Billy Vera and the Beaters
Rhino 74403

"I Can Take Care of Myself" / "Peanut Butter" (1987)
Billy Vera and the Beaters
Rhino 74404

"Let You Get Away" / "Anybody Seen Her?" (1987)
Billy Vera and the Beaters
Rhino 74405

"Hopeless Romantic" [no B-side] (1987)
Billy Vera
Rhino 74407

"I've Had Enough" / "My Girl Josephine" (1987)
Billy Vera
Macola 981

"She Ain't Johnnie" / "My Girl Josephine" (1987)
Billy Vera
Macola 9812

"Between Like and Love" / "Heart Be Still" (1988)
Billy Vera and the Beaters
Capitol 44149

"Ronnie's Song" / "Heart Be Still" (1988)
Billy Vera and the Beaters
Capitol 44200

"Enemies Like You and Me" [no B-side] (1988)
Billy Vera and Ruth Pointer
Epic 08115

ALBUMS

Storybook Children (1968)
Billy Vera and Judy Clay
Atlantic

With Pen in Hand (1968)
Billy Vera
Atlantic

Out of the Darkness (1977)
Billy Vera
Midsong

Billy and the Beaters (1981)
Alfa
Billy Vera and the Beaters

Billy Vera (1982)
Alfa
Billy Vera

Mystic Sound of Billy Vera (1984)
Mystic
Billy Vera

By Request (1986)
Billy Vera and the Beaters
Rhino

Blind Date Soundtrack (three songs) (1987)
Billy Vera and the Beaters
Rhino

The Atlantic Years (1987)
Billy Vera / Billy Vera and Judy Clay
Rhino

Retro Nuevo (1988)
Billy Vera and the Beaters
Capitol

You Have to Cry Sometime (1992)
Billy Vera and Nona Hendryx
Shanachie

Soul of R&B Review (three songs) (1993)
Billy Vera
Shanachie

Oh, What a Nite (1995)
Billy Vera and the Beaters
Pool Party

Not for Sale (1997)
Billy Vera
Chance

At This Moment: A Retrospective (2002)
Billy Vera and the Beaters
Varèse Sarabande

Good Stuff (2003)
Billy Vera and the Beaters
Vera-Cruz Music

The Best of Billy Vera and the Beaters (2008)
Shout Factory!

The Billy Vera Story (2011)
Rock Beat

Queen of Diamonds / Jack of Hearts (2014)
Billy Vera and Evie Sands
Train Wreck

Big Band Jazz (2015)
Billy Vera
Varèse Sarabande

INDEX